# A Theory of Personalism

# A Theory of Personalism

Thomas R. Rourke
and
Rosita A. Chazarreta Rourke

LEXINGTON BOOKS

A division of
ROWMAN & LITTLEFIELD PUBLISHERS, INC.
Lanham • Boulder • New York • Toronto • Plymouth, UK

LEXINGTON BOOKS

A division of Rowman & Littlefield Publishers, Inc.
A wholly owned subsidiary of The Rowman & Littlefield Publishing Group, Inc.
4501 Forbes Boulevard, Suite 200
Lanham, MD 20706

Estover Road
Plymouth PL6 7PY
United Kingdom

British Library Cataloguing in Publication Information Available

Library of Congress Control Number: 2005299928

ISBN: 0-7391-0121-8 / 978-0-7391-0121-6 (hardcover)
ISBN: 0-7391-2021-2 / 978-0-7391-2021-7 (paperback)

Printed in the United States of America

♾™ The paper used in this publication meets the minimum requirements of American
National Standard for Information Sciences—Permanence of Paper for Printed Library
Materials, ANSI/NISO Z39.48–1992.

# Table of Contents

# PREFACE

In terms of real participation or meaningful input into the political and economic decisions which govern our increasingly interrelated world, the percentage of people exercising substantive participation is small. This is most obviously true in the domain of economics. The political system increasingly accommodates the demands of the large corporations, and this at a global level. The problem is multiplied throughout much of the underdeveloped world, where economic policy is largely conditioned by the mandates of foreign creditors. Effectively in receivership, the governments of these poor nations have been largely stripped of their sovereignty; economic policy is conditioned by unelected economists working for international financial institutions such as the World Bank and the International Monetary Fund. It speaks poorly of what is left of our sense of the meaning of words such as "freedom," "democracy," and "sovereignty," when we predicate them of such hapless and manipulated regimes. Indeed, when we refer to such nations as free, democratic, and sovereign, we define our world in Orwellian fashion.

Concerning the related political system, the increasing dominance of the market mechanism itself reduces its scope and gives corporations an upper hand in all of their dealings with public policy makers. The problem of declining participation, however, does not end there. The majority of citizens eligible to vote in the United States, in fact up to two-thirds, do not even bother to cast a vote in an election during a nonpresidential year. Public opinion polls in the United States reveal that people feel alienated from politics and doubt that the outcome of elections will be to restore any substantive sense that they are the ones who govern this nation. More and more frequently, decisions are being made by unelected administrators and judges. Nor does this only occur on decisions of less importance. For example, both the World Trade Organization and the tribunal established to implement the North American Free Trade Agreement can effectively overrule national sovereignty, to declare laws governing trade illegal. They also permit corporations to sue in order to overturn regulatory laws passed to protect the health of the public. These decisions are not subject to review at the national level. The tribunals are highly skewed in favor of corporate interests. In the moral arena, unelected judges have increasingly taken it upon themselves to alter the moral fabric of society in opposition to public opinion and in circumvention of the democratic process. This has predominantly taken the form of inventing rights that have no precedence. Extremely liberal abortion laws are the most frequently cited example. This is evolving into the realm of the absurd, as in the decision by a judge in France that there exists a "right not to be born" to be used as a basis for suing doctors guilty of no more than obedience to their Hippocratic Oath. In decisions of this kind we see the attempt to replace the rule of law by the blatantly irrational and arbitrary. This authoritarian, even tyrannical mind-set is repeatedly seen in the attempt to force nations in the Third World to obey the dictates of unelected UN bureaucrats who seek to impose by dictate a global regime of abortion and population control, the permissive culture which surrounds the promotion of such practices, and a perspective on family which is foreign even to most people in the developed world. What percentage of citizens in the United States can name the "five genders" the existence of which is the basis for UN documents on the subject?

Creeping authoritarianism is also manifest in the alternation of appeals to relativism and tolerance on the one hand and the need to impose authority on the other. The seasoned observer will note that tolerance is pulled out of the hat whenever the goal is to eliminate traditional religious influences on the culture. In the next breath, the same people will be supporting legislation which violates the conscience of those who advocate traditional morality. For example, Planned Parenthood receives tax money and uses it to promote abortion and population control around the world. It also promotes the acceptance of active sexual lives for teens. In Canada, it is no longer clear that to quote the Bible in opposition to the practice of homosexuality is a protected form of free speech.

When the current crisis is viewed in all of its depth, it is clear that the reigning ideologies are bankrupt as solutions. Both conservatives and liberals are deeply implicated in the current crisis, as are all of the contemporary "isms" which accompany them. Nor can it be otherwise, as neither the left nor the right has a viable moral philosophy nor even internal consistency. The right talks about some of the themes which will be emphasized in this book, such as the need for more local control, but tosses this value aside in arbitrary fashion when the topic turns to economics and the need to solve the pressing moral problem of dehumanizing poverty. They wish to impose their dogmas of free trade, antistatism and public benefits for corporations, and will go around democratic processes to do so. The left is no better. They love to appeal to freedom and toleration, but mostly as a battering ram against traditional morality. When they control the power of the state, they use it to impose their moral views, and will similarly attempt to bypass votes they would not win.

William Greider suggested a decade ago that the substance of democracy was being hollowed out. He was right, and the problem is only deepening and becoming more globalized. What makes the future so troubling is that the right is divided between a faction that cares about the maintenance of traditional morality and a faction that does not. Corporations increasingly succumb to the pressures of the moral-cultural left. The major global cultural industries are clearly enemies of traditional morality, seeing how much money can be made via the exploitation of sex and violence. Moreover, it is increasingly obvious that the faction within the right that cares about traditional morality is reduced to the position of having to bargain with those who side with the left on moral and cultural matters. For example, in the current Bush Administration and in the Congress, there are numerous people on "the right" who favor abortion. Within the opposition party, there are no such people in the Congress. If this trend prevails and becomes manifest in the international arena, we may realistically face the domination by the authoritarian dimensions of both the left and the right, the right prevailing on economic matters, and the left prevailing on moral and cultural ones. As both of these prefer to impose their causes without regard for the people and resort to nondemocratic procedures of decision-making, the outlook for an authentic renewal of substantive democracy looks grim.

The prospects for improvement are worsened when we take into account the fact that individualism prevails in the moral and cultural arena. Significant opposition remains, but it seems more and more to take the form of rearguard action. Even those who argue against the prevalence of individualism do so by employing individualist language. The "right to choose" is countered by a "right to life." The latter argument is indeed a sound one, but at times leaves unquestioned the deeper error that there is nothing at issue in the abortion debate other than individual rights. And this is not the only example. Communities justly seeking legal remedies for being abandoned by corporations to whom they have granted considerable favors over decades are forced to find an argument in terms of individual rights, and they can find none that can compete with the corporate claim; according to our Supreme Court, a corporation is a person but a community of people is not. Individualism's worst effect, however, is the corrosive impact it has on any substantive meaning of the common good. Public opinion polls reveal profound apathy with respect to politics, and it is this attitude of indifference which will deal the fatal blow. The minority, authoritarian forces on the right and left are well-funded, with elitist disregard for opinions other than their own. They are mobilized and determined. In a political system dominated by the interest groups they control, they can easily defeat the passive majority. They do so principally by stripping the people of their sovereignty with respect to the issue; better a court, a tribunal, or an unaccountable bureaucracy to make the key decisions.

Thoughtful people are increasingly disillusioned with the transparent facade of the appeals to democracy by both ideologies, realizing that neither really cares about the thinking of the majority, but they are not always clear as to how to diagnose the present ills nor where to go. Some mistakenly believe that the only answer lies in making alliances with the powers that be, so as to have a voice within them. Such an approach can never work, as the political and economic orders are already sealed off from substantial change. Others believe that we should focus primarily on the moral and cultural issues, hoping to refocus society's attention on losses in this area. Although laudable, such an approach is fundamentally flawed in that it assumes that the moral-cultural climate can be changed by ignoring the economic dimension of life which is a driving force behind public policy. A moral and cultural movement which leaves the economy to the authoritarian forces governing it will go nowhere, because the same self-centered individualism driving the economic arena is driving the moral and cultural one as well. Moreover, the right-to-life movement often lacks credible explanations as to why its proponents frequently speak only about abortion and euthanasia, while failing to address adequately other palpable threats to life, such as malnutrition, inadequate health care, war, and political violence. This is in no way to minimize or relativize the real need for an abolitionist movement against abortion. The pro-life movement is good and necessary, but unwittingly succumbs at times to the overarching liberal mentality which falsely encourages the separation of issues which are in fact related.

This book attempts to articulate a vision which is both old and new. The foundational principle of this book is that Western political thought and practice has for centuries been severing itself from one of its richest and morally ennobling insights, namely, that the entire political, economic, and social order should be centered around the human person. Although easily demonstrable, this insight is not commonly recognized today. Ideologies left and right claim to be in favor of the "individual," and few have come to understand the fundamental difference between this "individual" and the real human person. The concept of individual is distinctively modern and abstract. Although attempting to build on the moral capital accumulated by its predecessor, the person, it is different in kind. The person is concrete, historically and culturally situated, and a member of a specific community. The modern individual is detached from all of these connections. Possessing no real life or human depth, the individual would be no more than a useless abstraction if not for the political will to make it the repository of a wish list one hopes to enshrine in the social order. The individual is variously conceived as the beholder of incompatible rights claims: property rights vs. the right to a job and a family wage; a right to choose as opposed to a right to life; majority rights vs. minority rights; and so on.

It was my theological studies that brought to light the concept of person and its distinction from what political theorists called "the individual." Particularly as a result of reading theologians such as Henri de Lubac and Hans Urs Von Balthasar, I realized that there was a well-developed theological anthropology which could be of great service to political theory. Moreover, I saw how the theologically influenced concept of person played a central role in earlier Western thinking. From this vantage point, I saw for the first time the depth of the tragedy that had occurred in Western political and economic thought. The theologically influenced concept of person had been driving philosophers to focus on the human person as the image and likeness of God. Breakthroughs concerning such important matters as constitutional government, freedom, rights, popular sovereignty, and democracy, were in the making. Unfortunately, at a crucial time, the Enlightenment came along to undermine the theological influence. The democratic, theologically informed version of popular sovereignty came to be replaced by national sovereignty often under one form or another of absolutist rule. Of course, the presence of religion in society guaranteed the ongoing influence of thinking influenced by theological notions. Hence, for example, some of the rights-based thinking led to positive outcomes such as the increasing acceptance of freedom of conscience in religious matters. Even as late as forty years ago, the civil rights movement in the United States accomplished a great deal of good. Nonetheless, the rich concept of person as an image of the Trinity gave way in modern thought to the individual, and it is the ambiguities of the latter concept which have paved the way for the morass of contradictory and confused thinking prevailing today. Those who seek power almost always seek to justify themselves by reference to some version of this nebulous individual who seems to support mutually exclusive arguments.

Only the recovery of the meaning of what it means to be a human person, fully informed by the older, more spiritually rooted thinking, can overcome the impasses of today. The person unites what is worth saving in the existing ideologies and holds these elements together in a coherent way. Materialistic and utilitarian approaches can never do this, as they inevitably take one component of the person and play it off against another, as in, for example, the fruitless contemporary debates pitting personal autonomy against communal solidarity, and liberty in opposition to authority. Nothing other than a full recovery of personhood can establish again our thinking on solid grounds, showing the profound compatibility among all of the essential moral and political values.

This book argues in favor of decentralizing the dominant political and economic institutions, a reorganization of society from the person up. All institutions should be centered around the human person and recognize the latter as the integrating principle of the entire social order. As it is not clear to many why the existing order does not do so, a good part of the book will necessarily be a critique. It is a critique, however, which points to something better. Ultimately, the argument of the book is hopeful in that almost all of the proposals suggested for a decentralized political and economic life have been tried and proven to be viable. It is simply a matter of having the willpower to return to them and to reject the centralizing tendencies of our time.

The writing of this book has been an unusually solitary enterprise. Although I originally presented some of these ideas at academic conferences, I found that even among academics, the prejudices in favor of centralized institutions and against agrarian insights were so overwhelming that I really could not be heard. For example, the biases against small farms and the people who work them are so strong that many people simply assume that any argument in favor of decentralized farming must be made in terms of aesthetics, despite the long tradition of thought associating democracy with the kind of independence of character and self-subsistence engendered by agrarian life. I confess that I myself never gave much thought to such arguments. It was in the reading of agrarian thinkers such as Wendell Berry and Gene Logsdon that I underwent a change of mind. In conjunction with writers in the theological tradition, I began to form the personalist argument I present here. Ultimately, I found that on many subjects, theological authors and cultural critics have more valuable insights to offer concerning the contemporary political world than political scientists in the academy.

Much of my thanks must go to people whom I have never met, but deeply embody the personalist statement I make here. Wendell Berry of Kentucky—essayist, novelist, and agrarian writer—has profoundly impacted my thinking in a decentralist direction, and alerted me to the multiple dangers of corporate farming. Dorothy Day is one of the greatest personalists, along with Peter Maurin and the Catholic Worker movement. I was privileged to be a full-time Catholic Worker earlier in my life, and its philosophy is indelibly etched in my soul.

Of people I have met, I thank again Anthony O. Simon, director of the Yves R. Simon Institute and son of one of the greatest philosophical writers of this century, Yves R. Simon, for granting me permission to quote from his father's classic work, *Philosophy of Democratic Government.* This timeless masterpiece is getting more recognition as time goes on, but merits to be considered among the greatest attempts to articulate a systematic philosophy of government that is both democratic and appreciative of the insights of the classical and Christian worlds. This great work accompanied me throughout the writing of this book.

Portions of this book have been published previously. Parts of chapter three were taken from my first book, *A Conscience as Large as the World: Yves R. Simon Versus the Catholic Neoconservatives.* I thank David Schindler, the editor of the English edition of *Communio: International Catholic Review,* for permission to use portions of two articles previously published in this important journal. These are: "The Death Penalty and the Ontology of the Person: The Significance of *Evangelium Vitae," Communio: International Catholic Review,* Vol. 25, No. 3 (Fall 1998): 397-413; and "Contemporary Globalization: An Anthropological and Theological Evaluation, *Communio: International Catholic Review,* Vol. 27, No. 3 (Fall 2000): 490-510.

Last but not least, I thank my wife, Rosita A. Chazarreta Rourke, who collaborated with me in the writing of chapter five. She brings the voice of that culturally rich, beautiful, yet tortured land we know as Latin America. Sadly, most North Americans, and even those who adhere to the label "multicultural," still have no idea of all that they have to learn from their brothers and sisters to the south. She taught me to reject not only economic imperialism but cultural imperialism as well. Her literary background helped me to see that much of what I wanted to say about this fragmented world is well captured by artists to the south. I also owe to her and to Latin America the awareness of how bourgeois Catholicism in the United States has become. For all of its flaws, the Latin American Catholic Church remains more authentic, paradoxically both more spiritual and more earthy.

# 1

# Introduction:
# Personalism and Political Theory

The twentieth century was the age of ideology. By any reasonable estimate, it surpassed all others in the numbers of people killed through political violence and economic deprivation, despite a variety of other indicators of growth and prosperity. The central ideological conflict was that between various expressions of liberal capitalism, on the one hand, and state socialism on the other. There was always more to it than that, prompting people with other political, cultural, ethnic, and religious concerns to complain that the polarizing tendencies of the conflict left them outside, ignored, or passed over. Nevertheless, as each of the ideologies was represented by a superpower with enough weapons to wipe out all life on the planet, and each of these was determined to exercise its influence around the world, other concerns were forced to play secondary or tertiary roles in the central drama of the century. Beginning in the year 1989, and playing out over the next couple of years, the state socialist or Marxist ideology dramatically collapsed, done in largely by its own intrinsic flaws which finally made it insupportable, even to those in charge of leading it. In truth, the ideology supporting the former Soviet Union and Eastern Europe had died long before. Thus, at the dawn of the new century, capitalism had clearly won. In the decades of the 1950s through the 1980s, a disturbingly large number of the regimes promoting capitalism outside of the developed world were authoritarian, even militaristic regimes, prompting many to ponder the connection between capitalism as a global system and these "national-security states." However, by the end of the century, one of the most frequently cited positive signs was the disappearance of military regimes not subject to popular vote. Some even began to speak of "an end of history," suggesting that liberal democracy accompanied by the capitalist economic order had demonstrated itself to be the superior system, with no future evolution necessary or to be expected.

In attenuated form, such views are prevalent, appealing as they do to the politically significant elites in the developed world. However, once one leaves the halls of the prosperous in the developed world, a radically different picture emerges. A euphemism of convenience developed decades ago according to which most of the people on the planet were held to live in—something called "the developing world." The term was and remains a convenient one, embodying liberalism's selective sensibilities to cease offending potential allies in Latin America, the Middle East, Africa, and Asia. "Developing" sounds nonprejudicial and avoids the more disparaging implications of "Third World," "undeveloped," or just plain "poverty-stricken." Nevertheless, however enlightened it makes elites in wealthy nations feel to use it, the term masks the reality that many of those to whom the term applies are insolvent nations, in various forms of receivership to foreign creditors, with economies characterized by depression levels of unemployment and unprecedented numbers of people living in the most desperate poverty. True, most of the military governors have returned to their barracks, and elections are held on a more regular basis than ever before. Below the surface, however, there is little in the way of substantive democracy, by which I mean to say government of the people, by the people, and for the people. The transitions to "democracy" were rigged from the start to insure that there would be no more than marginal debate over many of the most important issues, particularly economic ones. Regardless of who runs, wins, or loses, the state will continue to manage the private and public debt by obeying the dictates of foreign creditors, with much of the actual management done by foreign bankers and economists elected by no one. The nations will encourage foreign investors by offering a wide range of public favors, including promises of low wages, agreements to suppress organized labor, tax breaks, subsidies, and a variety of exemptions from the law not granted to domestic producers. The folding of domestic enterprises and smaller businesses will be ignored, as will the structural unemployment that results. The public sector will remain largely gutted, as educational, health, and basic security decline. Illiteracy increases along with "poor man's diseases" such as cholera and viral hepatitis. Most of the major cities are riddled by increasing levels of violent crime. A distressingly large number of people will migrate, legally or illegally, and not only the poorest and most desperate. The young in large numbers seek to abandon their nations of origin. Indeed, a close look at these nations—beyond the bits and pieces seen by most tourists, foreign journalists, and academics—prompts the question, "If these nations are developing, what exactly are they developing into?" To label these regimes "democratic" is an insult not only to Jefferson and Lincoln, but to Aristotle and any serious philosopher of democracy. The desire to put a positive spin on this part of the world by calling it "developing," "democratic," or "emerging," is driven by the fact that the region poses fewer problems for the world's political and global managers than in previous decades, when economic nationalism and armed violence posed serious threats to their designs. Even the debt problem which threatened the stability of the global financial system twenty years ago is no longer termed a crisis, as the exposure of the banks has been reduced by debt-equity swaps. None of this, of course, means that conditions for people living within these nations have gotten better; *the crisis is in fact worse today than it was twenty years ago for the people actually living in these nations.* But, unless they happen to be terrorists, these are not the people who matter to international political and economic leaders; nor do they matter much to their own national leaders except on election day and as potential sources of disruption of their plans to integrate their nations into the global political economy, come what may.

This latter point was driven home in a rather poignant way within the last couple of years during which time I had the dual opportunity to write on the topic of the theology of liberation and to interview one of the original members of the Movement of Third World Priests which supported the movement, Father Amado Dip, of San Miguel de Tucumán, Argentina. After he explained to me that poverty in Argentina was worse than ever, far worse than during all those years of passionate ferment, I asked him about the movement. He indicated that there was essentially nothing left of it anywhere in Argentina. During the era of organization and popular uprising, conditions were considerably better than they are today when poverty grows rampant in the absence of any substantive resistance or movement for social change.

The crisis is by no means one which pertains to poor nations alone. Beyond the self-serving rhetoric of political and economic leaders, and a patriotism rooted far more in militarism than in local community development, clear signs of malaise exist in the wealthier nations as well. Although one could say that cynicism about politics and politicians is a part of the political tradition of the United States, my own experience teaching political science to undergraduates for the past thirteen years inclines me to agree with the observation that William Greider made a decade ago—that most Americans simply accept the fact that what we call our "democracy" does not literally mean a government of the people, by the people, and for the people. They accept as normal what Jefferson and Lincoln would have abhorred: a largely indifferent majority; a citizenry generally ignorant of politics and uninclined to participate in anything beyond voting; the widespread acceptance of concealing the truth as normal behavior for political leaders; and the acceptance of money as frequently the determining factor in politics. A majority of students accept the morally cynical, Machiavellian caricature of politics as an affair of power and double-dealing, and consider many of the ideals of Madison, Jefferson, and Lincoln—particularly participatory government, the need for virtue, and government by the people—as laudable remnants of days gone by, not models for today. The citizens of the United States have grown to accept the daily bombardment of news about the stock market as an important indicator of economic well being, although 60 percent of them have no money in that market. Many lament the loss of trillions of dollars in investments in the stock market in recent years, but relatively few question the wisdom of so much money invested there in the first place. Like the "free market," the stock market is one of the dogmas we are now supposed to believe in, part of a new repository of faith in a society which thoughtlessly accepts dogmas in the economic world, but not in the religious. The citizens of the United States today accept and will that their nation is strong and powerful in the world, able to impose its will on others, even if that might be against the will of the people of another nation. Departures from our stated principles, as in supporting big business over democracy, occasion only limited resistance. Most citizens see no contradiction between believing their nation is great while acknowledging that most of the nation's communities languish economically and culturally. They fully expect that trend to continue. They accept that most of the younger generation in most of the country's small towns will grow up to leave home, and consider where they came from an undesirable place to live. None of these trends matter as the sense of what constitutes the nation is increasingly embodied in political, economic, and cultural centers which are the only places that really matter. Finally, the United States is engulfed in a moral and cultural crisis which shows no signs of abating. Family breakup is normal. The educational system forms the majority of young people to accept the regnant ideology of tolerance which is essentially to go through life in the absence of strong moral convictions of the kind most likely to support the foundations of any healthy society—such as love of neighbor, self-sacrifice, self-discipline, and sexual restraint for the unmarried—and to be hostile toward those who reject this facile consensus. A frightful indifference to the foundations of our civilization and the requirements for maintaining it prevails, as though somehow civilization were a given. In the popularized understanding, our civilization is defined mostly by the term "democracy," the definition of which is largely reduced to rights. Rights themselves are increasingly indistinguishable from deeply felt desires. Students are taught to learn their rights and assert them, but broader formation in character is largely lacking in the schools, and increasingly so in the home. That our society might simply be unable to sustain in the long run the broader, unprecedented assault on morality and culture promoted by the global cultural industries is a thought occurring to relatively few.

The perception is more often of a malaise than a crisis because the prevailing intellectual milieu provides no integrated vision to link our obvious problems to their common sources in our spirits. We are accustomed to think of burgeoning public and private debt, divorce and family breakup, the AIDS epidemic, drug abuse, abortion, abandoned children, violent crime, dishonest politicians, and a host of other ills as isolated problems. We subject them to "policy analysis," which only encourages us to divorce the problems from their common roots in our own minds and hearts. Ironically, as we become more cynical about politics, we tend more and more to seek solutions to our character problems in political and social programs. We solve none of the disorders because we increasingly lack a public language of character and morality within which to properly identify such problems and propose solutions. Those who insist that there are no political solutions to such problems and that what we need is to change our ways are often thought of as intolerant, judgmental people, obstacles to the reconstructed definition of democracy as tolerance without formation in an objective sense of morality.

None of the ideologies which purport to diagnose and treat these symptoms is capable of doing so, and the inadequacies are increasingly glaring. For the purposes of classification, we can call the mainstream of conservatism in the United States neoclassical liberalism. Adherents to this point of view see the limitations of political approaches to our character problems and the corresponding social disorders. They realize that authentic love of neighbor and social solidarity are not the result of any government program. Some of those who are beholden to it recognize the depth of the moral problems. They rightly emphasize individual responsibility. However, in their individualism lies also their downfall. They fail to see the depth of the need for human solidarity and the ways the individualism they applaud resists the formation of real community. They fail to see that a sense of individual responsibility is a necessary but insufficient condition for social reform. They do not make the connection between the individualism they applaud and many of the anomalies they deplore. Their worst flaw, however, is their relatively uncritical support for the liberal, capitalist economic order which is now becoming globalized. They fail to see any connections between it and the proliferating poverty, unemployment, and cultural demise. Those among them inclined to theorize arbitrarily attribute our social problems to the cultural arena, as though the latter were not deeply impacted by liberal approaches to economic organization, production, and marketing.[1] As the cultural products and lifestyles prevalent in the United States and other Western superpowers spread to areas of the world where older cultural traditions dominate, they rightly cause resentment, particularly when accompanied by the invasion of the multinational corporations, including the ubiquitous cultural industries. Herein lies one of their deepest contradictions. They lament cultural decay and support the projection of the economic and military power around the world, blithely ignoring that the two trends are mutually reinforcing. If they were consistent, they would be sympathetic to the traditional religious leaders in the Moslem world who dislike the United States for the ways it spreads its moral decadence around the world. But they are not, and encourage instead warlike attitudes against people whose complaints against the economic and cultural influence of the United States are completely justified. They render themselves incapable of leading the world to a better future.

On the other side, the contending factions are led by various forms of modern liberalism and the remnants of socialism. As among conservatives, the adherents of these ideologies have their significant disagreements. Some of them have largely gone over to the other side on any number of issues. For example, on economic matters and with respect to the projection of American power around the globe, many contemporary Democrats are indistinguishable from self-proclaimed conservatives. Those who remain true to their ideology turn to the state to solve our abundant social disorders, impervious to the evidence that their approaches do not and will never work. For example, they seem never to realize that state-sponsored peddling of contraceptives, abortion, and sex education independent of moral tradition is utterly destructive, nor that attempts to impose these around the world are rightfully despised by self-respecting cultures everywhere, fueling global anti-U.S. sentiment; indeed, this form of imperialism they support whole-heartedly. Nor are they willing to contemplate the widespread havoc at home wrought by the sexual revolution they defend. On economic matters, they are right to criticize the inexorable and inevitable effects of liberal capitalism, but have only ameliorative measures or expensive, state-centered approaches to recommend as alternatives. Their worst flaw has become their uncritical acceptance of those who seek to reform the West by undermining its moral and cultural foundations, particularly in the area of the family and sexual ethics. That society may not be able to survive the destruction of its foundations in these key areas is a thought which apparently does not concern them.

### Enter the Person

The failures of contemporary political ideologies and political parties lie not ultimately in their proposals to organize the political, economic, and social orders. Although these suggestions are indeed misguided, the roots of the problem lie beneath politics in anthropology. The philosophical constructions which have been guiding us are all ultimately rooted in inadequate conceptions of what it means to be a person. The concept of person arose in a specifically theological context in Western social thought, as something required to explain the mysteries of the Trinity and the identity of Jesus Christ. As we will see in chapter two, "person" is a rich notion which reveals the depths of the interiority of the human being. The person as conceived in the light of theological anthropology is one who is an autonomous center of responsible activity, yet is relational to his very core, oriented to the most profound solidarity with others. The person so conceived is also a creature of reason as well as faith, exercising reason in the context of a broader framework of understanding in which reason is an important part but not the whole. This concept of person was in varying degrees introduced into and exercised influence over the emerging Western social and political thought through the Middle Ages and into the Renaissance. As the specific influence of theological tradition progressively waned as a result of the Enlightenment and the ensuing secularization of Western political thought, the person receded in significance. Although in specifically theological contexts it remained common to think in terms of the human person as an "image of the Trinity," created in the image and likeness of God, the full import of the theological concept of person was becoming lost in Western thought at precisely the time it was most needed to provide rich and sound approaches to rights, democracy, property, labor, and capital. What survived was the thinner, more secularized and abstract creature we have come to call the "individual." Of course, it was recognized by modern thinkers such as Kant, Hobbes, Locke, Rousseau, and Marx that these individuals had to coexist, congealing into social orders subject to moral and organizational principles. Nevertheless, in isolation from the concept of person, modern thought has never been able to hold together the various dimensions of the person. It is as though the person were fractured, various parts gathered up by different schools of modern thought, none of which possessed the whole. Therefore, the modern ideologies would attempt to understand the parts apart from the whole. Notions dependent on the person—such as individual rights, solidarity, authority, reason, and faith—perdured, but in truncated or distorted forms; parts disconnected from their integrating principle came to be interpreted in diverse and mutually contradictory ways. Elements of truth remained, strong enough to transform the ideologies into fighting faiths, but never strong enough to prompt reconsideration of what was wrong. Some promoted the individual in opposition to the collectivity; others chose the opposite. Some promoted authority as a unifying principle of the state; others wanted to dissolve the state altogether. Some fought for the prosperity of the one (the state); others for the many (the individuals). Some fought for a reason conceived in opposition to faith; others defended faith in opposition to reason. And on and on it went and continues to go.

Immediately after the devastation of the First World War, a body of thought began to emerge from a Paris group which recognized the depth of the crisis and the challenges facing the modern world. The movement was called personalism, and its principal exponent was a Frenchman named Emmanuel Mounier.[2] The personalist movement arose to challenge what it saw as the root causes of the crisis of modernity, at the center of which was the profound dehumanization—or better, depersonalization—which was taking place. The social order was dominated by economic and political megaprocesses and megastructures based on ways of thinking which abstracted from the person. To make matters worse, the modern ideologies of individualism, capitalism, communism, and fascism argued over the processes and structures, without ever addressing the deeper root of the problem in depersonalization. Mounier and the personalists also lamented the intellectual abstraction and closed philosophical systems which were regnant in the modern world. The personalists believed that a revolution of sorts was necessary, against capitalism and state socialism, liberal democracy, the bourgeois spirit, and nationalism. The person had to be reinserted into the center of history.

A central tenet of personalism was that it could never be a closed system. This accounts for the radically unsystematic character of Mounier's writings. There was more to this than idiosyncrasy. Mounier held that a person cannot be known from the outside in the manner of an object. As the inwardness of the person was inexhaustible, he could never be fully known even from within the depths of his own subjectivity, nor was this viewed as a problem to be solved. The goal, therefore, was not to construct a closed philosophical edifice in which the concept of person could be housed. For Mounier, a person was a living center of creative activity, communication, and commitment who comes to know himself across the bridge of action. Free, creative, and acting persons were to unite with others to create a society in which the structures, customs, and institutions are rooted in and revolve around the person as center.

A pure philosophical rationalism cannot grasp the phenomenon of person, as the latter unites what rationalism has divided. At the core of the personalist philosophy lies a double movement which rationalism will always fail to comprehend. On the one hand, personalism insisted on the person as an absolute whose nature could not be impinged upon in any way. As will be explained in chapter two, the entire created common good must serve the person, and under no pretext can personhood itself be violated in the name of the collective good. On the other hand, the concept of person called for the most profound solidarity, drawing all people together as one by the most deep and lasting bonds within themselves, a universal union of people transcending all conventional boundaries. It was only the notion of the person as rooted in the transcendent which held these poles together. Modern rationalism, for all of its empirical and logical sophistication, was unable to see into the depths of the person, where the poles of individualism and solidarity are forever united.

Five dispositions are central.[3] First, there must be a going out from the self, a self-dispossession by which the person "decentralizes [himself] in order to become available for others." This "ascetic of self-dispossession is the central ascetic of personal life."[4] Second, there is the demand to understand; that is, "ceasing to see myself from my own point of view, and looking at myself from the standpoint of others."[5] It is, moreover, a willingness to accept the singularity of others. Third, one must take upon oneself and share "the destiny, the troubles, the joy or the task of another; taking him 'upon one's heart.'"[6] Fourth, a person is one who gives, and this conditions the entire realm of economics. Mounier wrote, "The economic of personality is an economic of donation, not of compensation nor of calculation. Generosity . . . disarms refusal by offering to another what is of eminent value in his own estimation, at the very moment when he might expect to be over-ridden as an obstacle."[7] Generosity breaks down barriers and builds solidarity. Fifth, a person must be faithful, love being perfected only in continuity. Therefore, the love by which I give myself to another must be perpetually renewed. The personalist "program" was perhaps summed up best by Mounier when he wrote, "I love, therefore I am."[8]

Concerning economic organization, Mounier argued that capitalism needed to be replaced by socialist forms of organization that were not centered in the state, but the result of personalist initiatives that would develop within capitalism itself. For Mounier, a just economy would do the following: eliminate the proletarian condition, supersede profit, socialize industries most responsible for economic chaos, have an extensive series of cooperatives, rehabilitate labor by allowing workers to exercise personal responsibility in the workplace, and recognize the priority of labor over capital. On political matters, Mounier argued for statutory recognition of the person in law, constitutional limitations on the power of the state, a balance between national authority and local forms of government, rights of appeal, habeas corpus, limitations on police power, and independence of the judicial authority.

As personalism was a philosophy emphasizing action, four dimensions were crucial. First, in the act of making, or economic action, the person must find his dignity, an experience of solidarity with others, and a fulfillment transcending utility. This was accompanied by a strong warning against ushering in the age of technocrats who operate under the illusion that no more is involved than the fulfillment of objective laws.[9] Second, action should be judged not primarily by external factors but by the action's authenticity, the way it is being done, and its transformation of the acting person. The means even to a good end can never degrade the person. In language prefiguring John Paul II's *Laborem Exercens* more than thirty years later, Mounier wrote:

> From the moment that a man appears, his presence affects the entire situation. He alters it by the very quality of his presence. Material means themselves become human means, living factors in a human life which they modify, but by which they are modified in their turn, and the person integrates this interaction in the whole process of which it is a part.[10]

Third, action must be contemplative; that is, an incarnation of values, an aiming toward perfection and universality through the medium of finite and particular actions. Contemplative activity has two characteristics in opposition to mere pragmatism. First, it engages in activities that transcend immediate use-value. Secondly, contemplative activity is at other times prophetic, aiming directly to disrupt the current practice.[11] The final characteristic of activity is collective, a drawing together of people that relieves them of their loneliness and unites them in the highest pursuits. It is the failure of the modern world to properly treat individual loneliness and alienation that accounts for the appeal of communism and fascism.[12]

Personalism was a radical engagement with the problems of the day. In the pages of *Esprit* throughout the 1930s and 1940s were spirited criticisms of liberalism, capitalism, communism, and nationalism. Mounier inclined to pacifism, but was careful to disassociate himself from any vague idealism or moral purity that is no more than "[f]ussy counsels of perfection [that] commonly go with a lofty narcissism egocentrically preoccupied with an individual integrity cut off from the collective drama." At worst such attitudes "may dress up pusillanimity."[13] For Mounier, evil was real, indeed personal,[14] and could not be eliminated without firm decisions. He rejected Francoism, urging a neutral stance in the Spanish Civil War. Moreover, he derided France's imperialism moves in Indo-China.

Personalism was deeply Christian in inspiration. Mounier was a deeply committed Catholic, but for two reasons this disposition was not always ostensible. First, he had a profound respect for freedom of conscience, and never wished to impose his theological convictions; nor did he wish to exclude non-Catholics or even non-Christians from personalism. Second, he was deeply disappointed by his fellow Christians. He saw in them much of the explanation for why people had abandoned the Church. He was both incensed and dismayed by French Catholics in the face of Nazism and the Vichy regime. To him, the bourgeois spirit prevailed within the Church; faith, hope, and charity giving way to an ethic of "security, economy, [and] ambition." Bourgeois Christianity is one of hearts "circumspect and cautious." Bourgeois Christians are possessed by their goods, Mounier believed, devoted to their personal well-being largely defined by material comforts, and committed to nothing else. Such Christians would never lay down their lives for God or for their neighbor.[15] Although never rejecting the Church as an institution, he would always distinguish the Christianity of the Gospel and the saints from the predominant practice of the faith in his time.

The faith provided personalism with its central concept, the person, in its dual role as: (a) society's integrating principle, the absolute center around which society and all its institutions were to be organized and which served as the standard by which the latter were to be judged; and (b) the basis for proclaiming the absolute universality and solidarity among all peoples. Christianity's assertion of persons in God gave the human person, conceived as the image and likeness of God, his identity and dignity. This dignity was deepened by the doctrine of the Incarnation which proclaimed that human nature was concretely united to the Divine Person of Christ. Moreover, Christian faith is the heart of the personalist approach to action, the call to change the heart of our hearts, to undergo *metanoia* in the biblical sense of the term.[16] The person becomes a member of the kingdom, called to go forth to bring this kingdom everywhere. Finally, a decidedly Christian sense informs personalism's understanding of freedom as taking on responsibility for others. Moreover, Jacques Maritain was a member of the Paris circles in which personalism originated. His important work on the ontology of the person and the common good brought the traditional soundness of Thomism to the movement. Other Christian influences included Kierkegaard, who rejected the impersonalism and rationalist abstraction of Hegel. Mounier adopted Kierkegaard's insistence on the subjectivity of the person, his irreducible liberty before God, and his irreplaceable role as the subject of history.[17]

From non-Christian writers, personalism drew particularly on Maine de Biran, the nineteenth century French philosopher who denounced the mechanical mentality of the ideologues and the attempt on the part of modern philosophy to resolve human existence into the categories of thought. On the contrary, Maine de Biran contended that our true selves are discovered in our actions, through which we also discover our real relationship with the exterior and objective world. Other influences included Max Scheler and Karl Jaspers.[18]

Personalism was made known to a broader audience in the United States through the Catholic Worker movement, founded by Dorothy Day and Peter Maurin in 1933, a year after the founding of *Esprit*. Peter Maurin was himself a Frenchman familiar with the personalist current of thought. The "program" he proposed for the Catholic Worker movement was decidedly personalist in nature. He would frequently refer to articles published in *Esprit* in his own teachings. Maritain's closeness to both the personalist and Catholic Worker movements deepened the connection. The radicalism of the Catholic Worker was personalist, with the insistence, as Dorothy Day would frequently say, that love, and ever more love, was the solution to the problems the world faced. The Catholic Worker always insisted that we should take personal responsibility for the poor. Each home, thought Day and Maurin, should have an extra room, and every local parish a home to care for the destitute. The movement was always primarily associated with its establishment of soup kitchens and homes for the destitute. Maurin contributed the idea of the need for a return to the land, to establish "agronomic institutions," agrarian cooperative communities of farm and school combined, "where scholars can be workers and workers scholars."[19] Finally, there was to be a newspaper to disseminate the movement's perspective, and "roundtable discussions for the clarification of thought," a Maurin expression referring to weekly meetings in which the issues of the day were discussed, open to all who wished to come.

Personalism has also been predicated of the "Lublin School" in Poland, the most notable member of which was Karol Wojtyla, who became Pope John Paul II in 1978. Wojtyla sought to develop an ontology of the person with a particular focus on the person as concrete, existential, and acting, synthesizing Aristotelian-Thomist insights with those of phenomenology. His most important philosophical work expressing this orientation is *The Acting Person,* in which he gives a phenomenological description of the fundamental structures of the experience of the acting person.[20] Wojtyla emphasizes that all dimensions of human experience and action presuppose the underlying unity of the person over time, a unity unsustained by empirical and postmodern approaches. The acting person is characterized first of all by self-possession, by which he knows that he is the author of his own actions, a center of activity. Second, the person is self-governing, one who imposes order on his actions. This includes, in addition to traditional notions of self-control, making life-orienting decisions. Third, the person in action is self-determining. There is an irreducible subjectivity, even incommunicability, in human actions. Through acts, the person forms himself; he becomes objectified in his actions. Fourth, the capacity of the person to distinguish good from evil "presupposes the will's specific relation to truth." This reference of the will to truth is "an essential condition of choice and of the ability to make a choice as such." Moreover, it is this inherent orientation to truth that reveals the person's transcendence, or what Wojtyla calls "vertical transcendence." The person transcends his circumstances, all objects of his volition, and even the culture he lives in, when and only when he is grounded in the truth of moral goodness. "It is the essential surrender of the will to truth," he writes, "that seems finally to account for the person's transcendence in action."[21] In addition, there is a corresponding pole of integration which provides the substantial unity of the entire structure of self-possession, self-governance, self-determination, and transcendence. Faithful to the demands of each, the person forms himself into a free and responsible actor. Throughout, Wojtyla is aware that the person lives not in isolation, but as a person-with-others. The person develops precisely in relation to other persons, forming associations characterized by common goods which are never reducible to a mere sum of individual goods. People join in solidarity to attain common goods, with the common good always at the service of the person. The social order should never coerce people in a way that disrespects the nature of human freedom; this includes respecting the person's need for transcendence and integration, as well as the social forms which promote such needs.

In his work as a bishop, and after becoming Pope John Paul II in 1978, Wojtyla continued to bring his insights into the human person to bear upon a number of questions, including those of the social order. For example, his repeated endorsement of religious freedom is rooted in his understanding of the nature of the acting person. Possessed with reason and free will, the person seeks vertical transcendence when he seeks to know the truth and act in accord with it. To interfere arbitrarily with this search for the truth or to prevent one from acting on the demands of conscience is to deny people their right to responsible person-hood. Moreover, John Paul II has greatly advanced thinking about economics from a personalist perspective, most notably in an entire encyclical letter devoted to human work: *Laborem Exercens*. Here he insists that man must realize his humanity in and through his work. Work must be organized such that man experiences himself as the one who exercises dominion over things. When speaking of dominion, he is careful to emphasize that he is referring to the subjective dimension of work; that is, work as an exercise of the intellect and will of the worker, work as experienced by workers. The source of dignity of work is found primarily in this subjective dimension. The basis for determining the value of the work is the fact that the one doing it is a person. To treat human work as one force in the production process is to reverse the order of the Book of Genesis which mandates that the person exercise dominion. Moreover, he also reasserts strongly the priority of labor over capital. Capital itself is no more than the result of previous human labor, and can never be set up as something separate from human work, for the only legitimate title to the possession of capital is its service of labor and the fulfillment of genuine human needs. To consider labor primarily according to its objective purposes, as in state socialism and liberal capitalism, is to commit the error he terms "economism." In a subsequent encyclical, *Centesimus Annus*, John Paul II extends personalism to the entire society, insisting that modern societies respect the subject character of all social organization.

### Purpose and Approach of this Study

This work intends to present a theory of personalism in continuity with the historical movement that bears its name, keeping in mind the teachings and practice of important figures such as Emmanuel Mounier, Dorothy Day, Peter Maurin, and Jacques Maritain. Acknowledging the timeless contributions of these foundational figures, this work nonetheless is no mere attempt to paraphrase them. The theory presented here breaks new ground in three ways. First, while avoiding any pretense of comprehensiveness or closure, it does attempt to systematize personalism as a political and economic theory grounded in a sound philosophical anthropology which also provides the foundations of sound culture. This will be accomplished by laying out an ontology of the person which provides the metaphysical and ethical foundations for the ensuing discussion of the elements of social order. Second, this work presents personalism as a theory for the particular times in which we live; albeit under influences similar to those of Mounier's time, the contemporary period presents distinct challenges at both theoretical and practical levels. For instance, personalism must respond to globalization, multiculturalism, and philosophies of morality and culture characterized by radical subjectivism. Third, and very much in accord with the spirit of Mounier, this work imports insights from other thinkers who, although never identifying themselves as personalists, have a great deal to add to personalist reflection on the political and economic orders. Among these are Francisco Suárez and Robert Bellarmine, who were instrumental in the development of the doctrine of popular sovereignty which here will be linked with personalism. Moreover, although neither of them ever advocated the actual practice of direct democracy, the theory they articulated opens the door to it. Later, from a different starting point, Thomas Jefferson would explicitly recommend the practice. This work will argue that practices of direct democracy are essential to personalism. In addition, the great Thomist philosopher Yves R. Simon will be cited throughout this work. Ironically, he will be referred to more often than Jacques Maritain, who was in fact a part of the Paris circles out of which the movement grew. Although Simon never identified himself as a personalist, and clearly did not share the pacifist leanings of the movement, his treatment of the concept of person reveals a definite affinity with personalism in that he recognized the need to distinguish between the person and the individual. Moreover, throughout his classic work, *Philosophy of Democratic Government,* and elsewhere, Simon evinces a deep concern for promoting the dignity of the person, and, like Mounier and Dorothy Day, is aware of the long distance modern democracy and modern capitalism have yet to travel to attain this end. Another contemporary author with insights supporting personalism is agrarian writer Wendell Berry. It is no coincidence that thinkers as diverse as Berry, Simon, Thomas Jefferson, G.K. Chesterton, and the Catholic Worker founders all believe that there is a connection between agrarian life and a substantive democracy. These arguments are here taken seriously. Moreover, personalism has much to gain by considering the work of Louis Kelso and Norman Kurland of the Center for Economic and Social Justice.[22] Their proposals to reform capitalism through employee stock ownership programs and to use the credit system to promote broader ownership of the industrial base are ingenious and have been unjustly ignored and ridiculed by mainstream economists. Finally, some contemporary Latin American theologians associated with the theology of liberation, most notably Gustavo Gutiérrez, have recognized the value of popular, culture-specific religiosity in preserving the autonomy of peoples and cultures in an age threatened by the imposition of uniformity. For this reason, popular religiosity properly conceived needs to be integrated into personalism.

Any attempt to speak of a "theory of personalism" must address the fact that Mounier himself resisted systematization and generally spoke negatively of it as something against which personalism needed to contend. It is surely the case that to make of personalism one more academic political theory would indeed undermine the core ideal of the movement. Equally destructive would be to shift attention away from bringing personal love to the center of our social order. While recognizing these dangers, I contend that personalism, while never neglecting the primacy of action, needs to articulate itself in a more comprehensive and systematic way than in the past. This is so because personalists are indeed concerned with the implications of what it means to be a person for all dimensions of social life; they want to leave nothing out. Yet, if personalists wish to transform the social order, they need to explain in a clear and systematic way what a person is, and then proceed to make the connections between personhood and the social order. These connections are best made when the links are drawn in a consistent and orderly way.

Over and above any attempt to apologize for presenting a theory of personalism are two other considerations. First, Mounier's primary worry was not systematic thought itself. If it were, he would have rejected Saint Thomas Aquinas, which he surely did not. What he did reject was the temptation that any systematic work must face, and that is to construct a system that is *closed* in three senses: (a) closed to new insights that, experienced over time, may serve to reveal and illuminate; (b) rigid and unyielding with respect to working out the implications of the fundamental principles; and (c) reducing personalism to a theory rather than a call to action. These are among the most common errors in modern thought, particularly in the ideologies of left and right, and Mounier went out of his way to avoid them. Second, it must be said that there is nothing inherently wrong with systematic thought. If you are trying to change the world and articulate alternatives, there is a need to explain oneself. Mounier seems to have recognized this in his own attempts to articulate the meaning of personalism. Moreover, with respect to the relationship between theory and action, there is something to be learned from the debates concerning orthodoxy and orthopraxis which characterized the liberation theology movement.[23] Aside from the issue of whether or not liberation theologians breathed Marxist analysis into the meaning of orthopraxis, the truth is that every intentional action worthy of a human being aims at some end or purpose. Moreover, this specific end is related to other ends. The mature person is aware of both immediate and long-term goals. These are worthy only so long as they reflect goodness and truth. Hence, all intentional human action is at least implicitly based on an ontology, some overall vision of what is true and good. To explore this dimension, to make the ontology of the person thematic, and to attempt to work out the implications for a social order is no violation of personalism so long as it is sensitive to history and experience.

A fine line must be drawn between a theory which is too abstract and general to point in any specific direction, and one which descends to such a degree of detail that it makes personalism into a definitive program along the lines of an ideology. I concur with the traditional judgment that personalism cannot be reduced to a program, and that to do so would be to transform it into exactly the kind of impervious ideological system the movement was created to resist. In this book, I will go so far as to argue that personalism implies a definite political and economic direction, and I will explore some viable and concrete ways such a direction might be pursued. Nonetheless, the intention is also to avoid trying to prove too much, to leave open many of the details to the lessons of what will hopefully be the future experience of building a personalist society. My research and reflection incline me to concur strongly that personalism *as a theory* can only influence public policy from a distance; the specifics are so inherently matters of practical judgment related to multiple historical contingencies that they cannot be predetermined by any theory.

This work will draw on insights derived from the Christian tradition and philosophy. For this reason, it is important to address briefly the relationship between philosophy and Christian Revelation underlying this work. First, there is surely a distinction to be made between philosophy and theology, corresponding to the distinction between faith and reason. Philosophy strictly speaking examines questions in the light of reason; faith supplements reason by drawing on revealed principles unavailable to reason alone. The distinction, however, is not correctly understood to imply that it is best for philosophy to ignore theology. Rather, as written by John Paul II, there is an "indissoluble unity between the knowledge of reason and the knowledge of faith."[24] Moreover, as Etienne Gilson argues, "by passing along the road of revelation, reason sees truths which it might otherwise have overlooked."[25] The fact that Revelation opens up vistas for reason does not render what is seen any less real, true, or reasonable. It so happens that in the case of the concept of person, philosophy was driven by and informed by theological insights all along the way. That the concept of person came to be understood in the way it did is not properly separable from Revelation. We have here a splendid example of how Revelation improved the state of philosophical inquiry. Moreover, it is no coincidence that the decline of the centrality of the person in more recent philosophical inquiry is associated with the absence of the influence of Revelation. In addition, whenever we are speaking of politics as a practical discipline, that is, as a proximate guide to action, then any purely rational philosophy is essentially misleading. Even a Thomist most concerned to preserve the integrity of philosophy concedes this.[26] This is because, in matters of actual choice, one who accepts Revelation must act in light of his last end which he knows via Revelation; he cannot as a practical matter prescind from this knowledge. Hence, as practical disciplines, moral and political philosophy rightly borrow from moral theology. In light of these considerations, this work will be rooted in the concept of person as it appears in the theological context from which it came to us historically. The precise political and economic implications, however, will be developed along the lines of political theory and political economy.

Some will find both the direction of this work and the specific proposals it makes "unrealistic." If by unrealistic one means that, given the current alignments of political and economic power, political and economic systems are unlikely to evolve along the lines I suggest, then the charge has some merit. It is, nonetheless, intellectually and morally demeaning to expect people of conscience to accept the given conglomeration of power as a given. To write of democracy in

Stalinist Russia or Hitler's Germany would have been similarly unrealistic according to these Machiavellian criteria. It is the task of political philosophy to diagnose the errors of one's time and to propose a vision which is realistic in the sense that it conforms more to human dignity than the present order, and that history has demonstrated much of it to be possible. What is lacking is the will to do it, and this work hopes to provide some of the necessary motivation. Swept along by macroeconomic and political processes, contemporary humanity has perhaps never been more enthralled by the myth of historical inevitability that tells us that we must simply accept the forces of globalization, centralization, and uniformity. The truth is that such beliefs are no more than rationalizations of injustice mixed with profound despair. The traditional democratic belief is that the future is largely what we decide to make of it. All claims to the contrary are acts of cowardice by which we hand power over to those wealthy and powerful interests who want to make the future for us and who have a vested interest in our passive conformity. It is the heart and soul of personalism to remind us of these truths which so desperately need to be repeated in our time.

One school of thought which will largely be absent from this book is that which has named itself economic personalism. This school of thought originated in the 1980s when a group of Christian social ethicists sought dialog with free-market economic theorists to the end of integrating free-market economic theory with Christian social thought.[27] The economic personalists wish in one sense to broaden economic discussion by introducing deeper dimensions of praxeology, axiology, and anthropology. This is laudable. Moreover, they are particularly interested in bringing John Paul II's philosophical work on the acting person into the discussion, comparing it with the corresponding theory of economist Ludwig von Mises. This, too, is commendable. The economic personalists concede that free-market economic theory is fundamentally off base when it claims to be value-free when it is in fact value-laden. Moreover, they desire to nudge economic theory away from its utilitarian and materialistic trends, and emphasize that economic analysis itself is frequently an inadequate basis upon which to make decisions.

Despite these worthy goals, economic personalism is fundamentally at odds with the personalist movement as it was articulated by the historically existing movement as outlined above. Their use of the same term to describe a radically different way of thinking can be confusing, so I will attempt to clarify the divergencies here. The biggest and most obvious difference is that historical personalism embodied a radical critique of modern capitalism precisely because of the latter's acceptance of the predominance of nonpersonal factors such as the market and the predominance of technique. This is best summed up in a phrase frequently used by Father Robert Sirico to protect modern economic thought from moral critique: "Piety is no replacement for technique," which implies that "we must always work for moral objectives within the context of market realities."[28] A more radical rejection of personalism would be difficult to formulate. Mounier's position was clearly the opposite; the market or any other system must serve the person. This relates to a more fundamental philosophical point which is also part and parcel of Catholic social thought, which is that economics is inherently related to the broader human good and subject to it. Hence, practically speaking, there simply can be no such thing as an economics which is a technique bereft of reference to moral ends. Second, the discussion of capitalism by the economic personalists is effectively a hypothetical one; it is the capitalism of theory which makes few references to the grave moral problems of capitalism as it actually manifests itself in the world today. Problems related to the growth of the modern corporation and concentration of ownership are not discussed; on the basis of economic personalism, one would assume that there are no fundamental differences between small businesses and Wal-Mart. Moreover, the international debt crisis, the increasingly dominant influence of corporate power over public policy, the exploitation of women and children in the labor market, are not treated as important themes related to existing capitalism. This is because the economic personalists rather arbitrarily blame the moral failures of capitalism on culture and the moral failures of individuals. Yet, Plato made it clear centuries ago in *The Republic* that the soul and the regime are related. The person is influenced strongly by the political and economic structures in which he lives. Those concerned with justice, taking into account human weakness, should try to construct structures that encourage virtuous behavior and economically just results, and eschew those which do not. When seeing problems of dehumanizing poverty and low wages, it is simplistic to assert that all the blame is reducible to individual moral choices and to refuse to consider the ways in which modern capitalism itself, precisely as an economic system, contributes to these dehumanizing results. The pro-market assumptions of the economic personalists seem to preclude explorations along these lines. Moreover, it is surely not in the traditions of Catholic social thought to engage in such reductionism.

Although the economic personalists favorably cite Pope John Paul II, the only extensive analysis they give is to his earlier philosophical work, *The Acting Person*, which does not treat economic justice. They cite John Paul II as "economic personalism's intellectual progenitor," but engage in no extensive analysis of any of his papal encyclicals related to personalism and economics.[29] What is so striking about this omission is that John Paul II articulates a well-developed philosophy of human work in *Laborem Exercens* along personalist lines. This gap in their work cries out for an explanation. The truth is that John Paul II is not making the same theoretical moves as the economic personalists. He is not abandoning traditional Catholic critiques of capitalism.[30] He self-consciously reads his own work in continuity with the rest of that tradition. He nowhere claims that the contemporary free-market solutions to global economic problems are the correct responses. Moreover, when he condemns neoliberalism, he does so precisely in its capacity as a political economy, never reducing it to simply a problem of culture.[31] Economic personalism's engagement with John Paul II's philosophy of work, economics, and political economy is so minimal precisely because the Pope's thought rejects any approach which would "integrate" morality into economics by accepting that moral concerns are to be pursued within the hegemony of the market. For John Paul II, the opposite is true: Hegemony is with morality, and it is the market that must answer to the person.

Chapter two, "The Ontology of the Person in Light of Reason and Faith," lays out the ontological foundations of the person, explaining how Christian reflection brought the phenomenon of person into view, particularly through the development of doctrine in the areas of trinitarian theology and Christology. The picture of the person emerging from this background is one who is a responsible and autonomous center of activity, yet radically bound to and related to all others. The transcendent nature of the person as created, as one who is ontologically constituted so as to receive God's eternal life within him, is ultimately what grounds and renders possible both the autonomous and solidaristic poles of his constitution. In the absence of transcendence, both autonomy and solidarity are inevitably misunderstood and defined in opposition to one another. The Pauline doctrine of tripartite anthropology, that is, man as mind, body, and spirit, helps to complete the picture. This chapter also develops some of the immediate implications of personhood for grasping the relationships between (a) faith and reason, (b) nature and grace, (c) freedom and responsibility, and (d) the person and the common good.

Chapter three, "The Person and the Political Order," works out the implications of the person for the political order. The key historical development was the development of the Jesuit doctrine of popular sovereignty, which empowered the people by making them the ultimate repositories of political authority. Hence all political authority exists only to serve the preexisting community of persons. Furthermore, it explores the nature and limits of political authority with reference to the common good of the community. Next, it takes up the issue of which regime best reflects the nature of the person, and nudges the traditional doctrine of popular sovereignty in the direction of direct democracy. Although aware that a nation cannot be so governed, the chapter argues for the importance of concrete practices of direct democracy, particularly at the local level, and the need to preserve local autonomy in government. Finally, this chapter develops the doctrine of rights, relying on the historical development of rights theory to show the necessary connection between rights and natural law, while delineating the contributions of Bartolomé de Las Casas in the development of the understanding of rights as that which protects the weak and the downtrodden in the promotion, not of a shallow egoism and individualism, but of universal solidarity among all peoples.

Chapter four, "The Person and Political Economy," takes up more specifically economic organization, particularly as it relates to the state and society. A lengthy critique of contemporary globalization comes first, noting the antipersonal developments of concentrated economic power, technological reductionism, and free trade. The economic critique is linked to a broader criticism of the way that economic globalization compromises sovereignty via a global jobs auction which sets governments against one another in a destructive competition wherein social standards for economic activity are lowered. Moreover, contrary to multicultural rhetoric, globalization will be portrayed as a scheme for a multiethnic but unicultural world wherein all values standing in the way of contemporary capitalism are marginalized or eliminated. The second part undertakes the task of laying out the principles of a personalist political economy. Of great importance here is John Paul II's articulation of the primacy of labor over capital, the need to organize work so as to emphasize the subjective dimension whereby man experiences himself as exercising his intellect and will. Also developed here is the meaning of the virtue of social justice. Finally, the chapter rearticulates the traditional argument favoring a vibrant agrarian life, both to preserve economic autonomy and to preserve the substance of democracy. The last section will set forth the case for diffusing corporate ownership as in the work of Louis Kelso and Norman Kurland.

Chapter five focuses on select topics related to the cultural basis of the personalist society. Explored first is the issue of multiculturalism as an example of the problem of the one and the many. Through the doctrine of the Incarnation, Christianity highlights in a unique way that the particular can embody the universal, yet without sterile uniformity; as all followers of Christ are "new creations" in Him, Christianity promotes and celebrates an authentic diversity of culture and personal gifts, precisely by eschewing the relativizing tendencies of contemporary multiculturalism, which glorifies a diversity in which all cultures and religions are denied universality. Along similar lines, the chapter promotes interreligious dialog that truly respects the absolute claims of the various faiths, seeking the ample moral common ground, while rejecting a "dialog" which relativizes all faiths and strips them of their essential content. The chapter insists that any personalist culture must have a hard ontological core consisting of the imperative to fulfill objective ends. It must be a culture of discipline and work, within limits determined by the good of the person. Activities of expansion and free development are also necessary to culture, reflecting man's transcendence. The latter become destructive, however, when set apart from or defined in opposition to the ontological core. Finally, we look at selected narratives that capture the reality of social fragmentation while holding out hope for the future. Of particular importance is popular religion, which can be a most powerful way of reaffirming the dignity of all persons before God.

### Notes

1. This is the characteristic flaw of the Catholic neoconservatives, including the "economic personalism" of Rev. Robert Sirico and the Acton Institute for the Study of Religion and Liberty. See Richard John Neuhaus, *Doing Well and Doing Good: The Challenge to the Christian Capitalist* (New York: Doubleday, 1992).

2. The best one-volume summary of personalism is Emmanuel Mounier, *Personalism* (Notre Dame: University of Notre Dame Press, 1952). For a briefer summary, see William Miller, *A Harsh and Dreadful Love: Dorothy Day and the Catholic Worker Movement* (New York: Liveright, 1973), 5-8. Personalism was expressed via a series of French

journals in the 1930s, such as *L'Ordre Nouveau, L'Homme Nouveau, La Revue des vivants,* and, most notably, *Esprit,* which began in 1932, edited by Mounier. *Esprit* would emerge in the postwar world as one of France's most highly acclaimed journals, after being suppressed by the Vichy government during World War II. Mounier himself would come to be recognized as a leader of his generation.

3. Emmanuel Mounier, *Personalism,* 21-25.

4. Emmanuel Mounier, *Personalism,* 21.

5. Emmanuel Mounier, *Personalism,* 21.

6. Emmanuel Mounier, *Personalism,* 21-22.

7. Emmanuel Mounier, *Personalism,* 22.

8. Emmanuel Mounier, *Personalism,* 23.

9. Emmanuel Mounier, *Personalism,* 86.

10. Emmanuel Mounier, *Personalism,* 88.

11. Emmanuel Mounier, *Personalism,* 88-89.

12. Emmanuel Mounier, *Personalism,* 90.

13. Emmanuel Mounier, *Personalism,* 92.

14. Mounier writes, "For the Christian, evil is indeed a Person, as is the Good." Emmanuel Mounier, *Personalism,* 82.

15. Rufus William Rauch, Jr., in Preface to Emmanuel Mounier, *Personalism,* xi-xii.

16. Emmanuel Mounier, *Personalism,* xxi.

17. Emmanuel Mounier, *Personalism,* 63. Mounier drew also upon the existentialism of Gabriel Marcel.

18. As personalism was never articulated as a systematic philosophy with definite boundaries, various trends and movements can be said to be "personalist" in some sense. The exploration of these is not the purpose of the present work. For a review of trends in thought that drew on the notion of person in various ways, see Stephen J. Grabill, Christopher Westley, Patricia Donohue-White, and Gloria Zúñiga, *Human Nature and the Discipline of Economics: Personalist Anthropology and Economic Methodology* (Lanham, Boulder, New York, Oxford: Lexington Books, 2002), 11-42.

19. William D. Miller, *A Harsh and Dreadful Love,* 100. This dimension of the original program was always to be the least developed. Although the original Catholic Worker house in New York established a farm—Peter Maurin farm in Staten Island, then Maryfarm in Easton, Pennsylvania—this dimension of the program did not work out well, mostly due to the lack of dedicated people with farming skills.

20. Karol Wojtyla, *The Acting Person* (Dordrecht, the Netherlands, and Boston: D. Riedel, 1979). For my interpretation of the work, I rely on Kenneth L. Schmitz, *At the Center of the Human Drama: The Philosophical Anthropology of Karol Wojtyla* (Washington, D.C., 1993), and Gregory Beabout, Richard F. Crespo, Stephen J. Grabill, Kim Paffenroth, and Kyle Swan, *Beyond Self-Interest: A Personalist Approach to Human Action* (Lanham, New York, Boulder, Oxford: Lexington Books, 2002), 37-70.

21. Karol Wojtyla, *The Acting Person,* 137-139.

22. See, for example, the classic work, Mortimer Adler and Louis Kelso, *The Capitalist Manifesto* (New York: Random House, 1958). As Adler admits, the ideas are Kelso's; Louis Kelso and Patricia Hetter, *Democracy and Economic Power: Extending the ESOP Revolution* (Lanham, Md.: University Press of America, 1991). Norman Kurland has promoted Kelso's ideas through the Center for Economic and Social Justice for three decades. For an example of his work, see Norman Kurland, *An Illustrated Guide for Statesmen: A Two-Pronged Strategy for Implementing ESOP Privatizations in a Developing or Trans-*

*forming Economy* (Arlington: Center for Economic and Social Justice, 1991); and *The Community Investment Corporation (CIC): A Vehicle for Economic and Political Empowerment of Individual Citizens at the Community Level* (Arlington: Center for Economic and Social Justice, 1992). See also William Greider, *One World: Ready or Not: The Manic Logic of Global Capitalism* (New York: Simon and Schuster, 1997), 416-443.

23. See, for example, Gustavo Gutiérrez, *A Theology of Liberation* (Maryknoll: Orbis Books, 1973), 6-15; see also Cardinal Ratzinger's critique in *Instruction on Certain Aspects of the "Theology of Liberation,"* Sections 7, "Marxist Analysis," and 8, "Subversion of the Meaning of Truth and Violence."

24. John Paul II, *Fides et Ratio,* no. 16.

25. Etienne Gilson, *The Christian Philosophy of Saint Thomas Aquinas* (South Bend: University of Notre Dame Press, 1994), 19.

26. Yves R. Simon, *Practical Knowledge,* ed. Robert J. Mulvaney (New York: Fordham University Press, 1991), 95.

27. The ensuing discussion of economic personalism is based on the three-volume series *Foundations of Economic Personalism,* of which the volumes are: Gregory R. Beabout, Ricardo F. Crespo, Stephen J. Grabill, Kim Paffenroth, and Kyle Swan, *Beyond Self-Interest: A Personalist Approach to Human Action* (Lanham, Boulder, New York, Oxford: Lexington Books, 2002); Patricia Donohue-White, Stephen J. Grabill, Christopher Westley, and Gloria Zúñiga, *Human Nature and the Discipline of Economics* (Lanham, Boulder, New York, Oxford: Lexington Books, 2002); and Anthony Santelli, Jr., Jeffrey Sikkenga, Rev. Robert Sirico, Steven Yates, and Gloria Zuniga, *The Free Person and the Free Economy: A Personalist View of Economics* (Lanham, Boulder, New York, Oxford: Lexington Books, 2002). It is possible that the critiques advanced here do not apply to other works of these authors. However, my assumption is that this three-volume work recently published is their attempt as a group to formulate the philosophy of economic personalism. Therefore, I relied on it exclusively as the basis for evaluating their thought.

28. Anthony J. Santelli, et al. *The Free Person and the Free Economy,* 20.

29. Gregory R. Beabout, et al., *Beyond Self-Interest,* 69. There are a few references to *Centesimus Annus* in these volumes, as on pages 69-70 in this volume, but never any systematic treatment. Given their attempts to portray John Paul II as a champion of the free market, this omission is glaring.

30. Similar to the Catholic neoconservatives, the economic personalists attempt to get a lot of mileage out of selected quotes from *Centesimus Annus* while ignoring others in the same encyclical and bypassing much of the rest of the tradition, most notably *Laborem Exercens.* John Paul II did say that "the free market is the most efficient instrument for utilizing resources and effectively responding to needs" (*Centesimus Annus,* no. 34). Catholics proposing a fundamental change in attitudes toward the market are of course fond of quoting this passage. However, John Paul II immediately notes two systemic problems with reference to the existing capitalism: (a) Many people do not have purchasing power to buy what they need, and (b) all resources are not marketable at a satisfactory price (*Centesimus Annus,* no. 34). These problems are in no way reducible to problems of morality and culture; they are clearly problems of the economic order as well. In *Centesimus Annus,* Pope John Paul II continues the traditional Catholic calls for a family wage, explicitly rejected by the economic personalists as inflationary in Anthony Santelli, Jr., et al. *The Free Person and the Free Economy,* 20. He also calls for social insurance for old age and unemployment, protection for conditions of employment, trade unions, and the need for more international economic regulation (*Centesimus Annus,* nos. 34, 58). He rejects the

proposition that capitalism is the only model of economic organization after the downfall of socialism (no. 35). He clearly distinguishes between two understandings of capitalism, one which protects the "free and personal nature of human work," regulating capital via society and state, and one which does not. So different is this from what we commonly call capitalism that the Pope wisely prefers another name, such as a business, market, or free economy (no. 42). The real issue, then, is not the more popular, interminable debate as to whether or not *Centesimus Annus* supports capitalism, but the extent to which capitalism as it actually exists now is in accord with the qualified form endorsed by the encyclical. The implicit argument of the economic personalists appears to be that the Pope's qualified endorsement of a market economy under carefully qualified conditions somehow amounts to an endorsement of the existing system called capitalism. This is clearly not the Pope's intention.

31. John Paul II, *The Church in America,* no. 56.

# 2

# The Ontology of the Person in Light of Reason and Faith

We begin far from politics conventionally considered by reflecting on what it means to be a person in the broadest philosophical and human sense. Here the contemporary political philosopher must confront the fact that the development of the concept of person was not only driven by theological considerations but was formulated in a specifically theological way; the need to formulate the concept and delineate its constitutive characteristics arose precisely because of problems that arose in theological reflection.[1] As Cardinal Joseph Ratzinger explains, the origin of the concept "person" is known to us today, originating in a kind of scholarly exegesis used in Antiquity.[2] The word *prosopon* (the Greek equivalent of the Latin *persona,* the root of the English "person"), simply referred to a role, as in a play. As a dramatic device, to avoid the mere narration of events, the poets of Antiquity would create roles to depict action by way of dialog. Literary scholars would bring these various roles to light, explaining the dramatic purpose of each. This kind of interpretation is known as "prosopographic exegesis." Early Christian scholars discovered something similar in Scripture, where events also develop in dialog. Moreover, at times God speaks in the plural and at other times engages in dialog with Himself.[3] The Fathers of the Church approached this textual reality through prosopographic exegesis. Thus, for example, Justin Martyr makes reference to the sacred writers introducing different *prosopa,* or roles. However, in terms of faith in the revealed Word, the roles are realities. Prosopographic exegesis thus helped to uncover the reality of the divine persons who were behind the "roles." Approached in this way, the intradivine dialog and the references to God as "us" in Scripture gave birth to the notion of "person" as a concept much deeper and richer than a mere role in the creation of a drama! It is therefore fair to conclude, as Ratzinger does, that the concept "person" arose out of a need to make sense out of Scripture.

Early Christian theological reflection inevitably had to explore two questions: "What—or better—Who is God?" and "Who is Jesus Christ"? With reference to the former, the question arose for theological reflection: "How is it possible to reconcile the assertion that God is One and possesses absolute perfection with the belief that God subsists in three persons?" If the divine persons are in some way different, how can they each possess the same absolute perfection? The answer to the problem was to define the divine persons in terms of relation. Because of the background provided by prosopographic exegesis, Tertullian, writing around the year 213, was able to give the West the formula it was to use thereafter to speak of God, *"una substantia, tres personae,"* one being in three persons. Tertullian was also the first to use both the word *trinitas* to make reference to God and the word *persona* to explain the Trinity. He declares, "I always affirm that there is one substance in three united together." The Son is other than the Father "in the sense of person, not of substance, for distinctiveness, not for division." He also applies the term *persona* to the Holy Spirit.[4] In 675, the Eleventh Council of Toledo declared that "the three persons are spoken of relatively." The Council of Florence, drawing on Saint Anselm of Canterbury, declared that, in God, "all is one, wherever no obstacle is posed by the opposition of relation." What distinguishes the divine persons from one another is relation. This is what the traditional theological expression "The divine persons are subsistent relations" intends to communicate. Moreover, this formulation solves the problem of how to assert both the absolute perfection of God and the existence of three persons in God. To be in relationship does not constitute an imperfection or a distinction in essence. Each of the three persons is absolutely perfect, the relations which distinguish them notwithstanding. What distinguishes them is no imperfection in their being, nor any division, but relation. The three persons in relation constitute a community, and this communion of persons sharing the one divine essence is God.[5]

When Christian tradition defines the divine persons as relations, it means to deny that they are substances, or self-sufficient wholes standing alongside one another. If the latter eventuality were true, then we would have three divinities in relationship. This would imply that relationship is something added on to the personhood. It is precisely this point that the Christian understanding of person denies. As Cardinal Joseph Ratzinger puts it:

> Relation, being related, is not something superadded to the person, but it *is* the person itself. In its nature, the person exists only *as* relation. Put more concretely, the first person does not generate in the sense that the act of generating a Son is added to the already complete person, but the person *is* the deed of generating, of giving itself, of streaming itself forth. The person is identical with this act of self-donation. One could thus define the first person as self-donation in fruitful knowledge and love; it is not the one who gives himself, in whom the act of self-donation is found, but it is this self-donation, pure reality of act.[6]

Of course, the concept of person when predicated of God can never simply be transposed to apply to human persons. There is an infinite unlikeness between God and man; one can never apply univocally the concept of person to God and human beings. There are three fundamental differences. First, the divine persons are radically original and they are distinguished from one another by and in their origins. Among human persons, on the other hand, origin is not the source of their respective distinctions. They have, rather, a common origin, having been brought forth through creation by God. Second, the divine persons are distinguished exclusively through relation, for the divine nature is absolutely one. Human persons, on the other hand, are distinguished from one another not only through their relations; they differ also in that each person has a separate, individual nature, concretely different from all others. Third, in God, the relations among the persons are perfect and complete, while relation in the human person is radically imperfect and in need of development.[7]

These very real differences do not imply that there are no similarities. Human persons have been created in the image and likeness of the tripersonal God. In Thomistic vocabulary, humans participate in the pure act of being, which is tripersonal, according to a limited essence. Through this participation, there is a real and true analogy, or fundamental likeness, between the being of God and that of man. Created in God's image and likeness, our personhood is a reflection of the divine persons. If, in God, the constitutive feature of person is relation, then, according to the fundamental analogy between God and man, relation also constitutes the human person. If there were no fundamental analogy between the being of God and that of man, then we really could not speak of God as divine "persons," because we would have no idea of what the word even meant. Theologically, we can speak of divine persons because the reality of person is indeed stamped within us, however imperfectly and however inadequately grasped by our intellects. As Jean Galot puts it, "The very statement of the dogma of one God in three persons implies the value of the concept of person in the designation of the divine persons, and this value rests on our experience of the person in our own life."[8]

It is important to understand that the affirmation that human persons are constitutive relations in no way denies or compromises personal autonomy. Unfortunately, the ubiquitous influence of modern liberalism has conditioned us to see constitutive relatedness and autonomy as mutually exclusive. But this is not the sense of autonomy that a Christian anthropology yields. A human person is necessarily related to all other human persons. But this is not to say that a human person is nothing but a relationship to others. The person is also a substance; it exists in itself, not as a part of another being. The human person has an abiding "center" of identity which grounds all of its relations and other attributes and which distinguishes it ultimately from all other persons and beings. Norris Clarke explains:

> For the very meaning of relation implies that it is *between* two terms
> that it is connecting, between two relateds. A relation cannot relate

nothing. Thus a relat*ed* is not simply identical with its relat*ion.* . . . No relation can be self-supporting by itself. . . . There must be an in-itself somewhere along the line to ground the betweenness. . . . This is too often forgotten by [those who] tend to stress so exclusively the person as constituted by its relations with others that the inner depth and interiority of the person tend to get swallowed up in its extroverted relationships. The inseparable complementarity between in-itself and toward-others must be maintained.[9]

Regardless of the depths of his relationships, and no matter how open he is to being influenced and changed by them, he in a way transcends all of them by his ongoing capacity to choose what the character of these relations will be. He remains a responsible center of activity, a free subject, a solid core of identity. Karl Rahner summarizes:

Being a person, then, means the self-possession of a subject as such in a conscious and free relationship to the totality of itself. This relation-ship is the condition of possibility . . . for the fact that in his individ-ual empirical experiences and in his individual sciences man has to do with himself as one and as a whole. Because man's having responsi-bility for the totality of himself is the condition of his empirical expe-rience of self, it cannot be derived completely from this experience and its objectivities. Even when man would want to shift all responsibility for himself away from himself as someone totally determined from without and this would want to explain himself away, *he* is the one who does it knowingly and willingly. *He* is the one who encompasses the sum of all the possible elements of such an explanation, and thus *he* is the one who shows himself to be something other than the subsequent product of such individual elements. . . . To say that man is person and subject, therefore, means first of all that man is someone who cannot be derived, who cannot be produced completely from other elements at our disposal. He is that being who is responsible for himself. When he explains himself, analyzes himself, reduces himself back to the plu-rality of his origins, he is affirming himself as the subject who is doing this, and in so doing he experiences himself as something necessarily prior to and more original than this plurality.[10]

To be a person, therefore, is indeed to be a self, to have a unique identity, and to be a center of responsible action. Yet, in the view of the person informed by its trinitarian roots, all of this is always-already interiorly informed by the creature's constitutive relation to God and, in God, to other creatures. There is a self, then, but there is nothing in it that is not always-already related to God and to others.

To say that it is constitutive of the human person to be related has profound implications for the way we conceive of the relationship between person and society. So fundamental is the relational dimension of the person that it is well recognized even outside of the faith context. Indeed, as Henri de Lubac notes, there is a greater comprehension in our time that a human person is not simply an individual. Psychologists, for instance, recognize how deep our need for one another is. Yet de Lubac pushes this insight beyond the psychological to the ontological: "We must be *looked at* in order to be *enlightened,* and the eyes that are 'bringers of light' are not only those of the divinity." To be a person is "fundamentally to enter upon a relationship with others so as to converge upon a Whole," not only in time but in eternity.[11]

What emerges here is a radical notion of human community as ultimately rooted in the community of persons in God. Drawing on Augustine's principle that "between the soul and God there is no intermediary," de Lubac concludes, "Each person needs the mediation of all, but no one is kept at a distance by any intermediary." Moreover:

> By this principle, which Augustine saw so clearly in the light of his faith, the neo-Platonist idea . . . is completely transformed: the hierarchic vision of the world is replaced by that of the *Civitas Dei*—a vision by no means individualistic, but how much more truly spiritual! Between its different purposes, whatever their variety of gifts, the inequality of their "merits," there obtains no scale of the degrees of being, but in the likeness of the Trinity itself . . . a unity of circumincession. . . . It is clear, then, that each person . . . does not constitute a final end, is not a positive, independent little world: God does not love us as so many separate beings—*Sociale quiddam est humana natura.*[12]

In speaking of this "social something," de Lubac goes far beyond the much more frequently heard claim that human beings are by nature social, which is often taken to mean that in their primitive structure they are first individual selves who are nonetheless disposed to enter, in a second moment, into relations with other persons and thereby form a community. No, an authentic anthropology places relation at the very core of the ontology of the person. In order to be precise ontologically, we must say that the being that grounds the substance or in-itselfness of the created person, created in the image and likeness of the trinitarian God, is simultaneously both a "being from" (from God) and a "being for or toward" (God and other persons). In other words, the substantial being, or "being in-itself" of the created person, far from excluding relationship to God and others, includes them in its fundamental ontological and anthropological structure. We are said to be created in the image and likeness of God only through Jesus Christ, Who is Himself both a "being from" and a "being for or toward." Therefore, as what is created is an image and likeness of God, the human person must also be a "being from" and a "being for or toward." To exist in oneself, to exist from God, and to exist in relationship to God and other persons, all three are structured into the very being of the human person, all three ontologically prior to any use of our free will.[13]

Although the explication of the social and political consequences of this anthropology remain to be developed, we can already see how this rich relational understanding of the person stands in contrast to and corrects the ontologically dubious, individualistic view of the person as a self-contained monad that underlies what is unique in modern political philosophy, particularly liberalism. Such ontologically thin conceptions of the person may be detected in all of the versions of modern social contract theory, Hobbes, Locke, Rousseau, or, much later, Rawls and Nozick. Glaringly absent from this modern social contract theory is the essential relatedness of human persons. Indeed, considered in the light of the notion of person that emerges from Christian theology, the individuals who inhabit "the state of nature," think behind the "veil of ignorance," and speak in "ideal speech situations" are not real persons at all, but abstractions, for, analogously to the divine persons, a human person exists only as a relation to other persons. Jean Galot concludes:

> The mystery of the Trinity stands out as the most obvious refutation of every form of individualistic personalism. It is the most compelling attestation of the communitary aspect of the person. In particular it manifests that in God the three divine persons are not constituted prior to their community, as if they each formed an entity before opening toward each other. The divine persons are constituted by their mutual relations. . . . None of the "I's" of the divine persons precedes its relation to the others. . . . It follows, therefore, that the Trinitarian community is not subsequent to the persons; it has coexisted from all eternity with the three divine persons. The same holds true of human persons. They do not first exist each in their selfness, and then later enter into relations with other persons to form a community with them. Community and person exist simultaneously. A person exists only as a relation to other persons. The reality of the person is the reality of a relational being. An "I" has meaning only in relation to other "I's."[14]

Supplementing what we have learned about the human person from trinitarian theology with Christology, we can underscore and deepen our understanding of person as relation in community. We have already had occasion to consider some of the implications of the fundamental anthropological reality that human persons are created in the image and likeness of God. Now we must relate this to Christology. As Ruysbroeck affirms:

> The heavenly Father created all men in his image. His image is his Son, his eternal wisdom . . . who was before all creation. It is in this reference to this eternal image that we have all been created. It is to be found essentially and personally in all men; each one possesses it

whole and entire and undivided, and all together have no more than one. In this way we are all one, intimately united in our eternal image. . . .[15]

Although sin can never fully destroy this "natural unity of the human race," it radically affects it.[16] In fact, as both Scripture and the Fathers of the Church emphasize, a prime effect of sin is precisely division. Maximus the Confessor, for example, says that through sin "the one nature was shattered into a thousand pieces." The Fathers typically viewed persons born in original sin as "so many cores of natural opposition." Accordingly, they characterized sin both as a disruption of the soul's relation to God and of relations among persons sharing in human nature. Maximus writes that "man's tempter . . . had separated him in his will from God, had separated men from each other." De Lubac laments that a later theology unfortunately failed to place the same emphasis on this social dimension of sin as did the Fathers, but tended to locate sin simply within the individual.

Seen in the context of sin as division, the work of redemption appears as the restoration of a unity that was lost. Just as sin divides persons from God and from one another, so the redemption reunites them to God and to one another. From the beginning, the Incarnation is a work of unity and peace among persons, because Jesus bore all persons within himself. The Word of God did not just take on one human nature, but human nature per se. De Lubac expresses the point powerfully:

> He incorporated himself in our humanity, and incorporated it in himself. *Universitatis nostrae caro est factus.* [He became the flesh of our universal humanity.] In making a human nature, it is *human nature* that he united to himself, that he enclosed in himself. . . . *Naturam in se universae carnis adsumpsit.* [He assumed in himself the nature of all flesh.] Whole and entire he will bear it then to Calvary, whole and entire he will raise it from the dead, whole and entire he will save it. . . . Christ the Redeemer does not offer salvation merely to each one. . . . [We] are all in Christ . . . and the common personality of man is brought back to life by his assuming of it.[17]

As we have already gleaned from our reflections, it is the nature of the person to be in relation to others, and not merely in an ego-centered, selective way, but to be related to the whole. "To be a person," as Norris Clarke expresses it, "is to be intrinsically expansive, ordered toward self-manifestation and self-communication."[18] In fact, one comes to discover who one is precisely by going out from one's self. This fundamental principle of human existence is stated clearly in Matthew 10:39: "Whosoever would save his life will lose it; whosoever would lose his life for my sake will find it." This statement expresses the truth that the person grows as a person only by going out from himself, sacrificing whatever is merely of self-interest, to serve the needs of others and the common good of the society to which he or she belongs. To fail to enter into the dynamic of self-sacrifice and service is to deny one's personal nature and become a mere individual, an enclosed self. Moreover, Matthew 10:39 also directs the human person to God and therefore to his or her salvation. If we are saying that the person achieves his or her identity only through other persons, then ultimately the person achieves identity only through the ultimate person and source of personhood, God. The truth is here, as it often is in spiritual matters, paradoxical, and not simply derived from a linear rationality. Relativity toward the other constitutes personhood. God is the most perfect person in whom perfect relations subsist. Therefore, in order for the human person to achieve perfection in personhood, he or she must direct his or her relatedness at God, the wholly other. By doing so, he finds both God and himself.

With these anthropological and theological considerations in mind, we are ready to understand how Jesus Christ is both the Revelation of the divine person and the way of the human person. What Christ discloses is not only the truth about God but the truth about man as well. We do not fully understand what it means to be a human person apart from the disclosure manifest in the mystery of the Word made flesh. Hence, in a profound sense, Christology is the completion of anthropology. This is one of the most profound insights of Vatican Council II:

> In reality it is only in the mystery of the Word made flesh that the mystery of man truly becomes clear. Adam, the first man, was a type of him who was to come, Christ the Lord, Christ the new Adam, in the very Revelation of the mystery of the Father and of his love, fully reveals man to himself and brings to light his most high calling. . . . He who is the "image of the invisible God" (Col. 1:15), is himself the perfect man who has restored in the children of Adam that likeness to God which had been disfigured ever since the first sin. Human nature, by the very fact that it was assumed, not absorbed, in him, has been raised in us also to a dignity beyond compare. For, by his incarnation, he, the son of God, has in a certain way united himself with each man. . . . Born of the Virgin, Mary, he has truly been made one of us, like to us in all things except sin.[19]

What *Gaudium et Spes* is underlining here is no novelty but the meaning of the traditional Christology developed in the ancient Church which was crystallized at the Council of Chalcedon. In Christ, there are two natures, divine and human, and one person, the Word who has been with God and been God since the beginning. As a divine person, to be in relation to the other is realized perfectly in him; it is the ontological foundation of his entire existence. Of course, Christ's total being-with-the-other in no way compromises his unique identity, his "being-with-himself." The implications of this both for the concept of person and the understanding of human beings are well stated by Ratzinger, "In Christ, in the man who is completely with God, human existence is not canceled, but comes to its highest possibility, which consists in transcending itself into the absolute and in the integration of its own relativity into the absoluteness of divine love."[20] In Christ, we come to understand that to be a human person means to seek to realize the fullness of personhood in our lives by following Christ's path of love and self-denial.

The understanding of person which emerges from its Christian roots has radical implications for the way we understand all human relations. The consequence of the Incarnation is that the divine person, Christ, is intimately related to all human persons created in his image and likeness. Moreover, the Redemption restores the original solidarity among all persons. Therefore, Jesus Christ is the ultimate "You" to whom all love and failure to love is ultimately directed. Jesus himself explicitly taught this doctrine, and it is recorded in the dramatic narrative of the final judgment in Matthew 25. Here Christ teaches that on the day of judgment we will be judged according to how we have treated him. "For I was hungry and you gave me to eat, thirsty and you gave me to drink, naked and you clothed me, in prison and you visited me." In response to the question, "When, Lord, did we see you hungry, thirsty, naked, or in prison?" Jesus responds, "Insofar as you did it to one of these, the least of my brethren, you did it to me." Jean Galot underlines the point that there is no question here of "as if," that is, a suggestion on the part of Christ that we should treat the hungry, thirsty, homeless, poor, and imprisoned "as if" they were Christ. No, the statement is more radical, asserting that the "You" of Christ is present in each and every person and is the "term of every act of love or every refusal to love." The real point of Matthew 25 is to declare that we touch Jesus personally in all of our contact with other human persons. This is the "ontological core" of the command to love our neighbor. As Galot summarizes, *"The presence of the 'You' of Christ within each human person, with the right to be loved, is an ontological presence."*[21] What Matthew 25 also underlines is that, as a relational being, Jesus is never indifferent to any human suffering; it is the "You" of Christ who is crying out for help. This ontological presence of Christ is not simply in his disciples and friends who heed his call. The emphasis is rather on his presence wherever there is human suffering. Moreover, not even evil behavior changes the profound respect owed to every human person as a true presence of Christ in the world. Even those who are in prison for crimes they have committed bear this presence within them, and Jesus bids us to go and comfort them as well (Matthew 25:43).

Trinitarian theology and Christology also add and underline the significance of "we," in addition to "you" and "I." The difference is not merely semantic. Jesus taught his apostles to address the Father in prayer as "our Father" for a reason. Only Jesus is by nature the Son of God. Human persons become sons and daughters of God, in Saint Paul's language, "by adoption"; we are incorporated into sonship in relation to the Father through Christ, as a result of the Incarnation and Redemption. It is the Incarnation which makes the human family a "we" at the deepest level. From the beginning, the Incarnation is a work of reuniting what was divided. Christ bears all men within himself. When the Word became flesh, it did not simply take on a body; as Saint Hilary said, the Incarnation is a *concorporatio,* a taking on of all flesh. He incorporated himself in our humanity so we could be incorporated into his divinity. Whether we speak of human or divine persons, there is always more involved than an "I-thou" relationship. The human "I," caught up in the dynamic of the Incarnation, gathers with all other human "I's" in Christ in relation to the "You" of God. That is why human persons most properly refer to the Father as *"our"* Father. Yet, even God is not a simple "You," but the "We" of Father, Son, and Holy Spirit. Christ is here the "we" into which Love, namely the Holy Spirit, gathers us and which means simultaneously being bound to each other and being directed to the Father. Unfortunately, in modern thought, with the loss of the sense of the person as informed by trinitarian theology and Christology, we have increasingly tended to reduce relationality to "I" and "thou" relations. Yet "I" and "you" apart from "we" tends to become an individualism *á deux,* and so to narrow itself until the "you," together with the essential relatedness of persons, is lost.[22]

Other dimensions of anthropology viewed in the light of Revelation and ontology include: (a) the biblical concept of tripartite anthropology, (b) human nature and grace, (c) faith and reason, (d) freedom, (e) the common good, and (f) subjectivity. As these will be important for the subsequent treatment of the political, economic, and cultural orders, we take them up here in order.

### Tripartite Anthropology

Saint Paul made a significant contribution to anthropology.[23] In I Thessalonians, we read, "May the God of peace sanctify you wholly; and may your spirit and soul and body be kept sound and blameless at the coming of our Lord Jesus Christ" (I Thessalonians 5:23). Although this Pauline notion of the human person as composed of spirit, soul, and body is not developed thematically by Paul, the text was significant in ancient Christianity when the patristic writers developed the theology of the person. What Paul means by body and soul is fairly clear. Most of the controversy has been about the meaning of spirit, or *pneuma.* The note on this text in *The Jerusalem Bible* introduces the ambiguity:

> Paul seems to have developed no coherent system of anthropology: this is the only place he mentions a tripartite division of body (cf. Rm 7:24+), soul (cf. 1 Co 15:44+) and spirit (which can be taken in two ways: as the divine presence in a human being, giving him new life in union with Christ, Rm 5:5+, or more probably as the innermost depths of the human being, open and awake to the Spirit, cf. Rm 1:9+).[24]

Whatever difficulties the interpretation of spirit would present, there can be no doubt that Paul meant to distinguish between the soul and the spirit. In Hebrews 4:12, we read, "For the word of God is living and active, sharper than any two-edged sword, piercing to the division of soul and spirit . . . and discerning the thoughts and intentions of the heart." What, then, is this spirit which is distinguished from the human soul? A review of the scriptural passages and the patristic exegesis reveals texts which refer to the "spirit" as simply part of the human composite; other texts seem to identify it more simply as the "spirit of God."[25] For Irenaeus, the soul "receives 'the spirit of the Father'; the man is called 'spiritual' insofar as he receives participation of the Spirit, and this participation makes him to be not only in the image but in the resemblance of God; finally, if this man is 'perfect,' it is because . . . he 'possesses the spirit of God.' "[26] In light of such a passage, it would be untenable to reduce the spirit simply to a component of the human person serving to distinguish man from God. Summarizing Paul, Irenaeus, and Origen, de Lubac, without attempting a full resolution of the matter, concludes:

> the *pneuma* that is "in man," in every man, assures a certain hidden transcendence of the man over himself, a certain opening, a certain received continuity between man and God. Not that there is the least identity of essence between the one and the other . . . ; but it is, at the heart of man, the privileged place, always intact, of their encounter.[27]

In other words, despite the distance between the essences of God and man, there is nonetheless, in the depths of the human person, this point of contact with God, which, through divine grace, permits the human person to participate in the divine light itself. Of course, whether or not this occurs depends upon the choices made by the soul. The soul in Saint Paul is "the very seat of personality, the reasoning and self-willed being, which judges and freely determines itself. It is the place of decision." It is the source from which comes our moral life, oriented toward virtue or vice. Paul, following the tradition from Psalm 1, clearly distinguishes between two paths the soul can choose: life according to the flesh (*sarx*), or life according to the spirit (*pneuma*). To choose the former is to live as though this world and the things in it were in themselves the ultimate realities, and in this lies the turning of the soul from God, its true end. In contrast, life according to the spirit, patterned after the life of Christ, allows one to receive the "spirit of God" and thereby participate in the transcendent, divine life. The soul is the part of our being that has to choose between the two ways. Here again, we see the difficulty of simple identification of the spirit with man. That is why Saint Irenaeus most frequently considers the spirit to be the personal spirit of God, the same spirit which Christ promised as a gift to those who believe in Him. So much does this spirit of God become one with the person who receives it fully that the distinction between the spirit as part of man and the spirit of God becomes indistinguishable. This can be seen in the following passage from Saint Irenaeus:

> Now the soul and the spirit are certainly part of the man, but certainly not the man; for the perfect man consists of the commingling and the union of the soul receiving the Spirit of the Father, and the mixture of that fleshly nature which was also molded after the image of God. . . .
> But when the spirit here blended with the soul is united to the body,

the man becomes spiritual and perfect because of the outpouring of the
Spirit, and this is he who was made in the image and likeness of God.
. . . [T]he commingling and union of all three [body, soul, and spirit]
constitutes the perfect man.[28]

The passage clearly suggests that we can open ourselves to the spirit of God
and thereby receive it such that this spirit becomes a part of us in a way that completes us. What, then, of those who do not choose the way of the spirit? Irenaeus
responds:

But if the spirit be wanting to the soul, he who is such indeed is of an
animal nature, and being left carnal, shall be an imperfect being, possessing indeed the image of God in his formation, but not receiving the
similitude through the Spirit; and thus is this being imperfect.[29]

Three implications emerge from tripartite anthropology which are constitutive for any authentic Christian approach to the human person and the social
order. First, without attempting to give a theoretically neat and complete definition of spirit, its presence within man does necessarily mean that transcendence
is written into man's very nature. Christianity can brook no compromise with any
philosophy or ideology which denies such transcendence either in theory or in
practice. This would include any attempt to "bracket" transcendence as in liberalism; to do so would be to imply that we can construct an adequate moral or
political philosophy without it. We cannot. Jean Danielou highlights the point:

There is in us a certain root that plunges into the depths of the Trinity.
We are these complex beings who exist on successive levels, on an animal and biological level, on an intellectual and human level and on an
ultimate level in those very abysses that are those of the life of God and
those of the Trinity. This is why we have the right to say that Christianity is an integral humanism, which is to say, which develops man on all
the levels of his experience. We must always be in defiance of all the
attempts to reduce the space in which our existence moves. We breathe
fully in the measure to which we do not let ourselves be enclosed in the
prison of the rational and psychological world but to which a part of us
emerges into these great spaces that are those of the Trinity.[30]

A second implication of tripartite anthropology is that the Christian must
reject any notion of "pure nature." The radical rootedness of the person in God
permits the reception of the spirit of God; it is the end for which the person's
nature is created. Man, created in the image and likeness of God, is oriented to
God from the very inception of his personhood. Therefore, the order of grace, by
which God imparts divine life to man, is completely necessary for man. It is only
with reference to grace that an adequate account of human nature can be given.

Third, the unity of mind, body, and spirit implies a unity among religion, morality, and mysticism. The New Testament, as embodied in the ancient and medieval Christian tradition, emphasizes the point. Objectively, there can be no separation or conflict among these. It is true that the tradition has indeed at times made a problem of it, at times suggesting that mysticism is for the few. However, in the ancient church, the matter was straightforward, along the lines laid out by Saint Paul. For Paul, the action of the spirit within us transforms us, bringing us into a true union with Christ, a full participation in the divine life, as in, "I live now, not I, but Christ lives in me." Similarly, Irenaeus, Origen, and Augustine speak of mystical union of the human soul with God as though it were the normal result of growth in the Christian life. As we have already seen, Irenaeus refers to the perfect man as one who has received fully the Spirit of God, causing union among spirit, mind, and body. Origen, interpreting the Canticle of Canticles as a metaphor of the relationship between the Divine Logos and the human soul, speaks of the "mystical marriage" between God and the soul.[31] Augustine emphasizes that in the summit of the spiritual life the image of God in man is made perfect precisely by being made a supernatural image: "The likeness to God will be perfect in this image when the vision of God will be perfect."[32] At the same time, there is no leaving morality behind in this mystical ascent; indeed the attempt to do so has always characterized false mysticism. The moral life focuses on the acquisition of the virtues through which the soul becomes good. At the same time, and as a result of the same life in the spirit, these virtues become elements of the soul's own being. The soul transformed by grace is united with the spirit of God.[33]

Surely, the language of "freedom of spirit," when not balanced by morality, has been the source of endless problems. Nonetheless, false mysticism is not the only problem. Whenever the spirit is stifled or negated, or when the soul fails to recognize the orientation of its powers to reason and to choose the transcendent, the result is a truncated and erroneous understanding of the human person, with pernicious results. We can say that the threats to the authentic Christian balance come in two ways. On the one hand, all positivism's rationalisms and psychologisms negate the existence of spirit either in theory or in practice. They fail to see the deeper context of the spirit within which the mind and body are situated and operate; the soul is therefore imprisoned. On the other hand, there are those who, in the hope of saving religion and morality from both false mysticism and the onslaughts of these modern "isms," negate the life and gifts of the spirit. The danger of this latter approach, all too prevalent in the twentieth century, is that the stifled spirit seeks to emerge outside the context of moral norms; false mysticisms will proliferate outside the boundaries of the Church.[34] To summarize, even though morality must always penetrate the spiritual life, the latter does transcend, without leaving behind, reason and the moral life. The equilibrium established by Christianity is lost on the one hand by forgetting the soul, which leads to the spurious mysticism of trying to experience God without the requisite moral discipline; on the other, it is lost by forgetting the spirit, reducing religion to a lifeless, spiritless obedience to moral laws.

## Person, Nature, and Grace

If we keep the ontological presence of Christ in the human person in mind, then we will stay on the right road in understanding the relationship between nature and grace and in understanding the person in light of that relationship. To be avoided at all costs is any form of dualism between nature and grace. The meaning of such dualism is perhaps best summed up in a metaphor suggested by Karl Rahner, in which grace would be an upper story of a building added to a lower one (nature) such that the lower, maintaining its original structure, serves as a foundation on which the higher is built.[35] Although a variegated phenomenon, extrinsicism in all its forms holds that nature and grace are external to one another, mutually impenetrable, with grace "coming from without" to be added on to nature.[36] This dualism underlies the "extrinsicist" position that was attacked decisively by Maurice Blondel. More fundamentally, extrinsicism was never the authentic Christian tradition. To be sure, human persons cannot acquire grace by their innate powers, and in this respect grace is indeed beyond nature. Nonetheless, nature and grace are not simply external to one another, nor is one superimposed on the other. Rather, grace penetrates the very depths of the human person who is open to it; it "leaves its mark *on* our nature and becomes in us a principle of life."[37] Grace divinizes the person without absorbing his or her identity. It is not added to the soul, but infused into it as a principle of life from within.

To reject extrinsicism is in no way to deny the real distinction between the order of creation and the order of redemption. For the Christian in the world, there will always be a radical distinction between the already and the not yet. That is, although we are already ordered to become children of God by nature, we do not possess the grace to which faith and baptism give us access. After all, the one end to which we are ordered, that is, participation in God's trinitarian life, exceeds the innate power of nature to attain. We are still in need of the grace of redemption. Baptism calls us beyond nature to our final end in God which transcends our nature. De Lubac's point, therefore, is in no way to negate the distinction between nature and grace, but to assert that nature is "ordered internally and from its creation toward the God revealed in Jesus Christ."[38]

An integrated view of nature and grace is extremely important for moral guidance, and particularly so for grasping the relationship between obeying the law of nature and participating in the divine life through the fullness of grace. For example, the law of nature forbids killing except in self-defense. The fifth beatitude reads, "Blest are they who show mercy; mercy shall be theirs" (Matthew 5:7). We are called both to respect the moral law and to have mercy on those who break it. The intrinsic relation between nature and grace rules out any juxtaposition of two separate laws—a law of nature and a law of grace—with unrelated sets of ethical demands. It suggests that there is instead simply the one law personalized in Jesus, which, however, already accounts from within its own unity for all of nature's immanent finalities, including those traditionally ascribed to the natural law. By the same token, we cannot reduce the commandments to an autonomous natural morality that we then separate from the requirements of the gospel. William Portier points out that the commandments and the beatitudes "cannot be related extrinsically as in the modern tendency to view charity as a kind of voluntary supplement to justice rather than its integral perfection."[39] As John Paul II explains in *Veritatis Splendor*, "Jesus shows that the commandments must not be understood as a minimum limit . . . but as a path involving a moral and spiritual journey toward perfection, at the heart of which is love." Moreover, Jesus "Himself becomes a living and personal law, who invites people to follow him."[40] Rather than there being somehow a law of nature and a law of grace, there is simply the one law of love personalized in Jesus. As John Paul II rightly says, both the commandments and the invitation to the fullness of the life of grace "stand at the service of a *single and indivisible charity.*"[41] Here we see the perfect integration of nature and grace.

To maintain an intrinsic relationship between nature and grace is no mere abstract theological concern. An extrinsicist view is dangerous, not because it holds to the existence of the natural law, which is indeed defended by the Church, but because it ends up pinning the natural law to a false autonomy of nature. For the logical burden of what is here called extrinsicism is that nature is primitively indifferent to grace, and, by implication, indifferent (or neutral) with respect to God. Hence, an extrinsicist reading of the relationship between nature and grace just so far seals nature against the claims of Revelation. In other words, extrinsicism affords no reason, logically speaking, why we may not construct a natural ethics against which Revelation can make no claims. Nor is this an idle concern.[42] Rather, extrinsicism opens Pandora's box in a number of respects. When we begin to think of the meaning of person apart from all that we have learned from Revelation, a lamentable spirit of abstraction begins to pervade our thinking which easily leads to depersonalization, graphically seen in so much of social contract theory where person as relation is replaced by autonomous, self-directing "individuals." A social ethics centered around person, relationship, and community is replaced by an endless and in principle unresolvable conflict between (a) claims based on rights on behalf of individuals, and (b) claims based on utility on behalf of the state. Finally, even for those who do not permit extrinsicism to compromise their faith so absolutely, the Gospel demands, which go beyond the law of nature, especially the call to mercy and forgiveness, tend to be viewed as optional supplements to our already established "natural ethics" concerning justice. Such supplements are held to be irrelevant to politics which must allegedly limit itself to the demands of this preconceived natural justice.

By way of contrast, de Lubac's rich understanding of the integral unity between nature and grace provides us with a solid paradigm to understand not only the relationship between nature and grace, but also between faith and reason, and even Church and state:

> The law of the relations between nature and grace, in its generality, is
> everywhere the same. It is from within that grace seizes nature, and,

far from diminishing nature, raises it up, in order to make it serve its (grace's) own ends. It is from within that faith transforms reason, that the Church influences the state. As the messenger of Christ, the Church is not the guardian of the state; on the contrary she ennobles it to be . . . more human.[43]

The case against extrinsicism is perhaps nowhere made more clear than reflecting on the traditional Christological formula of the Council of Chalcedon in 451, which states that the divine person who is the Second Person of the Trinity can appropriate a human nature without dilution of either his humanity or divinity, and that he possesses the fullness of grace and yet is fully human. By implication, the life of nature and the life of grace are intrinsically related in the person of Jesus Christ. On the other hand, the extrinsicist model implies that Jesus Christ had two lives going on within him, a divine and a human, that were not intrinsically related. Therefore, the unity that existed between them can only be the result of a special action on God's part completely unique to his case. Such a view undermines both the fullness of Christ's humanity and any humanly meaningful sense of a spiritual life rooted in following him. Jesus' manhood would not only be shared with an essentially alien life of divinity but united to it by an absolutely gratuitous and unique action of God—an act which united two unrelated forms of life. This is hard to square with the traditional doctrine that the spiritual life is based on following Christ, for in what sense could we follow someone whose ontological makeup was so far removed from our own? The Christ of extrinsicism is more akin to the kind of supernatural being found in science fiction than the fully human Christ of the gospels. Moreover, the extrinsicist view must forever imply that grace works "over the head" of nature, so to speak. This cannot help but suggest that nature should be denigrated in favor of something fundamentally other, that is, grace. The great irony is that such an approach cannot help but undermine any positive sense of the autonomy of nature that it purportedly set out to defend, for the autonomy of such a nature would hardly be something to be defended; it would be something to get rid of as soon as possible!

### Faith and Reason

Parallel to the relationship between nature and grace is that between faith and reason. In coming to grips with the orders of nature and reason, we consider the Prologue to the Gospel according to Saint John: "In the beginning was the Word, and the Word was with God, and the Word was God. He was in the beginning with God; all things were made through him, and without him was not anything made that was made (John 1:1-3)." From the biblical standpoint, or the standpoint of faith, it must be asserted without ambiguity that, ontologically considered, there is no reality that exists outside of the Divine Word; ontological autonomy from the Divine Word, the Logos, is not a property belonging to anything real; everything that is exists in Christ. Every truth to be known by the human intelligence is contained in that Divine Word.

The denial of ontological autonomy from the divine Logos is, however, no prelude to any kind of fundamentalism or fideism.[44] The ancient Christian tradition recognized earlier that reason and faith were two ways of appropriating truth, neither reducible to the other. This was a necessary conclusion drawn from reflection on the data of Revelation. In the Old Testament, for example, we see that the Wisdom Literature draws not only from Jewish but also from pagan sources. Saint Paul presumes a natural knowledge of morality available to the pagans, and uses it as a basis for insisting on the justice of God in condemning those who violate it. Such knowledge "is written on their hearts."[45] We can even go so far as to say that the relationship between faith and reason is no systemic problem in the Bible. The complications emerge later when some philosophers begin to insist on a reason that is autonomous with respect to faith and Revelation. In the face of such a claim, the question is not so much whether faith's claims are somehow unreasonable, but whether reason's claims are unreasonable.

John Paul II, in his encyclical letter, *Fides et Ratio,* suggests the lines along which we can find the answer. He writes that "there is a philosophy completely independent of the Gospel's Revelation: This is the stance adopted by philosophy as it took shape in history before the birth of the Redeemer and later in regions as yet untouched by the Gospel." In this effort to uncover truth through reason, the Pope sees "a valid aspiration to be an autonomous enterprise, obeying its own rules and employing the powers of reason alone." This aspiration, the Pope contends, "should be supported and strengthened." Furthermore, this aspiration should be "always open—at least implicitly—to the supernatural." To reject or refuse Revelation a priori would be to "preclude access to a deeper knowledge of the truth," thus damaging philosophy itself.[46] What is implied here is that the search for truth, which is intrinsic to reason, compels reason to be open to God's Revelation. With the coming of Revelation, especially in the person of Jesus Christ, reason is given a great boost in its search, being apprised of truths it could not have reached without divine assistance. Because of Revelation, philosophy has been given matter for its own development which would not have happened otherwise. This dynamic union between philosophy and Revelation the Pope terms "Christian philosophy."[47] It is no less philosophy for being Christian, as Etienne Gilson was wont to recall. The Christian philosophers, he contended, did a better job than their pagan counterparts.[48]

Insofar as morality is a practical matter, it can never be closed to Revelation. In the practical order, we are obliged to act, taking into account all goods and evils relevant to our decisions. Revelation contributes to our knowledge of those goods and evils, and makes demands upon us. Jesus' exhortation, "Come follow me," can only be obeyed or disobeyed in the practical order. It is not a moral theory and does not belong primarily to the speculative order. It must, however, be obeyed by anyone who would call himself a Christian. That is why someone such as Yves R. Simon, who insisted strongly on the distinction between philosophy and theology as theoretical sciences, could nonetheless conclude, "a purely rational philosophy is essentially misleading."[49] This is so for three reasons. First, all actions must be evaluated morally with reference to the ends we seek and the ends we are obliged to pursue. The most important practical question is that of our last or final end. Philosophy unaided by Revelation does not know what this end is, and hence would be unable to fulfill the purpose of a practical moral philosophy, that is, to direct our actions. Second, Revelation apprises us of duties we must fulfill that are unknown to unaided reason, such as the duty to worship God in specific ways at specific times. Third, Revelation demands that all of the natural virtues be interpreted in light of charity and our supernatural end. This will at times demand a different behavior than that determined by the natural reason alone.[50]

Much confusion could be avoided if we recall the foundations of theology and philosophy. As Ratzinger reminds us, theology is based upon the structure of the act of faith which justifies, even compels, a fusion between faith and reason. The Christianity of the New Testament itself assumes the existence of reason, most obviously in Saint John's Gospel, wherein it is affirmed, "In the beginning was the Logos," and that Christ is this Logos. The theology of this Gospel is rooted in the conviction that there is an ultimate reason behind the creation of the entire universe, and that this reason is manifest in all things made. All created things have their origin and end in the Divine Logos without which they would be unintelligible. This appears to be what Saint Thomas was getting at when he wrote, "All cognitive beings know God implicitly in whatever they know"; an implicit knowledge of the Logos is present in every act of knowing because the Logos is what makes the known to be and to be intelligible. Therefore, Revelation brings reason to light, even as it brings faith to light. Faith presupposes the existence of reason, that we live in a universe characterized by intelligibility, and that there are reasonable beings capable of understanding what is revealed. Moreover, reason itself assumes the foundation of the Logos, the source of the universe's intelligibility, the ultimate reasonableness of things which permits me to reason in the first place. The Logos, however, is an intelligibility which is inexhaustible and always itself a mystery beyond the comprehension of human reason. Hence, human reason needs the guidance of faith concerning those things which transcend reason yet never contradict it. With respect to matters of faith, reason has the function of rendering it more intelligible to us without compromising its final mystery. This mutual implication between faith and reason is what John Paul II was explaining in *Fides et Ratio:*

> The relationship between theology and philosophy is best construed as a circle. Theology's source and starting point must always be the word of God revealed in history, while its final goal will be an understanding of that word which increases with each passing generation. Yet, since God's word is truth (John 17:17), the human search for truth—philosophy, pursued in keeping with its own rules—can only help to understand God's word better. . . . Moving between the twin

poles of God's word and a better understanding of it, . . . reason is stirred to explore paths which of itself it would not even have suspected it could take. This circular relationship with the word of God leaves philosophy enriched, because reason discovers new and unsuspected horizons.[51]

The indispensability of seeing reason as self-limiting in light of the Logos can be seen from another angle. Reason must see the truth as the absolute to which it is ordered. Reason is to be valued precisely because it is a vehicle through which the truth can be apprehended. It is the truth which is absolute, not reason. When reason fails to recognize this and insists on its own absoluteness, then it will end up justifying the irrational and destroying any ground for obeying its dictates.[52] Let us suppose, for example, that we negate this proposition of the Logos, and argue simply that the universe began 13.7 billion years ago with the gigantic explosion we call "the big bang." Reason would, in such an account, have to be in some way a byproduct of this event. Since the event itself cannot be interpreted as the operation of any preexisting Logos, then it cannot be explained in terms of reason, and is simply a nonrational event. Reason, then, would be ultimately based on something nonrational. How could reason, a byproduct of an irrational event, assume the status of an ultimate standard of measure? It could not. The respect we owe to reason, and its privileged place in our moral, ethical, and philosophical affairs, is based on the assumption that there is a Logos, a reason, and an intelligibility in the universe, grounding our capacity to discover the truth of things through our reason. If the Logos is rejected, truth is rejected, and we are left with an absolute reason which for all that cannot provide us with grounds for acting in one way as opposed to another, and which cannot explain the universe we live in or its own place within it. Reason as absolute, negating the grounds of its own existence, can only appeal to the irrational. Any attempt to reassert morality on a reasonable basis can only come about by resurrecting the Logos. Martin Kriele writes:

> The idea that even before the big bang the Logos existed from which everything came into being and without which nothing came into being, and that in some way this Logos has its effects on human life— this or a similar assumption is today as it was before the minimum condition for respect for people. In the understanding of the political enlightenment 'human dignity' is a metaphysical concept. It becomes meaningless under the presupposition that man is 'merely' the result of accidental evolution.[53]

Yves R. Simon explains that it was the attempt to interpret nature in a mathematical way, based on the physical sciences, that influenced modern political philosophy and social science to abandon the role of the Logos in the universe. In a mathematical universe, composed of extension and motion, there are no final causes, no answers to the "whys" of things. The universe is nonteleological; it is no longer to be understood in terms of the ends or purposes contained in it, for mathematics can never tell us the end or the purpose of any of the beings that exist in nature. Simon writes:

> But a world that is both real and non-teleological is meaningless. It is a tale told by an idiot, signifying nothing. No Logos dwells in the universe of mechanism; it does not have any idea of its own. Man attempts an escape from meaninglessness by breathing words into things, but these man-uttered words never become the forms and souls of things; even when our effort to break away from nonsense is greatest, they remain mere value-judgments, in sharp contrast with judgments of reality.[54]

To conceive of human realities in terms of mechanism is precisely the flaw to be avoided when trying to clarify the relationship between faith and reason. It is the influence of a mechanistic model which prompts us to look at faith and reason as extrinsically related. According to this model, faith and reason have integrity only through their radical independence of one another and being defined in ways which are mutually exclusive. David Schindler argues that such a mechanistic approach cannot do justice either to faith or to reason, because it fails to understand them humanly. He suggests that the faith-reason relationship be made analogous to a love relationship. It is in a love relationship that we can understand that two entities can be both unified and distinct in such a way that deepening unity promotes distinctness and distinction is the product of deepening unity. Each finds integrity within the unity and never apart from it. Here, one would never wish to say that one partner became more himself or herself by being unrelated, or that deepening relatedness came as the result of destroying the uniqueness of each, and so it is with faith and reason understood as intrinsically related in the context of a person. Faith and reason are conceived of as an underlying unity in which faith grows to maturity by respecting that reason is distinct, and vice versa. Faith and reason deepen their unity precisely as each matures.

Those still reluctant to assert this kind of unity between faith and reason often remain suspicious that some violation is being made against reason; that at the root of all this is an act of faith which must always be, from the standpoint of reason, nothing other than an arbitrary choice. Such a view falsely assumes that the opponents of faith do not make choices equally "undemonstrable." In the practical order, where choices are demanded of us, we have to make a choice, whether or not we choose to be believers or unbelievers. Agnosticism is not a choice available in the practical order, for I must act either in accord with Revelation or not. Again, Christ's "Come follow me" is an imperative. It can only be obeyed or disobeyed. With the reason that we all possess, we must decide either to be open to the claims of Revelation or to refuse them, and again this has implications for the practical level where there are only yes or no answers. Moreover, the claims of Revelation have implications for how we understand ourselves and the world we live in. Rationalism tells us that we and the world we live in are normal, ontologically speaking. Revelation tells us that we are living in a fallen world plagued by sin which also implicates us. Again, we must decide, choosing between the two interpretations. Ultimately, the decision to be closed to God and to deny sin is a practical choice, similar in kind to that made by one who is open to God and chooses to believe that the human situation as it stands is the result of sin. Both make a choice which is not simply a dictate from reason. The one who rejects God and denies sin cannot honestly claim to know that God has not revealed himself, or to know that the human situation is not the result of sin. Both choose; neither choice is provable from the standpoint of pure reason.

Norris Clarke, in his reflection on *Fides et Ratio,* helps us to flesh out a bit further exactly why faith and reason are complementary, and what exactly they do for one another.[55] The possibility of learning from both faith and reason is grounded in the innate drive of the human mind both to know the truth and to live in accord with it. No partial truth will do. The mind strives for a comprehensive knowledge of the truth, and to live a life full of goodness. Faith contributes to this search for truth, and aids reason greatly whenever it demands conformity to the "great commission"; that is, "Go therefore and make disciples of all nations . . . teaching them to observe all that I have commanded you" (Matthew 28:19-20). This presupposes that there is a universal truth which encompasses all human beings, and that this truth is accessible to all and can be faithfully expressed to people of any and all cultures. As Clarke incisively concludes, this commission is itself a negation of relativism, historicism, postmodernism, skepticism, and deconstructionism, because it assumes a truth denied by all of these philosophical approaches. Philosophy is thereby strengthened to do its work in search of truth, emboldened by the knowledge that there is truth to be discovered and explained. Moreover, faith in divine Revelation opens reason to seek the highest human perfection in communion with others, modeled after the communion of persons in the Trinity. Philosophy itself thrives best in a communal search for truth, a community of friendship.

Philosophy, for its part, has much to offer faith. Faith needs to be explained. The truths it presents in narrative form often need to be put in terms of propositions. The truths of Revelation need to be put together, the connections among the parts being demonstrated. Moreover, the relationship between the truths of faith and reason need to be explicated, the compatibility among them clarified. Second, reason prevents our understanding of faith from being contaminated by superstition or other kinds of mere credulity. Third, faith needs reason to work out the details of its intelligibility, to explain the epistemological basis of faith. Faith by itself cannot fully answer the important issues of why we should believe in the first place and what justifies the act of faith epistemologically. Finally, faith benefits greatly from metaphysics, that philosophical discipline which explains and defends the mind's capacity to capture transcendent truths about our existence, provide an objective basis for morality, and come to the realization of a Supreme

Being. Metaphysics provides the most solid prelude for approaching the truths of faith. This is especially needed today when extremist philosophies of postmodernism and deconstruction undercut the entire idea of truth and objective morality which faith presupposes. John Paul II explains:

> We face a great challenge at the end of this millennium to move from *phenomenon to foundation,* a step as necessary as it is urgent. We cannot stop short at experience alone; even if experience does reveal the human being's interiority and spirituality, speculative thinking must penetrate to the spiritual core and ground from which it arises. Therefore, a philosophy which shuns metaphysics would be radically unsuited to the task of mediation in the understanding of Revelation. . . . If I insist so strongly on the metaphysical element, it is because I am convinced that it is the path to be taken in order to move beyond the crisis pervading large sectors of philosophy at the moment, and thus to correct certain mistaken modes of behavior now widespread in our society.[56]

Concerning the crisis in contemporary philosophy, it is appropriate to say a word about postmodernism, or better, the postmodern critique of modernity.[57] At the root of this project is the well-founded realization that so much of the modern world and the modern philosophy which undergirds it is a structure of oppression. The postmodernists claim that the problem begins with the very concept of modernity itself, which, in their understanding, is the beginning of a metanarrative; that is, an all-encompassing worldview through which we are to understand the world we live in. The metanarrative of modernity asserts a rationalist and scientific rationality according to which humanity is undergoing a process of evolution. Certain peoples and nations are more advanced; others remain "premodern." This justifies an entire hierarchy of nations and peoples, which further justifies the conviction that certain nations and peoples should lead, while others should follow. The postmodernists see in this way of thought nothing more than a Nietzchean "will to power" by which one group seeks to rationalize its domination of the other. For them, every unitary conception of history inevitably embodies a schema of oppression; the dominant group articulates the unitary history to its own advantage and to guarantee its dominance over "the other." The only solution, according to the postmodernists, is to attack each and every philosophy which purports to claim knowledge of the whole. The very foundations of universal reason, that is, all metaphysics, must be attacked in order to liberate those oppressed by universals. Moreover, we should celebrate difference and diversity and reject all appeals to any hierarchy of values, for the latter are merely a means by which some seek to assert their superiority over others.

The contribution of the postmodernists has been in the way they rightly question the structures of domination and the way of thinking which support them. The West has frequently resorted to universalistic schemes of thought as convenient ways of justifying oppression. One need only look at the conquest of the New World in both hemispheres to see how philosophy and even theology were brought in to rationalize the elimination of the rights of peoples deemed to be irrational, heathen, or "natural slaves." Moreover, ideologies of domination can function even at an unconscious level in those who may otherwise seek to dismantle unjust social structures. It is to the credit of the postmodernists that they relentlessly seek to expose ideologies of domination and to question the unexamined assumptions which frequently support them.

Although it has valid criticisms to make along the way, postmodernism is a fatally flawed philosophical approach because it undercuts the very moral foundations of human life which make moral progress conceivable in the first place. To respect differences concerning matters of conscience is one thing; to celebrate difference for its own sake with no reference to an objective sense of the moral good is quite another. Indeed, postmodernism ends up as arbitrary as any of the narratives it critiques.[58] To encourage difference systematically and to discourage dialog and unity among cultures can only terminate in an exacerbated individualism, even narcissism. A preoccupation with my own sense of being different is no basis for a culture of solidarity with those who may think differently. Moreover, the kind of moral relativism suggested by postmodernism is hardly a way of promoting any progress in areas such as "social justice" or "human rights," because these, too, have no meaning beyond the cultures which invented them, and hence cannot serve as a basis for progressive change. There is a cruel irony when the poor and the disadvantaged, having fought their way into decision-making structures, now discover that postmodern relativism has become fashionable in educational and political establishments. What the postmodernists fail to consider is that moral relativism ultimately undermines all arguments which appeal to an objective sense of justice, even those of the marginalized. Finally, the relativism so characteristic of postmodernism gives us no firm basis for respecting other cultures. There may be an argument for allowing the other to live and have his space, but there is no way to assert that any culture has any universal values of benefit to other cultures. In the end, postmodernism glorifies irrationality, individuality, and separation, to the destruction of both reason and faith. It is a formula for ongoing fragmentation both of knowledge and of society itself.

## Freedom

The discussion of freedom is most often conducted in a political context. However, such discussions are commonly unproductive because the ontological foundations of personal freedom are left unexplored. As is always the case when these roots are not held up for examination, hidden and erroneous assumptions inevitably plague the entire treatment of the issue. Therefore, we will here address freedom at its most fundamental, ontological level.[59]

The good to which voluntary actions are related is a completely nonparticular good. This is to say that the good transcends any and all particular actions in which it is embodied. In the language of Aristotle and Saint Thomas, the good serves as a form in all of the things in which it is found. Saint Thomas and his followers used the expression *bonum in communi* to designate this characteristic of the good. So as not to confuse such an expression with an abstraction inappropriate to questions of volition, we can translate this expression by the phrases "the good so understood as to include all goods" and "the all-embracing nature of the good."[60] Despite its transcendent character, this good is embodied in all particular, finite acts.

This distinctive feature of the voluntary act as related to this comprehensive sense of the good can be considered in another way; that is, as a relation to the final end. Reason requires that all contemplated actions demand the consideration of the ends that the contemplated action serves. Even actions undertaken abruptly, such as swerving a car to miss a dog, are teleological in nature. When a set of immediate purposes is identified with respect to a specific choice, rationality demands consideration of more fundamental purposes. In the example of the motorist swerving to avoid a dog, the end of avoiding the dog is not terminal in nature. The choice to swerve the car must consider the possibility of killing one or more human beings. And so it is in every act of deliberation. Immediate purposes are set in the context of more fundamental purposes until we reach the point of a final end in the light of which the choice is made. As Simon puts it, "the teleological process goes on until it reaches a thing that has unqualifiedly the character of a term, and this thing is what is called the last end." An act is not fully voluntary unless it partakes of this character. "An act," he says, "is not unqualifiedly voluntary unless it proceeds from a judgment which declares, in terminal manner, that it is good to act precisely in this way." Moreover, to declare in any specific case that it is *good* to act or not act in a specific way is precisely to involve the last end.[61]

One might object that concepts such as "the good" and "the last end" are abstract, that the particularities of the goods sought in concrete action are ignored in favor of a purely formal concept. Do people really act on the basis of concerns about the last end? We can resolve the problem by considering the distinction "between *that which* is loved and *that on account of which* what is loved is loved." This distinction is undoubtedly *real*. One man buys a piece of property because he loves the land and the intrinsic satisfactions the house in its particular location will bring him. Another buys a piece of property with no intention of living in it, but merely because he projects that its value will go up in the next decade and he can sell it. Both men may pursue their respective desires with the same fervor, but we all understand that there is a distinction in kind with respect to the wills of the two men. The first man loves the land concretely; the second loves money, and the property is desired under the character of an object which brings money. To love money as a final end is embodied in the specific desire to obtain this piece of property. Its influence on the man's behavior is anything but theoretical.

It may be the case that unreflective people may not have consciously formulated their final ends, even to themselves, and with these people in mind someone may wish to deny a role to the final end. The truth is that the lack of reflection in no way alters the fact that people do choose in the light of a final end. The choices we make on a daily basis are indeed directed toward some end; they are pointing us in some direction and away from all others. Each choice involves not only a yes but a no to every other possibility, and this series of daily "yesses" and "nos" are definitive. We could avoid choosing in light of a final end only by not choosing at all, and the real character of daily life forbids this option. If one were to go to the extreme of making a conscious choice to live without a final end, one would have to make a deliberate choice to live randomly, and thus randomness would assume the form of the final end.

With the distinction between that which is desired and that on account of which a thing is desired in mind, we can understand that to identify the object of the will with the comprehensive good is to say that, for a rational actor, any desirable aspect of a thing is desired on account of its participation in the quality of being good. It is this participation that is expressed whenever we claim that it was good that we acted in such-and-such a way.

Having argued that practical moral judgment involves the decision to pursue the comprehensive good through acts that participate in the form of this good, Simon further specifies two "poles" that order the activities of the intellect. One pole consists of judgments concerning "essential, intelligible, evident and necessary truths." This corresponds to the Aristotelian category of theoretical, or scientific, understanding; that is, it concerns truths that cannot be otherwise than they are. In such cases, it is absolutely necessary that the mind give assent inflexibly. For example, when one sees a right triangle with one leg three inches in length and the other four, we must conclude that the hypotenuse is five inches. This is *the pole of rational determination.* However, in most of the choices we have to make in daily life, this kind of objective necessity does not prevail. For example, in a teacher's choice of which topics to cover and how to cover them, a number of good and reasonable alternatives present themselves, none with the force of necessity. In such cases, the actual object which confronts my will has not the character to determine my will. The teacher, confronted with a series of possible topics to cover, is not compelled to choose one to the exclusion of others, at least in many cases. This reveals *the pole of practical indifference.* It is important to underline here that the absence of a uniquely determined judgment here is no defect or limitation. Even for the hero or the saint without defects of will, the same truth obtains: Most objects held out to us as possible choices are not of such a quality that they impel the will to choose them.

It is precisely the directedness of the free will to the comprehensive good that causes our wills to be undetermined in the face of practical objects of choice. It is because I must examine every particular good object in the light of the comprehensive good that I can say that my choices are not determined with respect to any particular object. We realize that every judgment must be referred to this broader good before being made. No particular good has an a priori determinate claim on my free will before being examined in context and in light of the comprehensive good. Therefore, the indifference of practical judgment in the face of particular objects is no simple indeterminism; the indifference is not simple indifference. It is the particular kind of indifference and indeterminism which exists because of the absolute character of the comprehensive good's claim on the will and the absolute determination of the free will to choose it no matter what the cost. This particular kind of determination Simon refers to as *superdetermination* so as to distinguish it from the lassitude of character and judgment suggested by indeterminism and indifference used in an unqualified sense. Again, the will, determined by the unrestricted drive to the comprehensive good, is necessarily indifferent to any particular good. It is this *superdetermination* of the rational mind to seek the good, and not any kind of indetermination, that necessitates the indifference of the practical judgment.

To be clear about the nature of the indifference that freedom involves, what has been termed *superdetermination,* let us compare it to passive indifference. The indifference which is superdetermination is a capacity to produce multiple effects; it is a kind of competence built up over time based on repeated decisions to realize the good, and it can do so in a number of ways. Passive indifference, on the other hand, is the mere capacity to receive influences. The former is a form of abundance, and its realization is a genuine human accomplishment. It is the capacity to master one's circumstances, to refuse to be determined by them, no matter what the circumstances are. This kind of indifference is present in an exalted way in the saint or hero who accepts death rather than renounce the good. On the other hand, passive indifference does not imply accomplishment or perfection at all. It is related to potentiality, not actuality. The predominance of this kind of indifference in a character ensures that the will remains indecisive, mastered by circumstances that it has not the resolution to overcome. This kind of indifference is well exemplified in one who has no commitment to the good. *This kind of indifference is the enemy of freedom.* Yes, there is an analogy between these two kinds of indifference in that in both cases the will is not determined by any particular good that confronts it. For this reason, freedom is often confused with passive indifference. Simon explains:

> As soon as man yields to the lure of decadence, he is tempted to substitute the delectations of a state of availability for the strong but costly joys of the mastery of one's self. In the heroes and saints the sense for freedom is accompanied by a sense of the unique worth of irrevocable decisions. The literary characters who seek mobility in order to avoid decisions do almost exactly the contrary of what the heroes and the saints do. They would be without prestige and without imitators if the cultivation of passive indifference did not procure a cheap substitute for freedom in intellectuals who no longer have any sense of freedom.[62]

When we see the true character of freedom as a superdeterminate force which propels the person to choose and to realize the good under any and all circumstances, and to refuse to be determined by them, then we realize that in authentically free acts, *causality* is indeed present. The more the freedom, the more there is causality. The subject of this causality is the free will that has determined to bring a definitive state of affairs into existence despite the obstacles which could easily have diverted it had freedom not been present.

In the light of reason, we see a person as possessing finite freedom oriented toward a comprehensive good which is infinite. Revelation personalizes this infinity; the tripersonal God is the good to which the finite, human person is oriented. As we have seen, the person is free insofar as he remains indifferent to all finite goods in his commitment to the infinite or comprehensive good. Through Revelation, we know that God alone is this infinite good to which we are directed from the very ground of our being. In God, on the other hand, the infinity of His being is perfectly directed to the good, thus giving Him an infinite as opposed to a limited freedom.

Revelation clarifies the relationship between the finite freedom of the human person and the infinite freedom of God. Reason allows us to recognize that within finite freedom there is an orientation to infinity that renders us indifferent to all particular goods. This good is ultimately beyond our grasp. There is an infinite distance, a gap which cannot be bridged by human effort. If we are not simply to be tormented by this unrealizable goal, then infinite freedom must assist finite freedom to maintain its practical commitment to the infinite good and to realize its ultimate end in God. The infinite freedom of God allows for finite freedom; in fact, it creates it in the first place. In order for finite freedom to realize itself and partake of infinite freedom, it follows that infinite freedom must be real, not merely an idea, and, furthermore, it cannot simply be divorced from finitude. Revelation tells us how God, the infinitely free, created human persons and entered into explicit relationship with them, so that they could attain the end for which they were created.

As finite freedom can only reach fulfillment in infinite freedom, there has to be a way for each somehow to take in the other; the infinite must take in the finite, and vice versa. Revelation makes known to us that the finite person and the infinite person are constituted precisely so as to permit this. The fulfillment of the human person is made possible because of the Incarnation and the Redemption; in Christ, infinite freedom takes on finite freedom, and finite freedom is perfected through union with the infinite. The formula of Chalcedon helps to clarify this. Christ creates no confusion between God and man; there is no mixing of natures. Rather, as Von Balthasar writes, in the one person of Jesus Christ, infinite freedom takes on finite freedom such that, while each retains its own nature, "infinite freedom indwells finite freedom, and so the finite is perfected in the infinite, without the infinite losing itself in the finite or the finite in the infinite."[63]

Clearly, human freedom has to attend to the infinite good which preserves its nature as free. Revelation is a great assistance to understanding what is required. The most foundational statement of Christian anthropology is that human persons are *created* in the image and likeness of God. We need to under-score the word *created*, and we can best do so by recalling the Prologue to John's Gospel previously cited (John 1:1-3). Paul's letter to the Colossians elaborates:

> He [Jesus] is the image of the invisible God, the first-born of all cre-ation; for in him all things were created, in heaven and on earth, visi-ble and invisible . . . all things were created through him and for him. He is before all things, and in him all things hold together. He is the head of the body, the church; he is the beginning, the first-born from the dead, that in everything he might be pre-eminent. For in him all the fullness of God was pleased to dwell, and through him to reconcile to himself all things, whether on earth or in heaven, making peace by the blood of the cross. (Colossians 1:15-20)

Moreover, the order of all creation, from God the Father through the Son, is suf-fused with love, such love personalized in the Holy Spirit. The point of all this for our discussion of freedom is that, prior to any choices, we must recognize that *our very being is something received through an act of love;* that is, the result of a choice made by God prior to any of our choices. John writes, "In this the love of God was made manifest among us, that God sent his only Son into the world, so that we might live through him. *In this is love, not that we loved God but that he loved us* and sent his Son to be the expiation of our sins" (I John 4:9-10). As our very being is constituted by God's love, it follows that the primary, quintessential human act and disposition must be *receptivity.* Our actions and choices are not ontologically primary, but secondary, and must always-already be oriented to the love of God.

Mary of Nazareth, the Mother of Jesus, has been held out for centuries as the model for Christian discipleship. Moreover, in John Paul II's words, as she is "totally dependent on Christ and completely directed toward him, [she] is the most perfect image of freedom and of the liberation of humanity."[64] She is so because she understood this primacy of receptivity. In the Annunciation narrative, she says, "Behold, I am the handmaid of the Lord; let it be done to me according to your Word" (Luke 1:38). Here she points to the primacy of God's initiative and her own need to be receptive in the face of God. Later, in the Magnificat, she pro-claims, "My soul proclaims the greatness of the Lord, and my spirit finds joy in God my Savior, for he has regarded the lowliness of his handmaiden" (Luke 1:46-47). Precisely because her entire life testifies to her emptiness before God and her willingness to respond freely to God's initiatives, she uniquely proclaims the greatness of God. She orients her freedom precisely to be a receptacle and reflec-tor of the divine image within her. She understands that her entire life is a gift and she offers herself back freely as a gift. It is her recognition of her ontological low-liness before God, her "emptiness," which permits her to be filled by divine life.

In order to be free, we have to become like children, in the biblical sense. Jesus says, "Truly I say to you, whoever does not receive the kingdom of God like a child shall not enter it" (Mark 10:15). What we have here is no pious sentimentality, but a central ontological claim. As all people are created through the Word of God, and as this Word receives everything from God the Father, we are in fact children of God in more than one sense: first, in that we receive our very being from God; second, in that we remain dependent on God for our ongoing reception of the gift of being; and third, in that we are called to radical trust in God. Von Balthasar notes that it is in our time, when the "makeability" and "autonomy" of man are emphasized as never before, when technocratic humanity seeks to govern and control everything, even life itself, that the mystery of childhood is being emptied of value. Therefore, it is now more than ever that "the contrasting Christian leitmotiv of birth from God—the childhood in God of even adult, active and inventive men—attains to its full and even increased validity."[65]

Within Scripture itself is a concept of freedom worth noting as well.[66] Again, the contrast with the modern concept of freedom as simple indeterminacy is clear. The Greek *eleutheria* in no way expresses the notion of freedom of choice. Rather, it meant participation, being a full member of a family, community, or social structure, with all attendant rights and privileges. This meant having a right to participate fully in the life of the community. In the New Testament, particularly in Paul, this takes on the deeper sense of having a share in the life of Jesus Christ, which obligates one to "fulfill the law of Christ" (Galatians 6:2). Those who "belong to Christ have crucified the flesh with its passions and desires" (Galatians 5:24). Saint Paul presents a list of fifteen vices to be avoided (Galatians 5:19-21). Again, we see freedom defined with reference to ultimate moral demands.

Through participation in Christ, the person ultimately participates in being itself, and this is the highest sense of freedom in Paul. It is to be the possessor, not merely the subject of being. This sheds further light on why God is infinite freedom; He is so because He alone fully possesses being, the pure act of being. We therefore become free through our choice to incorporate ourselves into God through Christ. But this is a long and arduous path, not the path of least resistance. Freedom thus understood includes being educated by way of the cross.

In conclusion, freedom considered both philosophically and theologically has an ontological foundation which orients it beyond itself to the infinite good which is God. Moreover, the free person must first of all appreciate that his own being is a gift which is the result of a choice not his own, that receptivity precedes our choices. Yet, much more than our own being is given! We must appreciate all the other "givens" that allowed us to come into being and remain in being: the gifts of nature from which we obtain the necessities of life, the gifts of family and community. Freedom must attend to these givens, whether they be physical, moral, or cultural. Prior to my acts of choice, I am rationally obligated to preserve all that which makes my life and the lives of all other human beings possible, such as the right to life, the preservation of the family, the protection of the moral and physical environment. Therefore, any philosophical perspective which prescinds from all this and asserts the primacy of an individual right to choose, as though that individual had no obligation to maintain the "givens" which sustain life, is a fundamentally false conception of freedom.

## Person, Individual, and the Common Good

As a prelude to the discussion of political philosophy, we need to consult the ontology of the person to clarify important issues regarding the relationship between the good of the person and the good of the community. We begin by recalling the two poles of personhood discussed above; namely, that the person has a pole of relationality and a pole of self-subsistence, neither of which is conceived of as prior or former. The relational pole orients the person to form relations with others and to enter thereby into a community, to create a "we." Here contemporary phenomenologists and personalists have made a great contribution to understanding the role played by interpersonal relations in the very process of coming to know ourselves. We need to encounter someone who, as another "I," will reach out to us as a "you," another center of freedom and intellect, and not simply as an object. In other words, the discovery of myself as an "I" is through relationship with other "I's" whom I encounter as "yous," that is, other centers of personality. As all people are similarly constituted, they form communities which themselves have a unique character. The community of persons itself has a good, the common good, to which all people are oriented and must contribute. In one sense, the relationship between the person and the community is as of a part to a whole. However, the character of a whole that is composed of persons is absolutely unique, and has special features we need now to delineate.

It is the ontological nature of a person to be ordained directly to God as to his final end. Persons are created, willed into existence by God, for their own sake. The created person is in direct relationship with God, and this personal contact is in no way mediated. Although, in the normal process of things, a person comes to know God through the goods of creation, the person transcends every created good in his direct orientation to God. Saint Thomas makes this clear. Human persons stand out in relation to other creatures "in the dignity of their end, for only the intellectual creature reaches the very ultimate end of the whole of things . . . which is the knowing and loving of God."[67] Moreover, as rational creatures they are masters of their own acts, able to provide for themselves through their own acts. "Therefore," Saint Thomas concludes, "intellectual creatures are so controlled by God, as objects of care for their own sakes . . . ; a rational creature exists under divine providence as a being governed and provided for in himself."[68] This is in contrast to the way God governs other creatures; that is, for the sake of the species. Saint Thomas argues that this special dignity of the person derives from his being created in the image and likeness of God, which places the person in a sense above the rest of the entire universe. Hence Saint Thomas writes, "The universe is more perfect in goodness than the intellectual creature as regards extension and diffusion; but intensively and collectively the likeness to the divine goodness is found rather in the intellectual creature, which has a capacity for the highest good."[69] (Of course, the person attains this highest good only through grace.) Therefore, Saint Thomas writes that "the good of grace in one is greater than the good of nature in the whole universe."[70]

As the final end is not attainable in this world, and transcends all created goods, it is a good that transcends human society altogether. In this life, the final end is most perfectly sought in the contemplation of God.[71] All other activities are subordinate to this and are ultimately ordered to it. It follows that the entire common good created by human activity, including the social, political, and economic orders, is inferior to the pursuit of contemplation. A properly ordered society will always respect this transcendence.

To affirm the primacy of the spiritual does not imply the reality of the material. Man is both, and our conception of the common good must take this into account. The human person is rooted in matter; it is matter that determines each person to be a specific individual, to occupy a particular space as opposed to any other. Matter gives our being a material pole. In and of itself, our material individuality, as a principle of distinction, tends to seek itself, even as its existence is threatened by the nature of matter as finite and subject to decay. On the other hand, man has a pole of personality which grants him the qualities previously discussed: interiority, self-subsistence, and an expansive relationality ultimately capable of and oriented to God. When man seeks to live in community with others, both poles of his being, material and personal, are involved. On the one hand, community life helps to serve his material needs. Moreover, community satisfies his needs both to discover himself and to give himself to others.

When a person enters community, he becomes in one sense a part of a whole. However, as a person, he is as a person already a whole unto himself. We can sort the multiple strands of the relationship between the person and the common good by coming to grips with two texts from Saint Thomas.[72] First, Saint Thomas states, "For, since one man is a part of the community, each man, in all that he is and has, belongs to the community; just as a part, in all that it is, belongs to the whole." However, Saint Thomas also says, "Man is not ordained to the body politic according to all that he is and has; and so it does not follow that every act of his acquires merit or demerit in relation to the body politic. But all that man is, and can, and has, must be referred to God. . . ."[73] There is, then, a significant distinction between saying, on the one hand, that man is a part of the community *in all that he is,* and, on the other, that man is a part of the community *because of all that he is;* the former is affirmed while the latter is denied. To assert that man in his entirety is engaged in the civil society is not to say that he is so engaged because of all that he is. Jacques Maritain explains using the following analogy: "A good runner engages the whole of himself in the race but not by reason of all the functions or all the finalities of his being. He engages the whole of himself in the race, but by reason of the neuromuscular machinery in him, not by reason of his knowledge of the Bible . . . or astronomy."[74] Similarly, the human person is engaged in his entirety in the civil society, but not by reason of everything in him. As we have already seen, by reason of some things in the person, he entirely transcends the civil society and its goods. So, we can say just as truly that man in his entirety is entirely above or transcendent to the civil society. Maritain clarifies further, "Man is a part of and inferior to the political community by reason of the things in and of him which, due as they are to the deficiencies of material individuality, depend on their very essence upon political society and which in turn may be used as a means to promote the temporal good of the society."[75] So, therefore, under common circumstances, I enjoy the material benefits of living in community in things such as roads, parks, and schools, and it is therefore entirely legitimate that the civil society requires me to contribute to paying for these goods. However, when it comes to the absolute and transcendent goods of the person, the community has no such authority. The state may not authorize the taking of life itself, or prevent citizens from ordering their lives to the love of God, for these concern the absolute goods of the person which completely transcend the community.

Following Maritain, we can draw conclusions concerning the relationship between the person and society:

> [J]ust as the person requires society both on account of its abundance or as a person, and on account of its poverty or as an individual, so the common good, by its very essence, directs itself to the persons as persons and directs the persons as individuals to itself. It directs itself to persons in a two-fold way: first, in so far as the persons are engaged in the social order, the common good by its essence must flow back over or redistribute itself to them; second, in so far as the persons transcend the social order and are directed to the transcendent Whole, the common good by its essence must favor their progress toward the absolute goods which transcend political society.[76]

That the common good flows back to the persons who comprise it is imperative and is a good practical test of whether we are talking about an authentic or a counterfeit common good. The common good is no mere addition of essentially individual goods. Nor is it an overarching entity that requires the parts to sacrifice itself to them. The common good is the good, fully human life of people in communion. It cannot therefore be something which subtracts from the lives of the members who comprise it. Consider such profound dimensions of the common good as the civic conscience, the sense of heritage and tradition which underlies a sense of human and civil rights, of spiritual riches. When these are genuine common goods, no one's life is diminished to create them! On the contrary, they enrich and build up the whole as well as all the parts. It is, moreover, the nature of the common good that its enjoyment by one does not prevent its enjoyment by others. The personal nature of society guarantees that its common good is something endlessly to be distributed to all of its members precisely so as to enrich them as persons. The common good is never something external to the persons who comprise the community.[77]

Having clarified the essential relationship between the person and the common good, it remains to address the problem of individualism, with respect to the way the latter is an inadequate replacement for the concept of person, and for the ways it leads to fundamental misinterpretations of the common good. False senses of the common good surround us on account of the enormous influence that the individualist turn of mind has come to exercise in modern societies.[78]

Individualism first of all insists that only the individual has the character of end, thus reducing any notion of the common good to a mere means, something useful for individuals as they pursue their respectively individual goals, but not desirable in its own right and not desired at all when failing to contribute to the attainment of properly individual goods. The emphasis on the individual has blinded societies to both the autonomous character and indeed the primacy of the common good in a just social order. Second, individualism in both economic and political theory came to be characterized by the belief that the good of the whole—in this case, society—was the result of the solitary determinations made by its units—in this case, individuals. This was traceable to the further assumption that the material causes of social effects are uniquely solitary individuals. Such assumptions fail to understand important dimensions of human community; there is a need for a concept which captures the unique manner in which a part is a member of the whole when the whole is a community of human beings. As we saw above, this concept is person, not the individual. As a member of a set, an individual is purely and simply a part. The concept of person, on the other hand, restricts the character of part because of its transcendent quality. Third, the notion of the individual utterly fails to capture the authentic sense of autonomy. What makes the individual most unique is personality. The basis of the claim that the individual should be autonomous, or self-governing, lies in considering aspects of personhood, such as, in Simon's words, "being possessed of rationality and integrity . . . an agent in control of his destiny . . . an agent which contains its own law . . . by way of understanding, voluntariness and freedom. . . ."[79] Although still a part with reference to the whole of society, the person is himself a whole, a substantial unity, even, in a way, all things; for rationality and liberty make the person a veritable universe. The person can understand the wholes of which he is a part, even, through the enterprise of ontology, the universe itself. Moreover, the person's adherence to the good as determined by the natural moral law written in his personhood has a character of absoluteness which, again, the notion of individual as a part cannot properly capture or convey. Finally, the autonomy of the person avoids isolated, atomistic interpretations to which the concept of individual is prone. Although a whole, the person has a social nature which demands existence as a part in society. Moreover, there are acts traceable to the sociability of the person as such, and these are the acts which most define and distinguish the person. These are acts characterized by self-disinterestedness and other-centeredness, where reason and freedom consciously operate so as to transcend subjectivity, where actions are gifts to another, proceeding from the core of reason and freedom in the depths of the person, motivated solely by the desire to give of one's very self.[80]

## Person and Subjectivity

It has always been an imperative of personalism however conceived to recapture the correct sense of subjectivity so profoundly threatened by the leading trends in Western philosophy since Descartes. Of these, one of the most important was surely the attack on scholastic metaphysics. Prior to modern thought, traditional metaphysics had posited a real interiority to all beings, though most especially to the human person. Kenneth Schmitz summarizes this well:

> For traditional metaphysics claimed for each and every being (and not just for spiritual or mental being) an ontological interiority and depth. This ontological interiority and depth was understood to be brought about by the principles and causes that constituted each being. For each being contained within it: its intrinsic formal and/or material principles, its finality, [teleology] and the primordial presence that remained in communicative continuity with each and every being. Indeed, each and every being was thought to be constituted by the intrinsic principles that flow from the originating communication of the manifest-yet-hidden God.[81]

In the sixteenth and seventeenth centuries, scholastic metaphysics and teleology were attacked—the principles of causality and teleology in particular. The metaphysical and teleological universe was replaced by a radically new universe of extension and motion to be understood in terms of mechanism. In this universe, nature is not composed of a variety of beings with different essences, causes, and ends. It is, rather, a nature of extension and motion to be interpreted mathematically. This modern science of nature completely rejected the interiority and metaphysical depth of every being. For it was not only that nature could be interpreted mechanistically, but that nature was actually constituted in the manner of a machine.[82]

The notion of modern subjectivity arose out of this transformation in the understanding of nature. Subjectivity as we know it came out of viewing nature as something external to our consciousness, as an object which confronts consciousness. As all of the interiority of the universe was jettisoned by the modern concept of nature as mechanism, interiority took refuge, so to speak, in the human subject as its only and ultimate repository. As the nonteleological universe is bereft of intrinsic significance, it was left to the human subject to create meaning and to determine ethical values and ultimately what is real. In other words, as human consciousness came to reduce or eliminate the role of the absolute, or God, in its understanding of nature, it absolutized itself, establishing the terms for what constitutes reality.

At first glance, this might seem to be a cause for celebration for a philosophy of personalism; the person becomes absolute. More careful investigation, however, reveals how ultimately depersonalizing the development is. First, the mechanistic view of nature quickly translates into a mechanistic view of society, with an overwhelming emphasis on the person as *one who serves a particular function with respect to the larger mechanism over which he exercises no control and to which he provides no personal input.* The great danger in the modern world is that, whether in the modern capitalist vision or the socialist vision, the person becomes an object, a cog in a wheel, and not a subject or person at all. The choice is reduced to whether one prefers to be depersonalized by a government bureaucracy or a corporate structure. Second, the assertion that the person is the source of value ultimately offers no relief to the threats posed by conceiving of society as a mechanism. Ultimately, regardless of the scheme of values one may create, the radically subjective and relative nature of the value claims more or less assures their impotence in the face of imposing structural mechanisms that increasingly take on a sense of imperatives to be realized. The prevalence in our own culture of referring to human beings and their tragedies in the antiseptic language of mechanism is testimony to this; the taking of lives is "collateral damage," while the destruction of human work is "downsizing" or "eliminating redundancies." The much vaunted "value creation" is actually allowed to influence only the periphery of society or the strictly private realm. The philosophy of "value creation" actually undermines the foundation of any moral imperative to alter the technocratic direction of the social order.

It is precisely these developments that occasioned the birth of the personalist movement at the conclusion of World War I. Personalism at its deepest root is a rebellion against the reduction of person to function or object in an overarching process that stands above the decisions of the hearts of free people. As Emmanuel Mounier wrote, "The profound purpose of human existence is not to assimilate itself to the abstract generality of Nature [or mechanism] . . . but to change the heart of its heart (metanoia), there to introduce, and thence to radiate over the world, a transfigured Kingdom."[83] The personalist movement wants to strip mechanism and process of their contemporary hegemony. The personalist idea, in the words of William Miller, is "that the primacy of Christian love should be brought from its position of limbo where human affairs are concerned and infused into the process of history. The central fact of existence should not be process . . . ; love should redeem process itself."[84] Another formulation comes from the pen of Nikolai Berdyaev, who participated in the earliest sessions of the personalists in Paris in the 1930s: "The end of history is the victory of . . . creative subjectivity over objectivization, of personality over the universal-common, of existential society over objectivized society."[85] This can only be accomplished when society is reoriented around the person as the transcendent center it must serve, allowing society to be created from the person up, thus preserving the essential subjectivity of the person and society.

## Notes

1. The following draws on Jean Galot, *The Person of Christ* (Rome: Gregorian University Press, 1981), 25-43, and Joseph Ratzinger, "Concerning the Notion of Person in Theology," *Communio* 17 (Fall 1990): 439-454.

2. Joseph Ratzinger, "Concerning the Notion of Person in Theology," 441-443.

3. For example, in the first three chapters of Genesis, we read, "Let us make man in our image and likeness. . . . Adam has become like one of us." In Psalm 110, we read, "the Lord said to my Lord."

4. Johannes Quasten, *Patrology,* Vol. II (Allen, Tex: Christian Classics), 324-325.

5. Jean Galot, *The Person of Christ,* 26-27.

6. Joseph Ratzinger, "Concerning the Notion of Person in Theology," 444.

7. Jean Galot, *The Person of Christ,* 31-35.

8. Jean Galot, *The Person of Christ,* 29-30.

9. Norris Clarke, *Person and Being* (Milwaukee: Marquette University Press, 1993), 16-17.

10. Karl Rahner, *Foundations of Christian Faith* (New York: Crossroads, 1987), 30-31.

11. Henri de Lubac, *Catholicism: Christ and the Common Dignity of Man* (San Francisco: Ignatius Press, 1988), 331. Emphasis in original.

12. Human nature is something social. Henri de Lubac, *Catholicism,* 334-335.

13. David Schindler, *Heart of the World, Center of the Church: Communio Ecclesiology, Liberalism, and Liberation* (Grand Rapids: William B. Eerdmans Publishing Co., 1996), 287-290.

14. Jean Galot, *The Person of Christ,* 36.

15. John Ruysbroeck, *Mirror of Eternal Salvation,* cited in Henri de Lubac, *Catholicism,* 30.

16. The following exposition concerning sin and redemption draws on Henri de Lubac, *Catholicism,* 33-40.

17. Henri de Lubac, *Catholicism,* 37-39.

18. Norris Clarke, *Person and Being,* 71.

19. *Gaudium et Spes,* no. 22, quoted in Michael Walsh and Brian Davies, eds., *Proclaiming Justice and Peace: Papal Documents from Rerum Novarum to Centesimus Annus* (Mystic, Conn.: Twenty-Third Publications, 1994), 172-173.

20. Joseph Ratzinger, "Concerning the Notion of Person in Theology," 452.

21. Jean Galot, *The Person of Christ,* 90. Emphasis mine.

22. Joseph Ratzinger, *Person in Theology,* 453-454.

23. The following draws on Henri de Lubac, *Theology in History* (San Francisco: Ignatius Press, 1996), 117-220. Readers interested in a thorough treatment of tripartite anthropology in Christian tradition should consult these pages.

24. *The Jerusalem Bible* (New York: Doubleday and Company, Inc., 1966) note 5.e., p. 354 of the New Testament section.

25. Such a review is undertaken in Henri de Lubac, *Theology in History,* 117-154.

26. Henri de Lubac, *Theology in History,* 133.

27. Henri de Lubac, *Theology in History,* 141.

28. Johannes Quasten, *Patrology,* Vol. I (Allen, Tex.: Christian Classics), 309.

29. Johannes Quasten, *Patrology,* Vol. I, 309.

30. Jean Danielou, quoted in Henri de Lubac, *Theology in History,* 200.

31. Johannes Quasten, *Patrology,* Vol. II, 98-100.

32. Johannes Quasten, *Patrology,* Vol. IV (Allen, Tex.: Christian Classics), 454.

33. William of St. Thierry, *Lettere,* no. 276, no. 249, as discussed in Henri de Lubac, *Theology in History,* 193, 192.

34. With respect to an emphasis on religion and morality which stifles the development of the spirit, de Lubac has in mind much of scholasticism after the Reformation, where an emphasis on doctrine and the fear of the subjective dimension of the spiritual life encouraged in many quarters an outright suspicion of mysticism. That mystical union with God was the normal result of spiritual development was infrequently heard, even in religious communities. To note the proliferation of Eastern mysticism and esoteric forms of spirituality in the twentieth century among people who were baptized seems to underscore the point de Lubac is making here.

35. Karl Rahner, quoted in Henri de Lubac, *A Brief Catechesis on Nature and Grace* (San Francisco: Ignatius Press, 1984), 35.

36. Henri de Lubac, *A Brief Catechesis on Nature and Grace,* 37-38.

37. Henri de Lubac, *A Brief Catechesis on Nature and Grace,* 37-38.

38. David Schindler, *Heart of the World, Center of the Church* (Grand Rapids: William B. Eerdmans, 1996), 78.

39. William Portier, "Are We Serious When We Ask God to Deliver Us from War?" *Communio* 23 (Spring 1996): 60-61.

40. *Veritatis Splendor,* no. 15

41. Quoted in Portier, "Deliver Us From War?", 61. Emphasis mine.

42. My presupposition, of course, is that it is not otiose to warn against extrinsicism; extrinsicism has not died in the post-Vatican II Church, but moved to a different address. For an excellent treatment of the practical problems caused by extrinsicism in the post-Vatican II Church see David L. Schindler, *Heart of the World, Center of the Church.*

43. Henri de Lubac, quoted in David Schindler, *Heart of the World, Center of the Church,* 78.

44. Fundamentalism here refers to the belief that all of Scripture is literally true. Fideism is the belief that faith is the sole source of truth.

45. Romans 1-2; Romans 2:15.

46. All quotations are from John Paul II, *Fides et Ratio,* no. 75.

47. The term is by no means new. Pope Leo XIII called for the renewal of Christian philosophy in his famous encyclical, *Aeterni Patris* in 1879. It was, moreover, the lifelong project of Etienne Gilson.

48. For an exposition of Gilson's views, see *Christian Philosophy: An Introduction* (Toronto: Pontifical Institute of Medieval Studies, 1993).

49. Yves R. Simon, *Practical Knowledge,* ed. Robert Mulvaney (New York: Fordham University Press), 95.

50. Yves R. Simon, *Practical Knowledge,* 90-95. Simon points out that in matters of strict justice, the conclusions of unaided reason and faith are the same. If John borrows twenty dollars from Bill, he owes him twenty dollars regardless of whether either one of them is a Christian or not. In matters where reason must make a judgment with reference to our final end, then differences may emerge between purely natural philosophy and a philosophy informed by Revelation. Concerning the virtue of temperance, Simon notes that many acts of asceticism performed by the saints appear unintelligible to philosophers. Indeed, extreme acts of asceticism and penitence make no sense from a purely natural perspective. This is because the judgment which directs them acts in light

of a supernatural end and an awareness of the need to make reparation to God for sin, neither of which is knowable through unaided reason.

51. John Paul II, *Fides et Ratio*, no. 73.

52. The following argument is taken from Joseph Ratzinger, *Church, Ecumenism and Politics* (New York: Crossroads, 1988), 152-155.

53. Martin Kriele, quoted in Joseph Ratzinger, *Church, Ecumenism and Politics*, note 2, p. 154.

54. Yves R. Simon, *Practical Knowledge*, 122.

55. Norris Clarke, "John Paul II: The Complementarity of Faith and Philosophy in the Search for Truth," *Communio* 26 (Fall 1999): 557-570.

56. John Paul II, *Fides et Ratio*, no. 83.

57. For a good summary of postmodern political thought, see Leslie Paul Thiele, *Thinking Politics: Perspectives in Ancient, Modern, and Postmodern Political Theory* (Chatham, N.J.: Chatham House, 1997).

58. The following critiques of postmodernism come from Gustavo Gutiérrez, *Dónde dormirán los pobres?* in Gustavo Gutiérrez, ed., *El rostro de Dios en la historia* (Lima: Centro de Estudios y Publicaciones, 1996), 37-45; and John Francis Burke: *Mestizo Democracy* (College Station: Texas A&M University Press, 2002), 138.

59. The following treatment of freedom is based on Yves R. Simon, *Freedom of Choice* (New York: Fordham University Press, 1969). It is taken from Thomas R. Rourke, *A Conscience as Large as the World* (Lanham: Rowman & Littlefield, 1997), 101-105.

60. Yves R. Simon, *Freedom of Choice*, 24.

61. Yves R. Simon, *Freedom of Choice*, 55-58.

62. Yves R. Simon, *Freedom of Choice*, 122.

63. The preceding discussion of finite vs. infinite freedom in light of revelation is taken from Hans Urs Von Balthasar, *Theo-Drama: Theological Dramatic Theory*, Vol. II, *The Dramatis Personae: Man in God* (San Francisco: Ignatius Press, 1990), 200-203.

64. John Paul II, *Redemptoris Mater*, no. 37.

65. Hans Urs Von Balthasar, *Unless You Become Like This Child* (San Francisco: Ignatius Press, 1991), 1.

66. The following discussion of the biblical concept of freedom is taken from Ratzinger, *Church, Ecumenism and Politics*, 196-201.

67. Thomas Aquinas, *Summa Contra Gentiles*, III, 111, 1. All quotations from the *Summa Contra Gentiles* come from Anton Pegis, ed., *On the Truth of the Catholic Faith: Summa Contra Gentiles*, Vols. I-IV (New York: Doubleday Image Books, 1955-57).

68. Thomas Aquinas, *Summa Contra Gentiles*, III, 112,1; III, 113, 1.

69. Thomas Aquinas, *Summa Theologiae*, I-II, 93, 2. All quotations from the *Summa Theologiae* are from *Basic Writings of Saint Thomas Aquinas*, Anton Pegis, ed., Vols. I-II (New York: Random House, 1945).

70. Thomas Aquinas, *Summa Theologiae*, I-II, 113, 9.

71. Thomas Aquinas, *Summa Contra Gentiles*, III, 37.

72. The following argument is taken from Jacques Maritain, *The Person and the Common Good* (New York: Scribners, 1947), 60-67.

73. Thomas Aquinas, *Summa Theologiae*, I-II, 21, 4.

74. Jacques Maritain, *The Person and the Common Good*, 62.

75. Jacques Maritain, *The Person and the Common Good*, 63.

76. Jacques Maritain, *The Person and the Common Good*, 66.

77. Yves R. Simon, *A General Theory of Authority* (Notre Dame: University of Notre Dame Press, 1980), 27.

78. The following draws on Yves R. Simon, *A General Theory of Authority*, 67-72.

79. Yves R. Simon, *A General Theory of Authority,* 71.

80. Yves R. Simon, *A General Theory of Authority,* 74-75.

81. Kenneth L. Schmitz, *At the Center of the Human Drama: The Philosophical Anthropology of Karol Wojtyla/Pope John Paul II* (Washington, D.C.: Catholic University of America Press, 1993), 131-132.

82. Kenneth L. Schmitz, *At the Center of the Human Drama,* 133.

83. Emmanuel Mounier, *Personalism,* xxi.

84. William Miller, *A Harsh and Dreadful Love: Dorothy Day and the Catholic Worker Movement* (New York: Liveright, 1973), 5-6

85. Nikolai Berdyaev, quoted in William Miller, *A Harsh and Dreadful Love,* 7.

# 3

# The Person and the Political Order

As we saw in chapter one, the ontology of the person is a discussion of "both-ands" rather than "either-ors." This is because the person is both spiritual and material, a creature of faith and reason, one who is concerned with both individual goods and the common good; a responsible, self-directing agent who is at the same time ordered to the most profound solidarity with others. This reflects the inner logic of the Incarnation; as Scripture and Christian tradition testify, "The Word became flesh and dwelt among us" (John 1:14). As a result, on the one hand, the transcendent and spiritual is approached through the natural and the earthly; on the other, the natural and the earthly reflect the transcendent and can only be properly understood with reference to it.

We have now begun to explore the implications of this concept of person for the formation and maintenance of common life in the civil order. Again, we will find that theology and natural law properly conceived provide us with the foundation stones and guidelines for arranging them so they can support a political structure. These foundations can accommodate a wide variety of particular structures, but cannot be made to accommodate any or all; incompatible ones are to be rejected. In other words, what is to be constructed here will not be a monolith, or a detailed, one-size-fits-all blueprint for all societies, but one which can coexist with a variety of cultures and traditions; although, again, not all.

## The Origins of Political Authority: The Social Contract and Popular Sovereignty

One of Christianity's most essential contributions to a personalist approach to politics lies in its "revolutionary" assertions about the limitations of the state and the entire political realm. As Jesus told Pontius Pilate, "My kingdom is not of this world" (John 18:36). Although the most obvious sense of this assertion is that the kingdom is transcendent, it is also a claim that politics is not the all-encompassing totality of human affairs. The end of the human person is the beatific vision, a good surely to be shared by others, but a common good that is completely transcendent to the entire created order. To attain this end, man lives by a faith and morality that transcend the political order absolutely. This particularly biblical claim was a decisive advance in political thinking, for even the best of the pagan thinkers tended to glorify politics as the highest realm. For instance, Aristotle held that politics was the highest science because it pertained to the highest good: the common good. The claim is a valid one as far as it goes, but, in the absence of Revelation, that highest good exists within the world and is political in nature. Despite Aristotle's intention to build politics on reason, even his philosophy inevitably glorifies politics and the state by placing all other goods beneath them. Therefore, Christianity's first and most fundamental contribution to politics is precisely to limit the latter's significance. That is why from the outset of the faith's presence in history, rulers wanting to be seen as divine, and states tending to absolutism, have seen Christianity as an enemy.

The paradoxical truth of the relationship between religion and politics in a Christian context is that faith promotes a politics based on reason, and politics without faith is likely to move in a totalitarian direction. Political reason in the context of faith is liberated to perform functions which are reasonable precisely because they are limited. On the other hand, the rejection of faith most likely leads to the rejection of politics based on reason and a return to a belief in political mythologies.[1] These can take a variety of forms, as in states based upon, variously: (a) the cult of a particular dictator, (b) religions which do not delimit the power of the state, or (c) totalitarian ideologies which purport to create an earthly paradise if we will only surrender our freedom to them. The most fundamental service Christianity can render to politics, therefore, is to liberate it from such all-embracing false claims which lead only to the enslavement of peoples. As the irrationality of political myths has been and continues to be the scourge of our time, this is by no means an insignificant contribution.

Let us begin by tracing the historical background of the Christian understanding of the relationship between church and state.[2] As historian Christopher Dawson points out, the early church conceived of itself as a real society, transcending distinctions established by politics, yet nonetheless a real community, with its own laws and system of authority.[3] Yet the church did not see itself as a replacement for the civil society. The church transcended the civil society, but did not negate it. From the outset, then, even in the absence of any fully articulated theory, the Christian church recognized a distinction between the religious and the temporal spheres. This distinction was manifest in the ancient church's rejection of both emperor-worship and caesaro-papism; the former violated the distinction between God and the secular authority while the latter violated the distinction between the religious authority and the state. The sacred-secular distinction was articulated in its most developed expression by Saint Augustine in the *Civitas Dei*. According to Augustine, the Christian is a resident of two cities, the earthly city and the city of God. Each city has its own valid authority, and the Christian was normally bound by both of them, so long as the secular authority did not transgress the temporal sphere. The state and other conventional social institutions came in with the Fall, but this was not to say that they were to be shunned or ignored by the Christian. They were indeed willed by God as partial remedies for sin; fallen human nature was in need of coercion and certain sins warranted punishment by the secular authorities. Thus the Christian, living as a member of the Christian community under the spiritual authority of the church, cooperates with the transfer of temporal sovereignty to the state, and becomes subject to the secular authority, in order that the latter might rule in accord with the moral ends of the natural order. The secular authority has the right to expect the obedience of the Christian so long as it recognizes those moral ends. Principal among these moral ends was the imperative to enact just laws and to serve the common good.

In the absence of deference to these moral ends, political sovereignty was lost. Implicit in all of this is a distinction between office and ruler. For the Christian, the office of the temporal sovereign was a manifestation of the will of God. A specific holder of office, however, could not claim that his decisions were necessarily the will of God. For the ruler was bound, as all people are, by the law of God and the law of nature.

The sacred-secular distinction and the accompanying limits on the sovereignty of the state were at the root of medieval political thought. For this reason, the sense of political absolutism that existed for the medieval ruler is different in kind from modern absolutism. Whatever absolutism the medieval ruler can be said to have possessed, it was an absolutism that was confined to a realm carefully circumscribed by the functions and duties of kings, which were themselves limited by the divine and natural law. The king was to judge according to the law, but he was not its author.

Saint Thomas was fully consistent with this tradition, and, as was usually the case, he clarified it even further. As Austen Ivereigh explains it:

> St. Thomas regarded the State as possessing a positive, moral function: the promotion of well-being and the securing of justice as well as the safeguarding of order. . . . St. Thomas therefore sees the state in a nuanced, carefully-balanced way: as at once pragmatic (not concerned with the fundamental ends of man's existence), moral (subject to the higher law of justice and the common good), positive (with a duty to secure justice and order) and curtailed (bound to its [secular] sphere).[4]

Saint Thomas' understanding of the role of the state is seen in his treatise on law. Eternal law "is the rational plan of divine wisdom considered as directing all actions and movements . . . the rational governance of everything on the part of God."[5] Moreover, "all laws, insofar as they partake of right reason, are derived from the eternal law."[6] The natural law "is nothing else the rational creature's participation of the eternal law."[7] It is, in other words, the part of the eternal law man can comprehend through the spark of reason in him whereby he can discern good from evil. Political authority is limited to the making of human laws. These are derived from the natural law in one of two ways: by a process of deduction from the principles of natural law or by way of applying the principle to suit the demands of a specific case. As the divine reason is only comprehended in a limited way by human reason, reason also benefits by the divine positive law, which is revealed by God. A valid regime, for Saint Thomas, is founded on the natural law, one of the most important principles of which is the common good. All human laws must be for the common good, and the common good is always defined in terms set by the natural law. The state, then, is not concerned with the final end of man nor does it determine the ends of the lives of its citizens. It is subject to all that is entailed by the natural law and the common good, and it is bound to the temporal sphere. Although Saint Thomas did not elaborate on the theory of popular sovereignty as his later followers did, he clearly stated it in principle:

> I answer that properly speaking, law has as its first and foremost purpose the ordering of the common good. To order something to the common good is the responsibility of the whole people, or of someone who represents the whole people. Therefore making law belongs either to the whole people or to the public personage who has the responsibility for the whole people.[8]

The tendency toward royal autocracy in the sixteenth and seventeenth centuries that accompanied the rise of the modern nation-state brought new challenges to the church and decisive developments in its political thinking. The Protestant Reformation in particular gave strong impetus to political absolutism, particularly in that theologians like Luther increasingly sough to exalt the royal power against papal authority. This would ultimately develop into the theory of the divine right of kings. As the great Anglican scholar J. Neville Figgis stated it, "Luther based royal authority upon divine right with practically no reservation."[9] Divine right theory radically rejected the entire preceding tradition by asserting novel teachings concerning the civil authority. Figgis summarized these as follows: First, monarchy is itself the divinely ordained governing institution. Second, the king himself, in his own person, receives authority to govern directly from God Himself. Third, the power is transmitted exclusively by way of heredity, and the right of the heir to the throne cannot be usurped for any reason. Fourth, the king is accountable to God alone, a proposition with two implications. First, royal authority has no legal limits. Law is the will of the sovereign, and no earthly institution can rightfully limit that will. Second, it is up to God alone to judge the king. The role of the people is simply to obey. If the king commands the people to act directly against God's law, they may in such a case disobey, but they would have to accept whatever penalty the sovereign ordered for their disobedience.[10]

The Jesuit writers Francisco Suárez and Robert Bellarmine were the two most important writers who attacked divine right theory. In arguing so, they were really doing two things: defending the long-standing teaching of the ancient and medieval church and developing it in response to the specific threats posed. In the process, they put down roots for a more specifically democratic theory of government which has been of great assistance to Christianity in the modern world.[11] To begin, Suárez reaffirmed the primacy of human community as a manifestation of human nature itself. According to Suárez, human society is both domestic and political. The former is in the highest degree natural, but lacks self-sufficiency; the further grouping of families into the political community is a natural development.[12] Of immense significance is that Suárez conceives of this community as *ontologically prior to the establishment of any political institution*. As we will see, this sets his theory apart from those who would simply equate human community with the formation of the state. Rather, in Suárez's version, the role of the state, though essential, is subordinate to the community; the state is bound to serve the community which precedes it.

The natural need for more of a self-sufficient community entails the creation of the power of civil government. As nature always provides for whatever is necessary to sustain it, and as life in community accords with our nature and reason, so also is the power to govern such a community in accord with nature and reason. There is, moreover, an a priori reason which supports this conclusion. Drawing on Saint Thomas, Suárez argues that the common good of the community cannot exist without a principle to bring it about and sustain it. The person as an individual naturally tends to procure his own particular goods which may be opposed to the common good. Moreover, goods necessary for the well-being of the community may not be produced at all by any particular person or group of persons within the community. Therefore, it is necessary to establish a public authority whose function is to realize the common good.[13]

To assert the necessity of political authority is to assert the necessity of human law which is also necessary for the common good. As a social being, the human person requires a civil life within which he realizes his proper nature as oriented to community. The person needs to live well, not simply in his capacity as a private individual but precisely as a member of the community. The community also has an end, a common good to which all contribute and from which all benefit. Arrangements related to the common good require particular care and attention. However, individuals find it difficult to know in what the common good consists. Therefore, there is a need for human laws to direct the person to the realization of the common good by specifying the concrete requirements of its realization both by compelling and forbidding specific behaviors.[14]

It is worth noting at this point that the common good serves as a substantive limitation on the power of human lawmakers and is therefore one of the foundation stones of the theory of limited government. It is of the very essence of law that it be only for the common good; laws contrary to the common good are no laws at all. As Saint Thomas put it, "law has as its first and foremost purpose the ordering of the common good."[15] Suárez reiterates that a law contrary to the common good is no law, is unjust, and cannot be obeyed.[16] In other words, civil law under any and all circumstances and regimes must always refer to and be bound by the preexisting body of natural law, and even to civil laws which are derived from the natural law.[17]

Both Suárez and Bellarmine contend that political authority is instituted by God. However, as the divine right theorists argued the same, it is important to explain the radical difference between their theory and what Suárez and Bellarmine are saying, for the latter forcefully deny the proposition that God mandates specific governing personnel, nor even the form or regime which political authority assumes. Their position will become clear when we understand that God can be said to confer a power in two ways: (a) the power can have an essential relation with the nature of a thing created by God, or (b) the power can be added to the nature of a thing by God. An example of (a) would be the creation of the powers of intellect and will whenever God creates a human soul. As it is the nature of the human soul to have the capacities of intellect and will, God's conferral of these powers is indistinguishable from the creation of the soul itself. The powers of intellect and will are conferred with the creation of each human soul. In case (b), however, God confers a power which is not intrinsic to the nature of a thing. This would be the case, for example, with ecclesiastical authority. No one can be said to be born with it; it is part of no man's nature. Ecclesiastical authority is something that must be added on to the nature of a person. Both Suárez and Bellarmine hold that the creation of political authority is according to (a). Therefore, we can say that *political authority flows from the very nature of the human person as such.* As Suárez words it, "Primarily, the supreme civil power, considered in itself, is given immediately by God. . . . [T]his does not take place by a peculiar and, as it were, positive disposition or by a donation entirely distinct from the production of such a nature; it takes place by way of a natural consequence from the first creation of such a nature."[18]

Bellarmine's argument is along the same lines. "It is certain," he writes, "that political authority comes from God." He refers to a number of Scriptural references to support the proposition, such as, "By me kings reign, and rulers decree what is just; by me princes rule, and nobles govern the earth" (Proverbs 8:14-15). From the New Testament, we have the reference "to render to Caesar the things that are Caesar's" (Luke 20:25), as well as Peter's command, "Honor the emperor" (I Peter 2:17). It seems particularly well brought out by Saint Paul in Romans where he writes, "Let every person be subject to the governing authorities. For there is no authority except from God, and those that exist have been instituted by God. Therefore he who resists the authorities resists what God has appointed. . . . For the same reason you also pay taxes, for the authorities are ministers of God. . . . Pay all of them their dues" (Roman 13:1-2; 6-7). Moreover, paralleling the argument of Suárez, Bellarmine contends further, "it is to be observed that political power, considered in general . . . proceeds from God alone; for it is necessarily annexed to human nature and emanates from Him who made that nature. Moreover, this power exists by the natural law . . . for whether they will or not they must be governed by someone lest they be willing to perish, which is not human." He adds, moreover, that the law of nature is here a divine law, "and by divine law, therefore, government has been introduced into the world." Regardless of the kind of regime, insofar as political authority is legitimate, the power comes from God.[19]

Having determined that political authority has its origin in God, Suárez proceeds to determine to whom God grants the authority to make laws which bind. This power, he contends, resides in the people, the human race as a whole. This is because human persons are by nature born free; no person can claim to have political authority over another, nor is there anything in the nature of the person that would cause one to have authority over another. To elaborate, Suárez writes:

> By the nature of things, this power resides only in the community, inasmuch as it is necessary to the preservation of the latter and inasmuch as it can be manifested by the judgment of the natural reason. But all that the natural reason shows is that this power is necessary in the community as a whole; it does not show that this is necessary in one person or in a senate; therefore, in so far as it is procured by nature, political power does not reside immediately in any subject except the community itself.[20]

Suárez notes that the multitude of mankind can be here viewed in two ways, corresponding to two different senses of political authority. It can be viewed as a mere aggregation lacking order or moral union. In the absence of any real common volition, there would be no political authority in any proper or formal sense. However, this is not the sense of the multitude of mankind which Suárez is speaking of here. He means it with respect to the common will by which they create the political community, bound by lasting ties to procure their common good. This is extremely important for two reasons. First, it clarifies the sense which Suárez attributes to the multitude: a body which is a unity. Hence it needs a power to promote and sustain that unity. In other words, *political authority exists in the very nature of the community of persons.* Second, we have here an explicit sense of a social contract, lying in that common consent by which people join together for the purpose of living a common life. This act of consent produces two things: the community itself and political authority, the latter being constitutive to the nature of the former. Suárez explains:

> For it is impossible to conceive of a unified political body without political government or disposition thereto; since, in the first place, this unity arises in a large measure, from subjection to one and the same rule and to some common superior power; while furthermore, if there were no such government, this body could not be directed towards one [common] end and the general welfare. It is, then, repugnant to natural reason to assume the existence of a group of human beings united in the form of a single political body, without postulat-

ing the existence of some common power which the individual members of the community are bound to obey; and therefore, if this power
does not reside in any specific individual, it must necessarily exist in
the community as a whole.[21]

For his part, Robert Bellarmine also articulates the theory of popular sovereignty.[22] "Political power," he writes, "resides immediately in the whole multitude
as in an organic unit. The divine law has not given this power to any particular
man; therefore, it has given it to the multitude." In the absence of any human law,
no one can claim any inherent right to govern another. Sovereignty derives from
the multitude itself constituted as a political community. As human society should
strive for the highest possible perfection, it must possess the power to preserve
itself and punish disturbers of the peace. Concerning Bellarmine's theory, John
Rager concludes, "The natural or divine law, which creates political power in general, creates and vests it immediately and directly, not in any individual, not in any
king, but in the multitude, the community, thought of as a political unit."[23]

Bellarmine devotes considerable attention to refuting the proposition that
God directly grants political authority per se to particular individuals. For example, concerning the kingship of Saul, Samuel says, "Has not the Lord anointed
you to be prince over his people Israel? And you shall reign over the people of the
Lord. . . ." (I Samuel 10:1). Bellarmine denies that there is any direct transfer of
power here on God's part. In the very same chapter, we read, "Samuel called the
people together to the Lord at Mizpah" (I Samuel 10:17); when all the tribes of
Israel were assembled, lots were taken and "Saul the son of Kish was taken by lot"
(I Samuel 10:21). Afterward, "Samuel told the people the rights and duties of the
kingship; and he wrote them in a book and laid it up before the Lord" (I Samuel
10:25). However, not all accepted Saul as king, "and they despised him, and
brought him no present" (I Samuel 10:27). After Saul defeats the Ammonites,
Samuel says to the people, "Come, let us go to Gilgal and there renew the kingdom. So all the people went to Gilgal, and there they made Saul king before the
Lord in Gilgal" (I Samuel 11:14-15). Bellarmine reads in this account a defense
of popular sovereignty. God did not bypass the authority of the people to choose
their own king. Rather, the decision fell to Saul by lot taken among the tribes of
Israel. Moreover, even after the lot is taken, disunity prompts Samuel to call yet
another assembly in which a more unified Israel could proclaim Saul king. Indeed
God's providence arranged it that Saul would win the lot. However, God did not
immediately grant kingly authority to Saul. Saul was chosen initially by lot and
later more perfectly through the inclination of the will of the people. At no point
did God bypass the consent of the people. Similarly, we have the case of Samuel's
anointing of David: "Then Samuel took the horn of oil, and anointed him in the
midst of his brothers; and the Spirit of the Lord came mightily upon David from
that day afterward" (I Samuel 16:13). David continues nonetheless to recognize
Saul as king so long as the latter lived. Nor did David assume the kingship immediately on Saul's death. Rather, David goes to Hebron in Judah. Then, "the men

of Judah came, and there they anointed David king over the house of Judah" (II Samuel 2:4). Later, all Israel acquiesces in the choice of David as king: "So all the elders of Israel came to the king at Hebron; and King David made a covenant with them at Hebron before the Lord, and they anointed David king over Israel" (II Samuel 5:3). Again, the principle of popular sovereignty could not be made more clear. God does not act in matters of political sovereignty without the consent of the people.

At this point, we can summarize the doctrine of popular sovereignty as follows. The community has precedence over the existence of any and all political institutions in that the latter are morally bound to serve the former; the state is an expression of the community and not the other way around. The compact which binds the community together affirms that the people as a whole are sovereign. This political authority, embedded in the people, is instituted by God in the creation of the human person himself. Obedience is due to the regime established by the people and to its laws so long as these are just; that is, in accord with pre-existing natural and divine law. By nature, no person has sovereignty over another. The regime the community creates has an authority delegated to it by the people, and it rules by their consent. Contrary to the absolutism of both divine right theory and Hobbes, authority is intrinsically related to the common good as the agent designated to *cause* it; in doing so, authority is also bound by it as all means are bound by the end they intend to promote. In this view, sovereignty is not so much a contract drawn up among individuals who are by nature autonomous, isolated, and unrelated, as it is a consensus arising from the unity of wills who seek to live in community in pursuit of a common good. Force here is an instrument of authority but not the source of authority. Authority derives from both God and the people simultaneously, God as the creator of the authority and the people as the repository. The consensus of the people is understood to be formed by the knowledge of natural law in society. Authority is therefore bound in its very origin by the consensus of the people and natural law. No subsequent political institution can claim to be the author of the law or the consensus under which the people live. Rather, the state would always have to answer to the higher law which stands above it. The proper role of political authority would be to provide for the common welfare. In the process, the state could legitimately pass a variety of laws so long as these too were in accord with the social consensus and the natural law. Should the state ever attempt to declare itself as the ultimate source of law, usurping the authority of the people, the state would lose its legitimacy, authority would immediately revert back to its original source in the people, and the citizens would no longer be bound by it.

The meaning and significance of the theory of popular sovereignty is illuminated by noting its enemies and the alternative theories that were advanced to explain the nature of sovereignty. Its most immediate enemy was the progenitor of all modern totalitarian theories of government: the divine right of kings, particularly as it developed under the Tudor monarchs Henry VIII, Edward VI, and Elizabeth I, reaching its nadir under James I, who acceded to the English throne in 1603. Since that time, all expressions of totalitarianism, both left and right, have of course similarly denied popular sovereignty. What is of greatest significance here is not the historical association but the philosophical one. Totalitarian theories *must* reject the theory, because it is not possible to base any theory of unlimited government on the theory of popular sovereignty so conceived.

Although totalitarianism in its most ostensible forms in regimes such as Hitler's Germany and the Stalinist Soviet Union have been the clearest opponents of popular sovereignty, it is important to notice the less obvious opponents, as these frequently assume the disguise of democracy. The movement away from the theory of popular sovereignty had already surfaced from the fourteenth century.[24] New national states confronting a weakened papacy wanted the recognition not of popular sovereignty but of *national sovereignty* which was increasingly indistinguishable from the sovereignty of kings. European monarchs wanted rights set forth in concordats with the Pope. Although the theory of two spheres and two swords perdured—the temporal sphere governed by the monarch and the spiritual sphere governed by the church—the tendency to national sovereignty blurred the distinction increasingly in favor of the crown precisely at a time when kings were demanding more authority. The explicit Catholicism of realms such as Spain often obscures the fact that the church was becoming subordinate to the state in a way never countenanced by the medieval practice. In Spain, the church was largely absorbed into the state. The Inquisition was a dramatic example of this: religious orthodoxy maintained by an institution of the state. A second example was the patronato, which granted the state the right to present or reject candidates for ecclesiastical office, levy ecclesiastical tithes, publish or not publish papal decrees, and grant or refuse permission to religious orders to expand or build. Later, non-Catholic monarchs would use such mechanisms to harness the church to political authority. At the same time, the political pluralism of medieval society was being eroded. By political pluralism, I mean to say that the medieval political authority was checked by a hierarchy of lesser, intermediate authorities, such as baronies, local governments, autonomies, and guilds. The rising nation-states did away with these checks on their authority as well.

By the second half of the eighteenth century, this centralizing political tendency had swept away most of the influence of the theory of popular sovereignty. Combined with the secularist philosophical influences of the Enlightenment, regimes governed by "enlightened absolutism" asserted more and more control over the church, expropriating lands, works of mercy, and, most of all, revenues; interfering with seminary formation and imposing regalist interpretations of the role of the Church. The goal was to create national churches which would be integrated in varying degrees with the state. Although the church was being invited to participate, the underlying goal was to strip the church of its independence and subordinate it to the state. The defense of both the doctrine of popular sovereignty and the independence of the church's spiritual authority was left to the lower clergy and, most of all, the Jesuits. Figgis recognized that the original sovereignty of the people was a Jesuit doctrine. And this was precisely what absolutist kings feared most of all, not the weakened papacy itself. No, the most virulent opposition was directed against those who, like Suárez and Bellarmine, sought to advance a Thomistic doctrine of a contractual, popular sovereignty and a firm commitment to the common good in opposition to the advancing tyranny. Concerning the latter, the most striking example was the famous missions in northeast Argentina and Paraguay, where the Jesuits helped the Guaraní Indians find refuge from European enslavers while building economically, politically, and culturally sophisticated civilizations. Eventually, the European monarchs would have no more of it, and the Jesuits were driven out of Europe and Latin America.

The Jesuit doctrine of popular sovereignty was soon to confront other challenges, this time in the form of social contract theories. These, too, opposed enlightened absolutism, but were nonetheless equally products of the Enlightenment and thus unwilling to propose anew the sovereignty of the people whom they took to be "unenlightened." Taking, for example, Rousseau's theory of the social contract, he agreed with Suárez and Bellarmine on the point that "no man has a natural authority over his fellow man."[25] However, unlike the Jesuit theorists, Rousseau does not find sovereignty as emerging from the nature of persons ordered to community; sovereignty simply does not exist by nature at all. Nor is there any real community. In radical departure from political philosophy rooted in the concept of person, Rousseau and other social contract theorists would deny the essential orientation of the person to others by asserting an irreducible individualism. Nonetheless, they eventually reach the point "where obstacles that are harmful to their maintenance in the state of nature gain the upper hand by their resistance to the forces that each individual can bring to bear to maintain himself in that state."[26] In other words, although Rousseau is unwilling to admit that community flows from the very nature of man, he concedes that "the human race would perish if it did not alter its mode of existence" from the individualist state of nature. Moreover, Rousseau is of all the classical social contract theorists the one who can least countenance the loss of any individual autonomy as it is alleged to exist in human nature. He states the problem as follows: "Find a form of association which defends and protects with all the common forces the person and goods of each associate, and by means of which each one, while uniting with all, nevertheless obeys himself and remains as free as before?" Rousseau believed he had found the solution in his ambiguous concept, the "general will." It is formed by "the total alienation of each associate, together with all of his rights, to the entire community. . . . Moreover, since the alienation is made without reservation, the union is as perfect as possible, and no associate has anything further to demand."[27] In Rousseau's conception, sovereignty arises completely and uniquely out of the general will which is the result of the social contract. As "the sovereign is formed entirely from the private individuals who make it up, it neither has nor could have a will contrary to theirs. . . . The sovereign, by the mere fact that it exists, is always all that it should be."[28] The establishment of the general will is a clarion call for the elimination of any limitation of the authority of the state by any lesser or intermediate associations. Rousseau speaks of all "partial associations" as "at the expense of the large association." Therefore, "For the general will to be well articulated, it is therefore important that there should be no partial society in the state. . . ." The state "ought to have a universal compulsory force to move and arrange each part in the manner best suited to the whole[;] the social compact gives the body politic an absolute power over all its members . . . the same power which . . . is directed by the general will and bears the name sovereignty."[29]

The contrast between the authentically personalist theory of popular sovereignty articulated by Suárez and that of Rousseau could not be more stark. First of all, in Rousseau, the state defers to no authority external to itself. There is no higher law, natural or divine, which has any political relevance and which could count as some kind of real limitation on the power of the state. The general will is the unified will of the totally associated community which brooks no opposition or limitation. Sovereignty in Rousseau's account derives exclusively from this general will. Unlike the society of Suárez and Bellarmine, wherein persons are always respected in their transcendent membership in the spiritual community, Rousseau's society eliminates effectively any real distinction between temporal and spiritual. Political society has become a total association encompassing both. In addition, the conceptions of sovereignty are radically opposed. For the Jesuit thinkers, sovereignty is the product of the moral union of wills; for Rousseau it is the result of the total association expressed by the general will. Moreover, the theory of popular sovereignty insists that the social compact precedes the formation of any political regime and is rooted in the nature of the person. For Rousseau, society comes into existence only with the social contract; hence, sovereignty and society are artificial constructs subject to no one and no law not of their own making. In addition, for Rousseau, the state creates society.

If we can continue to speak at all of a spiritual authority in Rousseau, it is Enlightenment reason as interpreted by political elites. Religion perdures in Rousseau as a kind of civil religion to serve the state. Austen Ivereigh captures well the totalitarian tendency involved:

> In its rejection of all distinction between state and citizen, temporal and spiritual, and between temporal allegiance and spiritual citizenship in the Church . . . the state is placed above the Church, absorbing it, and creating a secular theocracy. In Rousseau's conception, the nation becomes the framework of allegiance, the will of Man expressed in the state becomes the ultimate sovereign above which there is no higher authority. The State therefore becomes the source and sanction of morality, with no rights existing anterior to, outside or above the state. Political society—in the Suarezian conception, only a *part* of society—was in Rousseaunian theory society itself.[30]

This was clearly a step beyond even "enlightened absolutism." The latter, similarly, could tolerate no spiritual allegiance above it. However, the revolutionary contract theory of Rousseau went so far as to demand that the state instill the secular religion as a form of messianism. The French Revolution exhibited these tendencies clearly.

The other classically modern statements of social contract theory also stand in contrast to popular sovereignty and for the same reason: The concept of person as developed in the Christian tradition is similarly rejected. For Hobbes and Locke as well, human beings are conceived in their natural state as having no intrinsic ties to other persons. The forces that drive them together to form a political community are the inconveniences of living without settled law and government. Although Hobbes' account of human nature is decidedly more pessimistic than Locke's, both conceive of the person as essentially an individual, all subsequent ties instrumental and utilitarian in nature. In their respective accounts of human nature, the individual is sovereign over himself and there is no sovereignty in the community at all. Political sovereignty is an artificial creation which occurs when individuals come together to make the social contract. In Hobbes' version, the surrender of individual sovereignty is total and the absolutist state, the Leviathan, is created. Locke, on the other hand, insists that the transfer of sovereignty is limited. The deeper issue, however, is not the degree to which individual sovereignty is surrendered to create public sovereignty, but the very notion that sovereignty is created by such voluntaristic and individualistic acts in the first place. How can essentially private powers create public ones? As Aquinas had said centuries before, no private person can create a law. Lawmaking is a part of no man's nature, and is therefore not an individual power that can be transferred to some artificial entity created by man. At the root of this erroneous thinking are the false assumptions that (a) individual, private contracts can create public rights, and (b) the common good is nothing more than an addition of private ones.

With the loss of the authentic sense of popular sovereignty which had developed over centuries, Western political thinking would move in troublesome directions. Of course, the theory of popular sovereignty was grounded in the authentic concept of person as it had developed in the Christian tradition. The person was *both* a free center of responsible activity *and* intrinsically ordered to community and to the common good. Both poles of the person were always to be understood with reference to one another. The transcendence of the person deriving from his spiritual nature is what holds the two poles together. As this specifically Christian influence waned, it was replaced by more materialistic concepts of the individual as in the theories described above. Invariably, modern political thought tended in one of two directions. It would either follow the Anglo-American liberalism which negated the communal orientation of the person and made the individual autonomous in the sense of not oriented to any substantive common good. This has led to two growing and intractable problems: (a) the difficulty of defending any firm conception of public morality rooted in the common good, and (b) the accumulation of an enormous degree of public power in private hands, particularly on the part of modern business corporations and wealthy individuals, justified in the name of preserving individual liberty. With respect to the latter, of course, those who lose out in the competition for wealth frequently end up with little real liberty. But as the theory sees nothing beyond individuals, there is little effective recourse, for interference with the economic and political privileges of wealth is judged by the latter to be an infringement of their liberty. The other option was the Rousseaunian and later Marxist versions which tried to solve the problems of liberalism through concentrating power in the state as embodying the "will of the people." We have already seen the inevitably totalitarian nature of such approaches.

The individualist and statist tendencies in modern political thought frequently converge in the threats against life occasioned by usurpations of power by judicial authorities. Legalized abortion, brought about by judicial fiat, is an excellent example of the erosion of the elimination of popular sovereignty under the guise of expanding individual rights. In the United States, for example, it was brought about by the *Roe* vs. *Wade* Supreme Court decision which changed the content of the law with no consultation whatsoever with the people or the other branches of government—this in a nation which is purportedly based on the principle that the laws have the "consent of the governed." The Supreme Court, however, would continually deny the right to life to the infant in the womb in opposition to the sovereign right of the people to preserve life. Judges today continue to legislate their own preferences, bound by neither natural nor divine law. When the Court assumes the right to interpret the Constitution without respect for the will of the people, it follows that the people lose their sovereign authority to govern themselves. What is most interesting is that it is precisely those most inclined to appeal to "rights" as the most characteristic feature of democracy who are most likely to deny this most basic right of all to the most vulnerable. It is, therefore, no surprise that the proponents of a woman's "right to choose" are the least likely to resist the trend by which the state takes on the very power to define life itself, to determine who has the right to live or not. That to place such powers in the hands of government is a sure sign of encroaching absolutism is a truth which escapes many of today's self-conscious campaigners for "the expansion of rights."

In the final analysis, the loss of the concept of person in political theory inevitably undermined popular sovereignty, and with it the most substantive core of democracy. (This will be made clearer in ensuing discussions of regimes and political economy.) Hans Urs Von Balthasar sums up the developments deftly:

> [I]n the development of the Modern Age . . . the philosophical "independence" of the person sought first to define itself as subjective self-consciousness (Descartes), and this independence then absolutized itself very soon (Spinoza, Hegel) so that the individuals had to give themselves up to this Absolute (Rousseau, Marx). Kant's attempt to save the dignity of the person could not halt this drift. For even though it was demanded that the other person be respected, the absoluteness of the person was anchored simply in his ethical freedom. Thus there was nothing preserved of a fundamental interrelatedness of persons—

as a meaningfully understood *imago Trinitatis* would have demanded. . . . The world situation today shows clearly enough that whoever discards this Christian or at least biblical view . . . must in one way or another find a personless collectivism or individualism (which converge upon one another) his downfall.[31]

## Political Authority and the Common Good of Persons

Political authority, as we have seen, derives from God and is ordered to the good of the community of persons. Pope John XXIII summarized the point well:

> Human society can be neither well-ordered nor prosperous without the presence of those, who, invested with legal authority, preserve its institutions and do all that is necessary to sponsor actively the interests of all its members. And they derive their authority from God, for, as Saint Paul teaches, 'there is no power but from God.' In his commentary on this passage, St. John Chrysostom writes . . . 'I am not now talking about individual rulers, but about authority as such. My contention is that the existence of a ruling authority . . . is a provision of divine wisdom.' God has created men social by nature, and a society cannot 'hold together unless someone is in command to give effective direction and unity of purpose. Hence every civilized community must have a ruling authority, and this authority, no less than society itself, has its source in nature, and consequently has God for its author.'[32]

We have now to clarify the nature of this common good of the community of persons to which authority is related. Although few would question the relationship between authority and the common good, modern discussions of the subject are most frequently plagued by lack of philosophical clarification, resulting in the bad name that authority has come to have.[33] Perhaps the most common of these errors is to reduce the concept of the common good to mean no more than a shorthand way of referring to a collection or addition of individual goods. For example, we add the incomes of every member of the community together, the so-called gross domestic product, and refer to this as a common good. Such thinking is fundamentally flawed, however, for there is a qualitative difference between an individual good and a common good. This difference is disclosed first of all when we consider that the common good enables people to create and share common material goods, values, and experiences. It makes this sharing possible over an extended period of time and in a greater variety and diversity than would be possible were society to exist solely for the satisfaction of individual desires and needs. The common good is therefore a compact across generations, ultimately irreducible to the good even of all the present members. Yves R. Simon makes the point, "The law of generation and corruption covers the whole universe of nature. This law is transcended in a very proper sense by the . . . immortality of human association. . . . Human communities are the highest attainments of nature, for they are virtually unlimited with regard to diversity of perfections, and virtually immortal."[34] Perhaps the best illustration of this point is when individual persons sacrifice their very lives for the good of the community, even when such sacrifices clearly terminate the pursuit of individual goods. It is only the assertion of a common good qualitatively superior to any and all individual goods that makes such sacrifices morally intelligible.

Yves R. Simon further clarifies the meaning of the common good by distinguishing in three ways a community, which is a society relative to a common good, and a mere partnership, wherein individuals pursue individual goods, albeit in some kind of coordinated fashion.[35] Simon refers to "collective causality," "communion-in-immanent action," and "communion-causing communications" as criteria of communities not present in mere partnerships. Collective causality is present whenever social effects are wrought by actions traceable ultimately to the collective and not to the individuals who comprise it. Simon cites armies, sport teams, and teams of workers as examples of communities. With respect to their actions, Simon writes:

> Such operations do not necessarily involve the actual participation of [each individual]; an act exercised by some remains the act of the whole if those who are actually engaged act as agents of the whole. This is plainly what happens in the case of an attacking army: the attack is traceable to the army as to the cause of which it is the action; yet members of the army, possibly many, are waiting, watching, resting, healing their wounds, not attacking. In mere partnership each action is traceable to some partner . . . none is traceable to the partnership itself.[36]

A second criterion for a community, "communion-in-immanent action," refers to the combination of common intention and common action which accompanies the pursuit of any properly common good. There must be a mutual knowledge of the end to be realized by the common action and common participation in the desire that this end be realized precisely by the common action. Materialistic and utilitarian influences encourage us to overlook this element, prompting us to refer to any effect caused by a group effort as a common good. But such a point of view is antipersonal, because the common good of persons flows from the deepest wells of the spirit of the person, and must engage the depths of both intellect and will; hence the requirement that the common good be an object of both cognition and volition. Moreover, it is essential to the good of all persons that they have a lived experience of participating in the pursuit of genuine common goods. In the contemporary emphasis on subjective needs, the simple but profound truth that human beings have a need to give and to contribute to something beyond themselves is sadly overlooked with often devastating consequences. Simon explains:

Communion implies, in addition to immanent acts relative to the same object, my knowing that the others know and desire the same object and want it to be effected by the action of our community. Communions in immanent action make up the most profound part of social reality; theirs is a world of peace where ennui is possible and where death itself can be sweet—there alone the individual is freed from solitude and anxiety. Mere partnership, on the other hand, does not do anything to put an end to the solitude of the partners. They may be better off as a result of their contract, but their contract will not relieve their lonesomeness. There is not, between them, any communion in an immanent action. It may be that in our time mere partnership plays too great a role in the life of men at work; according to certain criticisms, this would be a major cause of the anxiety prevalent in our societies.[37]

The third criteria distinguishing a community from a partnership of individuals is "communion-causing communications." The purpose of these communications is to cause particular cognitions and emotions accompanied by the awareness that these are shared by the other members of the community. They bind the members together and may mobilize them to act in specific ways. Such communications can be words, gestures, ceremonies, or even silences.

Any civil society worthy of the name clearly has these characteristics. This is not to claim that all causality, intention, and communication are common; merely that collective causality, communion-in-immanent actions, and communion-causing communications are consistently present and represent the most profound dimension of social reality. For example, as effects of collective causality, we can cite national security, treaty commitments with other nations, the distribution of ownership, the education system, and the entire system of law itself. Under the category of communion, consider the sentiments of patriotism and national loyalty, particularly when expressed in public ceremonies. These latter also provide the material of communion-causing communications, as in inaugurations, parades, funerals, even daily flag-raising ceremonies.[38]

Counterfeit common goods abound. The most dangerous of these are the ones that imitate or take on actual dimensions of the common good while negating others. Liberal and utilitarian theories tend to reduce the common good to a mere instrument of individual welfare. A variety of associations resulting in mutual benefit, particularly financial benefit, are frequently thought of as common goods. The danger in this is not simply the faulty theory; indeed the practice can be more profound than the theory employed to explain it. Rather, the problem is that political authority is ultimately only justifiable with reference to a properly common good. In the absence of the latter, there is properly no political authority. Hence societies patterned more and more after individualistic models will lose the sense of the justification for authority altogether, and will fail to appreciate the unique goods authority alone provides. For example, political authority, when properly constituted and genuinely ordered to the common good, plays an irreplaceable role in promoting moral conscience and the willingness of people to prefer right to wrong. In the absence of political authority, history continues to offer examples of formerly law-abiding citizens participating in the most hideous crimes, even genocide. One only need think of Bosnia, Rwanda, and even the Los Angeles riots to see how much is owed to political authority for the maintenance of social conscience. Clearly, social conscience is no mere individualistic matter to be maintained voluntaristically by individual choices. Rather, social conscience and the resistance to evil that it brings about are "goods of such nature as to be pursued in common and procured by the distinct causality [here termed collective causality] that belongs to a multitude, differentiated and stabilized in its differentiated unity."[39] Political authority remains the indispensable element in keeping this particular kind of causality alive and well.

A second kind of counterfeit common good results when the sense of the interiority of the person is obscured and people succumb to the temptation to believe that the common good is patterned after the creation of goods *external to man*. Here the materialistic threat to personalism is most powerful, for the common good of people can never be found in anything that is strictly external to the good of persons as such. A clarification, however, is in order. External goods can indeed surely be a part of society's common good, when they are in proper relationship and subordinated to the good of persons. Magnificent structures, aesthetically appealing cities, canals, and roads can be part of the common good. The problem comes when they are conceived as such without reference to their purely instrumental character; they are common goods only when in proper relation to other goods and put to good use on behalf of the community. In the absence of these criteria, such goods would be external to persons and hence no part of their common good. For example, the building of the pyramids involved the sacrifice of the tens of thousands of lives for a good in which the people had no participation. Goods external to persons can be created by vicious and exploitive behavior unrelated to the true common good. The authentic common good is characterized by its constant distribution to persons and their full and personal participation in it as a good.[40]

Much of the reason for the abandonment of the common good in contemporary thinking is that it seems to many of our contemporaries to imply an absolutist and unified scheme of moral judgments used to evaluate all private and public behaviors. It seems to be static and insensitive to contemporary sensitivities which would emphasize the proliferation of a diversity of goods and the recognition of the resulting plurality as a value. The notion of the common good seems, moreover, to require that there be no valid conflicting claims of interest in opposition to the common good and no valid conflicting claims among personal goods. Finally, the common good seems to precede the formulation of any personal claims of interest. The assertion of a common good seems therefore to be far removed from the actual experience of democratic politics, where there is a proliferation of diverse goods and interest claims, even in opposition to political authority. Any implementation of a common good would seem to have hopelessly undemocratic, authoritarian overtones.

Properly understood, the notions of both the common good and authority, far from threatening autonomy and the proliferation of particular personal goods, actually are the only authentic bases for their existence. This requires some clarification of both the common good and authority, the two being so essentially related. To begin, in a partnership, wherein there is no more than a set of individual goods, there is no essential need for authority. Civil society, however, is a society relative to a common good. The well-being of the political community at times necessitates common action. The unity of common action cannot, however, be guaranteed without a firm and stable cause to bring about such unity. Such unity consists of a unity of practical judgments. Obviously, a factory could not operate if the workers did not agree that a particular schedule be observed. A nation could not survive in the absence of common action to defend it. Unanimity is one way of arriving at the unity of practical judgments. However, whenever the means to the common good are not uniquely determined, and the genuine plurality of means renders unanimity impossible, then unanimity is not a sufficient cause for guaranteeing united action. Here authority plays the first of its essential functions. Authority is the power which causes united common action. This means that all members of the society, insofar as they are engaged in common action, agree to follow one judgment that is determined by authority to be the rule for all.

Beyond the question of the means by which to achieve the common good, there is the question of the relation between authority and the intention of the common good. Does the intention of the common good require authority, or would a sufficiently virtuous citizenry itself intend the common good without the operation of political authority? Clearly, good citizens love the common good and subordinate themselves to its requirements. But is such love sufficient to bring about the common good? Let us consider the case of a man condemned to life in prison for murder. Saint Thomas argues, "Now a thing may be considered in various ways by the reason, so as to appear good from one point of view, and not good from another point of view."[41] In this case, the judge issues the sentence as a way of protecting the common welfare, and from that standpoint the decision is a good one. On the other hand, the condemned man's wife and family first consider the good of their family, and from this standpoint the decision is harmful. A husband, father, and chief provider will be permanently absent from the family, causing immense harm. Their desire that he not be sentenced to life in prison involves no moral irregularity nor lack of concern for the common good. The point is a crucial one for understanding both authority and the common good. Saint Thomas holds that it is perfectly acceptable for individuals to will particular goods, even when these goods are not in conformity with the common good. However, he argues further, "a man's will is not right in willing a particular good, unless he refer it to the common good as an end." In other words, when individuals' particular desires would hurt the common good, they agree to forego the legitimate goods attached to those desires. Saint Thomas completes the explanation as follows:

> Now it is the end that supplies the formal reason, as it were, of willing
> whatever is directed to the end. Consequently, in order that a man will
> some particular good with a right will, he must will that particular
> good materially, and the [common] good, formally. Therefore, the
> human will is bound to be conformed to the [common good], as to that
> which is willed formally, for it is bound to will the [common good];
> but not as to that which is willed materially, for the reason given
> above.[42]

With reference to the case at hand, the murderer's wife and family, in willing that
he remain at home, does exactly what the common good demands. Their dis-
agreement with the common good is only under its material aspect. By submit-
ting to its demands, they will the common good under its formal aspect, which is
all that is required of them.

We can actually carry the reasoning one step further, and assert that particular goods are willed because of the common good. Simon gives an example from
military life, wherein issues of authority are given a particular clarity. A lower-
level officer is ordered to hold a particular piece of territory. As a good soldier,
he desires the common good of both the army and his nation. It is in light of the
end of the common good that he desires to hold this particular piece of territory.
As Simon puts it, "Thus the particular good . . . is willed because of the common
good, on the ground of the common good, under a determination supplied by the
common good."[43]

Two important conclusions emerge for a personalist approach to authority
and the common good. First, both the common good and the authority which pro-
cures it are ultimately rooted in the good of each person who is a member of the
civil society. Both encourage and require that particular persons pursue the particular goods appropriate to them. As Simon states it, "*That particular goods be
properly defended by particular persons matters greatly for the common good
itself.*"[44] It is important to understand here the ontological dimension, for it
involves the fundamental relationship between the one and the many. Although
unity is essential for the pursuit of the common good, it is important to keep in
mind that there is a unity appropriate to a multitude and a unity appropriate to a
person. The unity of the former is less than the unity of the latter. To confuse the
two and conceive of the unity of the multitude in the manner of the unity of an
individual is a philosophical blunder which creates political disaster, as in totalitarian states. The error consists in ignoring the role that the many is meant to play
in the context of a community. The many exists to serve the purpose of plenitude.
It matters greatly for the common good that there be an abundance of goods pursued and a plethora of perfections attained by persons acting both alone and in
concert. Such plenitude arises only where there is an abundance of freedom and
where particular persons focus on the pursuit of particular goods and perfections.

By way of analogy, consider a symphony in which everyone played exactly the same instrument and played the same notes. Contrast that with the beauty and vivacity of Beethoven's Ninth Symphony, in which a multitude of instruments with particular patterns of notes combine to create a unity which is ever so much richer for its multiplicity! Simon goes so far as to say that it is appropriate for a person to be so caught up in his or her particular good that other goods may be lost sight of. He cites the example of the Latin scholar who seems so caught up in Virgil that he seems to ignore the value of other pursuits. He approves of this zeal because a society in which some people can and do read Virgil is better than a society where none can. This dedicated Latin teacher serves society well precisely through his zeal for his particular excellence and contribution to the plenitude of his society. On the other hand, Simon laments the type of teacher, who, lacking enthusiasm for his particular field, refrains from appearing zealous on its behalf. This extinguishing of zeal for the particular is customarily defended by an appeal to keeping everything in its place. This thinking is wrongheaded, however, in that it suggests that the ideal is somehow achieved when all particular enthusiasms and excellences, which require single-minded dedication, are extinguished. In truth, the common good flourishes only when there is a plenitude of enthusiasms for particular goods. Simon writes, "A society in which none intends . . . a particular good is like a dead world. . . . Common good cannot exist unless it exists as the good of a multitude; but there is no good 'of a multitude' unless particular goods are intended by particular appetites and taken care of by particular agents."[45]

A second conclusion flows directly from the first. If private citizens should pursue a genuine plurality of particular goods, and indeed such a plenitude of goods is crucial to the common good itself, it follows that to will the common good in its material sense is not the role of the person qua citizen. It is the role of the person to adhere to the common good formally considered, which is to say that he is willing to restrain his pursuit of individual goods at the point when such pursuit is contrary to the common good. This adherence does not mean that the person determines what materially constitutes the common good. This is the function of authority. In Simon's words, "The most essential function of authority is the issuance and carrying out of rules expressing the requirements of the common good considered materially."[46]

Authority, then, in a personalist account, is necessary precisely because the primary concern of persons is to pursue particular, personal goods. Clearly, such pursuits can and do conflict with one another and with the common good. For example, my pursuit of property and other forms of wealth may come to the point where it is in conflict with the good of society. Therefore, over and above my willingness to limit my pursuit of individual goods on behalf of the common good, the common good requires that someone or some institution attend to the common capacity materially considered.

There is a second and equally important sense in which the particularity of a good requires authority. A good can be particular by being a good of an entire society but only a *part* of the common good. For example, consider public health or national defense, goods which are clearly common in nature. Yet neither of them are *the* common good; they are particular goods which are part of the broader common good. This kind of particularity necessitates authority as well. Concern for either public health or national defense could be pursued in ways injurious to the common welfare. Consider the results of bankrupting the nation to pay for health care, or abandoning the nation's democratic character so as to build a militarized state. It is also an essential function of political authority that the pursuit of all particular goods, even those which themselves are common goods, be regulated and ordered to the common good broadly considered.

To conclude on authority, Simon emphasizes that it is essentially connected with the pursuit of excellence and the preservation of autonomy. This involves both encouraging the pursuit of personal excellences and protecting people from overzealous pursuit of particular common goods. Contrary to its modern reputation, therefore, it is clear that authority is actually a protection of autonomy properly considered. Simon writes, "Let it be emphasized . . . that the theory of authority as agency wholly concerned with the common good is connected with the excellence of particularity. Insofar as the particularity involved is that of the [person], not that of the function, the theory of authority comprises a vindication of autonomy at all levels."[47]

At this point it is worth introducing the principle of subsidiarity, for it is central to any personalist theory of politics. The classical formulation was given by Pius XI in his encyclical, *Quadragesimo Anno:*

> Just as it is gravely wrong to take from individuals what they can accomplish by their own initiative and industry and give it to the community, so also it is an injustice and at the same time a grave evil and disturbance of right order to assign to a greater and higher association what lesser and subordinate organizations can do. For every social activity ought of its very nature to furnish help to the members of the body social, and never destroy and absorb them. The supreme authority of the State ought, therefore, to let subordinate groups handle matters and concerns of lesser importance, which would otherwise dissipate its efforts greatly.[48]

The principle of subsidiarity preserves the subjectivity of society; that is, in Komonchok's words "the priority of the person as origin and purpose of society."[49] Moreover, with the same end in mind, it regulates the relationship between higher and lower-level communities, preserving the autonomy of the latter from the former. The state and its agencies should encourage families, local communities, and their respective systems of self-government in their efforts to maintain self-sufficiency and must never prevent them from exercising the functions appropriate to them. Intervention should only occur to fulfill necessary functions that a lower-level community cannot perform on its own behalf. Subsidiarity therefore preserves the conditions for the proliferation of social, cultural, and economic goods. John Paul II underlines the connection between subsidiarity and personalism:

> Apart from the family, other intermediate communities exercise primary functions and give life to specific networks of solidarity. These develop as real communities of persons and strengthen the social fabric, preventing society from becoming an autonomous and impersonal mass as unfortunately often happens today. It is in interrelationships on many levels that a person lives and that society becomes more 'personalized.'[50]

The related theories of the common good and authority preserve both of the poles of personhood as well as the person's transcendence. In fact, in a personalist society, both the common good and authority will always be at the service of the person, and never vice versa. On the one hand, the common good is about promoting and preserving the essential relatedness of the person and building a culture of solidarity. On the other hand, it is about the priority of the person, a self-directing, free, and autonomous agent. When the theories of common good and authority respect the transcendence of the person, the poles of personhood will be correctly viewed as complementary. Authentic autonomy is preserved only when the person is committed to self-transcendence and the good of the community. Authentic solidarity is promoted only when it is the result of the free choices of persons. Both solidarity and autonomy, moreover, must always look to the long-term good of the community over time.

A personalist theory of the state must distance itself from both of the predominant ideological approaches of our time. It critiques conservatism, because conservatives have frequently denied the need for authority, particularly with respect to economic matters. As Simon puts it, "In their fight against the modern state, against the growing tendency to treat issues by the method of distinct functions and to let public powers assume a growing multitude of functional duties, in their fight for the preservation of independent management by strongly organized families, conservatives displayed almost anarchic dispositions."[51] Modern methods of mass production and the rise of the modern corporation have occasioned the need for larger organization, and it was right for the state to take on more regulatory functions with respect to it. The Bishops of the Second Vatican Council affirmed as much when they wrote, "The complex circumstances of our day make it necessary for public authority to intervene more often in social, economic and cultural matters in order to bring about favorable conditions which will give more effective help to citizens and groups in their free pursuit of man's total well-being."[52] One need only think of the necessary role that antitrust legislation, laws protecting unions, workmen's compensation laws, social security programs, and consumer protection legislation played in promoting the common good. Nor is this merely a concern of the past. John Paul II laments that so many families find themselves "without the necessary support of the state and without sufficient

resources. It is urgent therefore to promote not only family policies, but also those
social policies which have the family as their principal object, policies which
assist the family by providing adequate resources and efficient means of support
. . ."[53] On the other hand, the perennial danger remains that the state will seek to
expand its legitimate sphere of activity and trample down the autonomy of persons and the associations they form on their own initiative. Sound personalist
social philosophy will always prefer action for the common good to be undertaken by associations closest to the person: voluntary associations. State intervention always runs the risk of overriding the proper functions of families and
local communities, and stifling the initiative and creativity needed to find solutions to pressing social problems such as poverty. Moreover, because of its distance from the person, the state also tends to emphasize the material dimensions
of problems and to treat people as subjects more than persons. Although never
criticizing the state's important contributions to social welfare, John Paul II
writes:

> By intervening directly and depriving society of its responsibility, the
> social assistance state leads to a loss of human energies and an inordi-
> nate increase of public agencies which are dominated more by bureau-
> cratic ways of thinking than by concern for serving their clients and
> which are accompanied by an enormous increase in spending. In fact,
> it would appear that needs are best understood and satisfied by people
> who are closest to them and who act as neighbors to those in need. It
> should be added that certain kinds of demands often call for a response
> . . . which is capable of perceiving the deeper human need. One thinks
> of the condition of refugees, immigrants, the elderly, the sick. . . . All
> these people can be helped effectively only by those who offer them
> genuine fraternal support. . . .[54]

One of the most important contributions personalist thinking about the state
can contribute to the contemporary ideological impasses is precisely to remind
people that so often what is proposed to them are two wrong solutions, as though
the only real choices were between a social order dominated by the marketplace
and the large corporations which predominate therein, or one dominated by the
heavy, intervening hand of the state! John Paul II reminds us of the properly personalist response:

> The individual today is often suffocated between two poles repre-
> sented by the state and the marketplace. At times it seems as though he
> exists only as a producer and consumer of goods or as an object of
> state administration. People lose sight of the fact that life in society has
> neither the market nor the state as its final purpose, since life itself has
> a unique value which the state and the market must serve.[55]

## The Regime of Personalism

Having delineated the nature and function of authority, we proceed now to look more specifically at the issue of the regime, for what has been said to this point would apply equally to any kind of regime, be it a democracy, aristocracy, or monarchy, or any combination thereof. The question to be answered is, "What kind of regime is most compatible with the person?" In asking this question, we must reject the temptation to search for an ideal regime independent of the social, cultural, and historical contingencies with which politics as a practical science is perpetually obliged to take into account. Moreover, there is no one regime which can be called personalist to the exclusion of all others. This is so first of all because no form of regime can itself ever guarantee the realization of the moral principles of personalism. A monarchy governed by a saintly king may be far more personalist than a democracy. Nonetheless, it is necessary for personalist philosophy to treat the issue of regime at some level of specificity, because the person does require that authority be exercised in some ways and not in others. Although there is no one personalist regime, there are many regimes which are clearly antipersonalist. Therefore, what follows should not be taken as a "one size fits all" proposal, but as a serious attempt to work out the implications of personhood for the establishment of a political order.

We begin by treating the issue of the transmission of authority. As we have already seen, political authority rests by nature with the people considered as a whole. This does not, however, mean that such authority remains in this original condition. Aquinas, Bellarmine, and Suárez all concurred in the judgment that authority would not simply remain in its original state, but would be transferred to a regime. In other words, the people must consent to the transfer of their authority. This issue of transference has been the occasion for a great deal of misunderstanding, for it cannot be denied that the theory of popular sovereignty irrevocably holds that the power of the people is the highest and ultimate repository of political power. That is why, for example, a corrupt king who flaunts the natural law and the divine law and deprives people of their long-held rights can be legitimately deposed by the people. What, then, is the nature of this act of transmission? It suspends the capacity of the people to exercise their power and places them in a relation of obedience to the created regime so long as the latter exercises authority in accord with the limitations incumbent on any legitimate political authority.[56] In other words, the transmission must be a genuine one. If the people choose to transmit their sovereignty to a specific regime of distinct personnel, and do so through acts of fundamental law, then any attempt under normal circumstances to refuse obedience or make the transfer ungenuine is fundamentally unethical and can never be countenanced, for attempts to seize a power that has been lawfully transmitted is inherently arbitrary and lacking criteria by which the will of the people could be authentically and reliably determined. The people may not transfer their power to a regime of distinct governing personnel, but, having done so, they are bound to obey them in accord with the law of the land; the transmission of authority must be real or not at all.

To which regime should the people transmit their authority? Saint Thomas, who was the first to argue that lawmaking "belongs either to the whole people or to the public personage who has the responsibility for the whole people,"[57] argued that "all should have a share in the government," so that "peace is preserved among the people." The best constitution is one "in which one person governs in accordance with virtue, and under him there are others who govern in accordance with virtue, and all have some part in government because they are all eligible to govern and those who govern are chosen by all."[58] In this, he was following Aristotle's preference for a mixed regime of monarchy, aristocracy, and democracy. Aquinas goes further to contend that this was the form of government established by the divine law itself, seeing it in the government of the people of Israel, wherein Moses and his successors governed along with seventy-two wise elders who were chosen by the people.[59]

Robert Bellarmine similarly contended for a combination of regimes. His analysis is considerably more rooted in history, as he examines concrete examples of regimes. Concerning monarchy, he notes the constant tendency to arbitrary and unchecked use of power. Even holy men like Saul, David, and Solomon were deeply corrupted by the powers of kingship. Concerning aristocracy, he notes that it helps to distribute the responsibilities of government, but it also leads to dissensions, divisions, and factions that ultimately divide society and corrupt government. Concerning democracy, he was convinced that in its pure form it would degenerate into mob rule and tyranny, along the lines suggested by Plato in *The Republic*. Bellarmine concludes that a combination of the simple forms of government is best, so as to include their respective virtues yet eliminate their vices. A monarchy, he argues, promotes order, peace, strength, stability, and efficiency in administration. He sees in the distribution of power among legislative, executive, and judicial branches elements of aristocracy. Finally, from democracy he would borrow the principle that the people must consent to whatever regime they transfer authority to. Moreover, he believes that the regime may legitimately be subject to a referendum by the people. The people have the right to select their rulers, determine the form of government, and depose rulers in extreme circumstances.[60]

Francisco Suárez, for his part, similarly prefers that political authority be transmitted, but he introduces a clarification about the nature of political authority in its original state that nudges the theory of popular sovereignty in the direction of democracy in a way that is particularly significant for a personalist democratic theory. According to Suárez, natural reason does not determine that power should be transferred to any particular regime. Is this to say that democracy, or popular sovereignty in its original, natural form, is the law of nature? Yes, if we mean here by democracy a natural institution and not a specific regime. Recall that nature itself mandates *no* specific regime. Nonetheless, there is an important distinction to be made between democracy on the one hand and any other kind of regime on the other, and that is that the latter only comes into existence as the result of what Suárez calls a "positive disposition," that is, the consequence of political enactment, whereas democracy derives its existence from nature itself. Suárez explains:

> [D]emocracy can exist without any positive disposition, as a result of a merely natural establishment or process, without any addition being required except the negation of a new or positive disposition, for the natural reason states that the supreme political power follows upon [the gathering of men into] a perfect community and that, by virtue of this same reason, it belongs to the whole community unless it is transferred by a new disposition. . . . [T]hus the perfect civil community is free by law of nature and it is not subjected to any man external to itself; considered as a whole, it has power over itself, and, *if no change takes place, this power will be democracy.* Yet . . . through the will of the community itself . . . political power can be taken away from it and transferred to some person or senate. From which it can be concluded that no king ever had political authority immediately from God or through divine institution . . . but through the intermediary of human will and human disposition.[61]

It is clearly not Suárez's intention here to develop the theme of direct rule by the people, but he introduces an important theme which was later developed by the practice of direct democracy, especially in the United States. Although direct democracy cannot be practiced in its pure form at the level of the nation-state, it is central to any personalist conception of politics, for it is and must always be the exemplar of democracy. Moreover, in a democracy, power is never completely transmitted. As Simon writes, "*Every democracy remains, in varying degrees, a direct democracy.*"[62] That the transmission of the original sovereignty is not complete is evidenced by the following: (a) The governing personnel must render accounts to the people and are subject to being voted out of office; (b) the practice of referendum maintains the direct lawmaking functions of the people; (c) the people as a whole maintain the character of an assembly;[63] and (d) the people may on occasion depose someone in public office for just cause.[64]

Direct democracy is important to personalism because in its absence the tendency is for the regime to compromise the centrality of the person. When power gravitates away from its original holders to a regime, the perpetual problem is how to insure that the governing personnel remain in communion with the people. The problem of the communion between governing personnel and the people, particularly the largest and least wealthy segment of the people, is the central problem of what has been called "the democracy of the common man." In strong terms, Simon indicts modern democracy for the degree to which it is led by elites, men of property, wealth, and education, who remain unaware of much of what occurs on the other end of society. Despite what were undoubtedly sincere efforts in many cases to serve the poor and downtrodden, the widespread outbreak of revolutionary violence in our century revealed the stark inadequacy of such measures, and "revealed to the world that modern democracy had remained, to an unsuspected degree, the concern of the happy few."[65] Evidence abounds that things are getting no better, that what passes for "pluralist democracy" in the United States is subject to E.E. Shattschneider's famous critique, "The flaw in the pluralist heaven is that the heavenly chorus sings with a decidedly upper-class accent."[66] Under such conditions, society remains governed by an elite who are perceived as outsiders by the masses of nonelites, staged attempts to appear with the common people notwithstanding. Because these elites generally lack the experience of what it is like to be unemployed, to lose a home or farm, and to wear rags, they tend to lack real solidarity with these people. Although it is not strictly essential for leaders to belong to the groups they govern, communion of intention with them is. Leaders from outside a group are perceived as distant and unrepresentative. "The common man," Simon writes, "dislikes to be ruled by outsiders because he is afraid of a ruler who would not feel his . . . rags on his back, whose feet would not be hurt by his worn-out shoes, and whose anger would not be aroused by the injustices that he undergoes in labor and business relations."[67] As a result, to achieve intentional communion with those of a fundamentally different social class is no frequent occurrence.[68] For this reason, a personalist approach to politics must continue to seek remedies to reform modern democracy.

Simon contends that direct democracy remains the exemplar of democracy. "The archetype of democracy," he writes, "is a government without a distinct governing personnel, without any representative assembly. No representation is needed: the people gather, and they are the government."[69] That direct democracy is the permanent paradigm and exemplar of democracy should be affirmed by personalists as central, for no other theory fully underlines the dignity of each person, promotes concrete solidarity of intention and practice, fully educates the person to embrace the common good, and thereby becomes the ideal school to learn to be a person. Although modern nations cannot be simply governed in this fashion, *it is of central importance to personalism that the actual experience of direct democracy be revived within modern democracies.* Direct democracy cannot realistically remain the paradigm of democracy in the absence of any lived experience of it. In the world of politics, the theory tends to follow the practice. If the people have no real experience of self-government, the proposition that democracy in fact is self-government will travel the road within the popular mind from lived practice to former practice to an historical curiosity completely unrealistic for today. This latter point may indeed have already been reached.

It is at this point worth recalling the mind of Thomas Jefferson on this subject. Jefferson remained concerned throughout his life to promote direct democracy, and it is useful for personalists to study him carefully here. Jefferson understood that the passage of the Constitution of the United States left important questions unresolved. Jefferson was concerned that authentic popular sovereignty might be lost with the creation of the new, federal government. We needed to be fortified, he argued, "against the degeneracy of one government, and the concentration of all its powers in the hands of one, the few, the well-born or the many."[70] Jefferson feared the loss of popular sovereignty, having the perspicacity to realize that a written Constitution is a necessary but insufficient cause of its preservation. Moreover, he wanted to create a space for the exercise of the personal civic virtue which he rightly believed to be the core of a healthy political order, a space which the Constitution itself neither creates nor forbids. Similar to the Federalists of his day, he believed in a political pyramid composed of counties, states, and the federal government. Where he differed from his centralizing colleagues, however, was in his belief that authority should remain in its original base within the people as a whole instead of flowing away from them to the federal government.

The solution Jefferson sought was to make the people the repository of power by creating a system of government in which local government would be vital, substantive, and characterized by universal participation. This was to be accomplished through the creation of what he called "ward republics," which would be the base of popular sovereignty, organically linked to higher and more centralized state and federal governments, but with the understanding that the people would vote for and be represented by delegates in these more centralized governments. Let us allow Jefferson to speak for himself on the matter:

> The way to have good and safe government, is not to trust it all to one, but to divide it among the many, distributing to every one exactly the functions he is competent to. Let the national government be entrusted with the defense of the nation, and its foreign and federal relations; the State governments with the civil rights, laws, police and administration of what concerns the State generally; the counties with the local concerns of the counties, and each ward direct the interests within itself.[71]

> The elementary republics of the wards, the county republics, the States republics, and the republic of the Union, would form a gradation of authorities, standing each on the basis of law, holding every one its delegated share of powers, and constituting truly a system of fundamental balances and checks for the government. Where every man is a sharer in the direction of his ward-republic, or of some of the higher ones, and feels that he is a participator in the government of affairs, not merely at an election one day in the year, but every day.[72]

> Divide the counties into wards of such size as that every citizen can attend, when called on, and act in person. Ascribe to them the government of their wards in all things relating to themselves exclusively. . . . These wards, called townships in New England, are the vital principle of their governments, and have proved themselves the wisest invention ever devised by the wit of man for the perfect exercise of self-government, and for its preservation. . . . [I]n government, as well

as in every other business of life, it is by division and subdivision of duties alone, that all matters, great and small, can be managed to perfection. And the whole is cemented by giving to every citizen, personally, a share in the administration of the public affairs.[73]

Three features of Jefferson's proposals are worth noting from the perspective of personalism. First, it is a system marvelously suited to preserving the subjectivity, the personal nature, of society. It underlines that government is *by the people* with its emphasis on universal participation. It prevents any gap from opening up between the people and their governing personnel, keeping authority legitimate in its exercise. Second, Jefferson's system of ward republics tends to promote the authentic common good as previously outlined. Because accountability is promoted at every step, it is unlikely that pseudo-common goods would ever be foisted on the people: that is, goods external to persons. Moreover, universal participation tends constantly to invigorate the sense of communion in intention. At the same time, it encourages the necessary distribution of the common good to all. Third, the ward republic system inculcates the civic virtue which strengthens the person's healthy sense of competence and autonomy while at the same time instilling solidarity. Finally, it is a most excellent way of preserving the principle and practice of subsidiarity.[74]

A question can be raised here as to whether or not Jefferson's formulation supports the theory of authority outlined above, which insists that the transmission of authority be real, and, when accomplished and written into law, not be withdrawn. It must be conceded that the ward republic system, accompanied by the emphasis on preserving popular sovereignty, lends itself to being exploited as an insincere transmission of authority, and it is likely that many would try to use it simply to resist authority. It must, however, be recalled that the tendency to rebel against legitimate authority is by no means limited to those who would embrace ward republics! Moreover, there is nothing inherent in the theory that causes the transmission of authority to be ungenuine. Properly understood, Jefferson's proposals do involve real transmission of authority. What distinguishes them from others is the degree to which they emphasize the preservation of popular sovereignty as an actual practice. Jefferson was aware that American citizens could not participate in all levels of government. The solution to preserving popular sovereignty at the higher levels was representation. When the people could not meet to conduct their business, they reserve the right to select those who will conduct it, and those selected remain accountable to them. Ultimately, the Jeffersonian republic consisted of the following elements:

> . . . direct action by citizens at the township level; representation or agency as the concerns of the polity escaped local bounds; a federal system based upon representation to accommodate the functions of State and nation; a vertical system of checks and balances to prevent concentration, usurpation, or abuse of power; and shades or gradations

of republicanism as representation moved up the pyramid and became more remote.[75]

In none of these elements do we find any failure to transmit authority. For example, insofar as questions of fundamental human rights are concerned, clearly such questions need a clarification at the federal level which would be binding at the lower. However, in accord with the principle of subsidiarity, authority is removed from the local level only when the local level is inappropriate to the task.

The challenge that of course would be raised is that Jefferson's theory of ward republics, whatever its merits in its day, is simply impossible, our political system having centralized a long time ago. Moreover, many would undoubtedly see in this centralization political development. Would not such diffusion of power back to the base of the pyramid simply result in unacceptable degrees of fragmentation and division? In a compelling book, Gary Hart has argued convincingly not only that ward republics are possible but they respond uniquely to the political problems of our time.[76] Hart is primarily interested in reviving the classical republican ideal, but there are many points of overlap with personalism, particularly as both focus on preserving popular sovereignty, the common good, and the importance of personal virtue. Hart, reflecting on Jefferson's concerns over the centralization of authority, sees the problem as far more acute in our own time, and believes that the United States needs Jefferson's vision far more today than in his own time. Local communities, he contends, need to be reinvigorated, and this can only be done if real authority is handed over to the local level. Three areas he addresses in particular are education, social welfare, and national defense.[77] In education, we have witnessed the expansion of national standardization. While this can help to insure quality, Hart laments the disjuncture between the expansion of national mandates and the decline of local responsibility. Hart believes that local involvement in the kind and quality of education can help in two ways to revitalize education, turning it away from its current overpreoccupation with socializing people to find their place in the market society to revitalizing active citizenship. First, the curriculum of the school would be revised to include training in citizenship as a central component. Second, the very involvement of the citizens in the process would reengage them as active agents of self-government involved in local affairs. With respect to the maintenance of national standards, Hart sees no reason why local communities cannot be as concerned about them and as effective in their realization as higher-level bureaucrats. In the area of social welfare, Hart believes that relief programs are best delivered locally. The involvement of the local community promotes a needed flexibility in methods and better identification of actual needs. To the extent that federal resources are used, these can be deployed in creative new ways by local initiatives; job-training programs would similarly benefit through local involvement. As in education, local accountability is the most effective and least expensive. Finally, in national defense, Hart thinks our post-September 11 era is particularly adapted to Jefferson's proposal of local militias. Even in the early years of the American republic, Jefferson saw such militias under the control of the various states as the most constitutional way of promoting national defense. Obscured by the obvious need for a national army for so long, local militias are perhaps now to have their day, when the threats are no longer from armies organized at the national level but from informal terrorist organizations looking to attack particular cites. Clearly, vigilance by the army, navy, and air force is insufficient, as we were attacked on September 11 by people with box cutters. "No public service," Hart writes, "more immediately and vividly demonstrates civic virtue than the citizen's defense of the homeland. . . . Nothing more immediately engages the citizen's attention and energies than a threat to the well-being of family, community and nation." Moreover, those entrusted with the defense of the homeland are most likely to be interested in the well-being of their local community. Hart cites evidence to demonstrate that military units with strong bonds of solidarity are the most effective. In addition, tightly knit local communities respond best to unexpected threats and crises.[78]

The real threat to democracy today comes not from the likelihood of returning substantive political authority to the local level and the alleged fragmentation that might result therefrom. The real menace is the actual concentration of political power in a developing regime of national governments in collusion with monied interests, most notably corporations, and a developing international regime subservient to the former. This is principally the result of two intersecting trends: the tendency to shift power to the center, that is, the federal government, and the openness of the latter to lobbying and other forms of influence buying on the part of monied interests. As components of these developments, we will consider, in order, fragmentation, regulation, privatization, and national sovereignty.

Taking the fragmentation claim first, the truth is that fragmentation has already occurred, but has nothing to do with popular sovereignty. A functional fragmentation of lower levels of government, resulting in declining accountability to the people, has accompanied the consolidation of power in Washington. There has also been a geographic fragmentation at the local level as new instruments of government proliferate and other semigovernment entities have sprouted to administer a variety of federal government programs.[79] Richard Dagger comments:

> Superimposed on the layer of municipal governments in the metropolis are a number of other jurisdictions—school districts, police and fire protection districts, sewer districts, cultural districts, transit districts, port authorities, metropolitan councils, and so on. According to the 1977 Census of Governments, the 272 Standard Metropolitan Statistical Areas (SMSAs) in the United States had a total of 25,869 "local governments," or an average of 95.1 each.[80]

Hart contends that the revival of the Jeffersonian ward republics would actually contribute to reducing the fragmentation that exists. A properly reconstituted local government with real authority could consolidate all of this government and quasi-government activity under one roof and make it accountable locally, at the same time providing a common forum in which citizens could discuss and resolve all of the interrelated issues involved.[81]

Concerning regulation and deregulation, a properly personalist perspective would want to evaluate such activity in terms of subsidiarity as well as its contribution to the common good. Recent trends have been negative. The federal government has progressively abandoned important components of regulation in order to pursue a deregulation which seems to respond to special-interest, particularly corporate, influence. Personalism need not question the basic thrust to national regulation which slowly accompanied the Industrial Revolution. The development of national-level industry required a significant measure of corresponding regulatory legislation; there is no inherent violation of subsidiarity here. Antitrust legislation, Progressive Era reforms, and laws guaranteeing labor rights and consumer and workplace safety, were essentially needed reforms. The major problem that has developed has been the increased influence that monied interests have over the process. Ironically, the development of the regulatory state, originally the result of democratic pressures, was over time captured to a significant degree by the interests which were supposed to be regulated. Once corporations and other lobbies realized that the game was being played in Washington, they moved their focus there, developing cooperative relations and privileged access to both Congress and the burgeoning federal bureaucracy, to the point where the formally regulative relationship degenerated into a "grand bazaar" of deal-making and negotiating between corporate advocates and government actors. Regulatory law became riddled with loopholes to respond to corporate advocacy. Laws were often hollow in content. When they were not, the regulatory agencies themselves began to respond to pressures to alter standards, allow for exceptions and delays in implementation of the law, or impose penalties too insignificant to alter corporate behavior substantially. In another area, we seldom witness antitrust law dealing with any more than the most egregious cases of monopolization. Two examples are telling. First, consider the fate of the Clean Air Act of 1970. Amidst a great deal of publicity, this act was passed into law accompanied by a widespread hope that substantive change would occur. Twenty years later, Congress passed additional clean air legislation the net effect of which was to postpone the realization of standards set by the initial law until 2010! More noticeable perhaps was the debacle that developed over the deregulation of the savings and loan banks. Savings and loans were creations of New Deal legislation designed to expand home ownership among lower-income families. This was accomplished by subsidizing low-interest home mortgages while keeping the smaller and lower-profit banks out of risky markets like commercial real estate. The legislation accomplished its purpose—witness the steady expansion of home ownership for decades. The savings and loan succumbed to the deregulatory trend of the early 1980s, particularly lobbying by their long-term foes, the commercial banks, who resented them as a source of subsidized competition. The results were notorious. Through the 1980s, S & L's became increasingly insolvent because of bad loans, some of which were the result of criminal violations. Moreover, the end of the subsidized mortgages meant a reversal of the trend of expanding home ownership. Political leaders refrained from calling the initially two-hundred-billion-dollar default the crisis they knew it was until after the 1988 election, when the newly elected Bush regime engineered the taxpayer bailout the American public is still paying. Clearly, deregulation was the central cause of the crisis, but lobbying on the part of the commercial banks prevented any reconsideration of the issue as part of the solution.[82] Considering the cases of both the Clean Air Act and the deregulation of the S & L's, the culprit in both cases is unaccountable, centralized power. The real issue is never simply to regulate or to deregulate, as the simplistic ideologies of left and right suggest, but to promote policies for the common good without violating the principle of subsidiarity, and to insure that the federal government remains accountable to the people. A regime of ward republics would not deny the need for national standards for clean air, but it would involve local government in implementing the regulations and thereby avoid the corrupting influence of lobbying in Washington. Moreover, the elimination of the influence-buying in Washington would most likely have kept the savings and loans properly regulated.

The process of privatization has followed the same pattern of advantages for business and lack of accountability to local communities. As with federal deregulation, it is not inherently wrong. Exercised in accord with subsidiarity and accountable to the people to be served, privatizations may be laudable. However, if we examine the widespread privatizations of recent decades, particularly in the developing world, they most frequently result in transferring ownership from government to big business without expanding the broader pool of ownership.[83] They frequently cause increases of unemployment. The "efficiencies" they undoubtedly promote simply transform them into profit-making enterprises. This does not necessarily make them better public servants, as "privatization" conventionally understood does not preclude the possibility of reducing public services for many citizens. Privatizations also negatively impact workers. Corporations securing so-called "outsourcing" contracts from local governments customarily guarantee significant profits for themselves, high salaries for their executives, even an advertising budget; they save by reducing salaries and benefits for their workers. Such privatizations involve what are effectually subsidies to corporations.[84]

Above and beyond any properly national developments, contemporary internationalization of the flow of goods, investment, and finance has resulted in the accumulation of economic power increasingly beyond the control of even national governments. A CIA report published in January 2000 summed up the situation well when it pointed to two conflicting trends: the components of globalization—free flow of capital, goods, services, information, people, and expanded power for nonstate actors—will undermine the authority of national governments at precisely the same time that more international cooperation will be needed to solve these same problems.[85] Two points are worth noting here. First, it is clear that if the authority of governments everywhere is to be challenged, then there will be a declining accountability for those who control the information flows, capital, goods, and services. Second, the increasing cooperation referred to will take place over the heads of the people; it will be a coordination among corporations and various public agencies increasingly unaccountable to the people. Not only popular sovereignty, but the sovereignty of nation-states themselves may ultimately be in question. A new regime of international regulation is emerging, but it is disturbingly undemocratic in character, evidenced by institutions such as the European Union, NAFTA, and the World Trade Organization (WTO). The decision-making processes internal to them seem to be made by bargaining among unaccountable entities such as corporations and government bureaucrats. Corporate profits and the expansion of markets seem to be the guiding principles. Examples abound. Concerning NAFTA, Chapter Eleven of the agreement has "investor rights" provisions which permit foreign corporations to challenge perfectly legitimate verdicts of state and local courts. The Loewen Group, a Canadian-based funeral home conglomerate, was sued and fined for its illegal attempts to monopolize the market in Mississippi. They challenged the judgment in an international trade tribunal created by NAFTA. The case was not even subject to a court in the United States. The claim frequently made by corporations is that exercises of sovereignty on the part of even national governments in the form of regulations or fines are expropriations of their investors' assets. In 1998, Canada settled out of court a lawsuit brought by the Virginia-based Ethyl Corporation, which claimed that a Canadian law banning a gasoline additive (MMT) similarly was an expropriation of their investors' profits. Canadian taxpayers paid out $251 million while the Canadian government apologized, even though they had evidence that the additive is harmful to human health. The government of Massachusetts was sued by an organization representing a conglomeration of corporate lobbyists, the National Foreign Trade Council (NFTC), for the state's decision to purchase no product from any corporation doing business with the government of Burma, for the latter's egregious human rights record. Although the case was heard in a U.S. federal court, the real issue was undoubtedly the corporate belief that the Massachusetts law violated the WTO. Massachusetts lost the case, meaning in effect that a state may not use its purchasing power to reflect the moral concerns of its citizens.[86] If these trends continue, the only sovereignty remaining will be corporate sovereignty.

The centralization of power in the most powerful of the governments of the nation-states, working in conjunction with the largest business corporations, raises concerns of a moral and cultural nature which today are particularly alarming. Surely, the centralization of political power is an issue as old as politics itself, and from this perspective we are tempted to see nothing in contemporary developments but a new version of an old theme. However, a personalist perspective opens up other vistas which compel us to note disturbing and novel features of contemporary power.

One of these is the peculiar way in which the contemporary concentration of power is accompanied by a declining sense of personal responsibility for its use. In the past, it was easier to identify centralization as an explicitly and uniquely political issue. In the ancient tyrannies and in modern totalitarianisms, everyone knew that power was no longer with the people and had gravitated to identifiable governing personnel. Today, the concentrated power is more distinctly *impersonal* in that it is harder and harder to identify *which particular persons* have it. Three trends encourage this. First, there is the ever-growing technological imperative of our civilization. Fascinated by its capacities, the contemporary world increasingly organizes life around it. This is most obvious in the economic organization of society, wherein the quantity and quality of human work increasingly tends to be determined by ever-advancing technological capacities. As a result, job losses and the declining participation of workers in the organization and direction of their work are dismissed as mere side-effects of progress. Second, there is the growth of the utilitarian ethos, wherein the operational definition of what is good is what is deemed useful, and the overriding sense of what is useful is profit-making and the proliferation of goods and services. Third, accompanying the declining accountability in democracy is the increasing sense of democracy as *a process*. Indeed the one trend only reinforces the other. Society loses the personalist sense of the common good, that is, a substantive set of goods to be achieved through common effort and distributed to all members, through the agency of authority accountable to the people. This is replaced by the concept of democracy as the mere following of established "democratic" procedures. To make matters worse, one of the most important of these procedures is that elected officials rely on and ultimately pass off responsibility to unelected "experts" in a growing national and international bureaucracy. Perhaps the best illustration of the last point is to consider the fate of the majority of the people on our planet who live in what is popularly referred to as the developing world. There, the truly pressing problem is the absence of the goods necessary to sustain life; that is, food, clothing, shelter, and basic medical care. Understandably in such a context, economic policies are particularly important. Although the majority of these regimes meet the current definition of democracy as a process, their economic policies are largely determined by unelected economists from the United States and Europe who work for international banks or international institutions such as the International Monetary Fund and the World Bank.[87] There is almost a complete removal in such cases of any realistic sense of popular sovereignty. Each of these three trends illustrates the larger concern: the concentration of power away from the hands of people accompanied by a growing diffusion of any sense of responsibility for its use. To divorce power from persons in this way will ultimately undermine the notion of personal responsibility itself. As a result, respect for the person grows ever more feeble.[88]

Steadily growing technological capacities and centralization of power seem directly proportionate to declining responsibility for the outcomes. As Romano Guardini writes:

[T]here is a fateful inclination to utilize power ever more completely, both scientifically and technically, yet not to acknowledge it, preferring to hide it behind aspects of "utility," "welfare," "progress," and so forth. This is one reason why man governs without developing a corresponding ethos of government. Thus power has come to be exercised in a manner that is not ethically determined; the most telling example of this is the anonymous business corporation.[89]

As a result, contemporary man rightly feels more than ever vulnerable to domination by an autonomous technological, economic, and political power external to him as a person. Guardini perspicaciously notes that "power acquires characteristics only Revelation can interpret." As modern man feels increasingly that he no longer controls the impersonal processes that govern him, he "no longer feels that *he,* personally, is acting; that since the act originates with him he is responsible for it." He feels, rather, "like one element in a chain of events." As the situation is the same with others, "there is a growing sense of there being no one at all who acts, only [an] intangible, invisible, indefinable something which derides questioning." The vacuum created by the loss of personhood, does not, however, remain. The emptiness "is succeeded by a faithlessness which hardens into an attitude, and into this no man's land stalks another initiative, the demonic."[90]

Hans Urs Von Balthasar similarly refers to the demonic element in the contemporary processes by which power is centralized. "Wherever modern technological civilization penetrates . . . it also infuses a post-Christian, secular, atheistic consciousness as well." This is partially due to the technological developments themselves. As Von Balthasar puts it, "these new fetishes cast a previously unknown spell precisely because they are manipulable." Initially, the modern notion of progress referred only to the improvement of technology as a means to better the quality of the instruments man used to serve him. Over time, however, through the trends mentioned above, technological developments came to occupy center stage, and the dignity of the person was sacrificed to it. What undergirds the process is, again, the separation of power from the person. Von Balthasar states unequivocally that such power is simply evil. Yet, echoing Guardini, he acknowledges that its exercise is hidden:

> [T]his technocracy, this manipulation of things and of man (who has himself become a thing) can no longer be recognized as a phenomenon originating in power. For it is characteristic of the resultant manipulation that it does not actually apply force, nor does it confront man openly in the form of coercion; he is subject to it without violence and without external conflict. In contrast to all relationships based on power, modern manipulation simply ignores the aspect of free will in man; *thus it pursues a quasi-anonymous annihilation of personal exis-*

*tence that is even more radical than that undertaken by force. This is what makes the modern technocracies . . . much more menacing.*[91]

## Rights and the Person

The entire discussion of rights is grounded in the person's freedom, the ontological basis of which was explored in chapter one. Freedom authentically exercised can never be indifferent to the underlying grounds which make choice possible. The first of these is the gift-character of existence, the realization that my very existence is something given to me. Moreover, there are other "givens" which ground my capacity to choose, such as the family, the community, and the physical environment. Freedom must attend to these givens or stand vitiated in its very root. In addition, freedom is intrinsically linked to the attainment of moral goodness. The free person is not one of a flaccid and undetermined character, but one who has developed the inner capacities, virtues, needed to accomplish the good under diverse and difficult circumstances. Freedom so understood serves as the background for considering freedom politically and legally in the form of rights.

The historical origins of rights in Western political thought are inextricably linked to the concept of person as developed in Christianity. Because of the dignity of the person, Christianity came to argue in favor of rights. It is therefore worthwhile for a theory of personalism to revisit the historical context in which rights emerged. We begin by recalling that prior to the time that Christian theology formed the concept of person, the notion of citizens having subjective rights did not exist. The word "right" has its origins in the Latin *ius,* the Latin translation of the Greek word for justice, *dikaion,* which had two meanings in Aristotle: (a) justice as a moral virtue, and (b) a morally correct state of affairs. The same meanings devolved onto the Latin *ius.* Although an interpretation of *ius* as a subjective power inhering in individuals had already developed by the time of Saint Thomas, he did not himself use the term that way; he developed no explicit doctrine of subjective rights.[92] It was left to his followers, later scholastic writers, to do so. The issue of subjective rights and their relationship to natural law was forced on the attention of Spanish scholastics at the time of the conquest of the New World. The collision of two worlds inevitably raised practical questions concerning the respective rights of the indigenous peoples and the Spaniards. It was providential that the initial development of a doctrine of rights occurred in the context of asserting rights for the Indians, because the latter were being subject to such dehumanizing treatment and their very status as persons was questioned by thinkers such as Sepúlveda. As both the personhood and the rights of Indians needed to be established, the resulting arguments underlined the link between the two in a way that would have been less clear had the repositories of personhood and rights been more socially esteemed.

Francisco Vitoria developed a subjective sense of *ius* out of Saint Thomas' objective meaning. The transition is observable in the following: "[Aquinas] says therefore that right is that which is licit in accordance with the laws. And so we use the word when we speak. For we say, 'I have not the right of doing this,' that is, it is not licit for me; or again, 'I use my right,' that is, it is licit.' "[93] What begins as a statement of what is objectively right ends in an assertion of subjective rights. As Tierney explains it, Vitoria was relying on a concept of permissive law, an arena of choice in which the law neither mandated nor forbade specific action. A right, then, was a freedom to act within the framework of law. From here he linked *ius* to its already existing legal meaning as a faculty or power.[94]

In another work, Vitoria takes up explicitly the issue of the rights of the Indians.[95] Given that the Indians had clearly been living in the New World and possessed the land *de facto*, there were four possible justifications for denying them dominion: that they were either "sinners, unbelievers, madmen, or insensate." Vitoria's implicit argument is that all peoples have the right to own property unless hindered by some defect. Vitoria finds each of the justifications wanting. Even mortal sin would not deprive someone of his civil right to own. Vitoria notes that the argument to the contrary has no support in Scripture, and was explicitly rejected by the Council of Constance. Similarly, Scripture does not challenge the right of unbelievers to own land. As to the negation of the Indians' rationality and the assertion that they are mad, Vitoria states that the Indians have "judgment like other men," as evidenced by the ordering of their civil affairs via marriage, established cities, law, and commerce. Vitoria concludes that the Indians certainly possessed true dominion and had a valid right to the land.[96]

In the process of defending the Indians here, Vitoria affirmed a principle that became central to human rights theories; that is, the unique status of the human person. Earlier, he affirmed that "the foundation of dominion is the fact that we are formed in the image of God." This is to say that the basis of rights is the origin of the person in God. Therefore, only human persons can be bearers of rights. The insight appears commonplace, but other authorities, such as Conrad Summerhart and Silvestro Mazzolini de Priero, had likened the right of human persons to the dominion exercised by other creatures, the "right to use a thing for one's own benefit." From this perspective, an animal has a right to its prey and a star has a right to shine. Vitoria contended that there is no question of justice when dealing with other created beings. To deprive a lion of his prey would be no injustice to the beast; to draw the blinds is no offense against the sun.[97] What Vitoria sees unique is one of the qualities of personhood identified in chapter one, namely, that the human person is *sui generis,* master of his own actions, knowledgeable of the ends of his nature, and capable of directing his actions to reach those ends. This is what makes man free, and hence a bearer of rights. As a creature bestowed with reason, man also has dominion over the rest of nature. Again, God is ultimately the basis of the claim, dominion being exercised in the name of man's status as an image of God; man has a power with respect to other creatures analogous to God's absolute dominion.[98]

Another important contribution in the fight to grant dignity to the Indians was Vitoria's refutation of an argument which had become a popular rationalization among those who sought to enslave the Indians: the application of Aristotle's category of "natural slaves" to the Indians. Aristotle believed that some men were insufficiently rational by nature to govern themselves, and therefore needed to be governed by another. Those wishing to enslave the Indians found it a convenient argument, especially in that they could use the authority of Aristotle as a justification. Vitoria responded that Aristotle did not mean to say that some men belonged to others by nature and thereby lost their rights, for this could only be a civil and legal condition to which no one can belong by nature. Conceding that the Indians may indeed suffer from some "natural deficiency," this would only grant the Spaniards a position as governors and directors.[99] Whatever defects the Indians had in no way deprived them of their natural rights. As an interpretation of Aristotle, Vitoria was surely being creative here, but the significance of the point is that Vitoria is looking to the underlying personhood of the Indians, although clearly sharing some of the prejudices of his countrymen.

Bartolomé de Las Casas looked at rights from a far more personal perspective. He himself had been an *encomendero* and witnessed the Spaniards' depredations of the native peoples of the Indies. Through his lifelong commitment to defend the Indians, Las Casas insisted that the Indians were persons endowed with all of the corresponding rights. What is especially rich in Las Casas is the theological context which alone reveals what it means to be a person in its transcendent fullness as an image of the divine. He echoed many of the same themes as Vitoria; like his countryman and fellow Dominican, he grafted a theory of natural rights onto Saint Thomas' natural law theory. But in his insistence that the Indians were persons, equal to all others, and in his determination to root the claims in God, his contribution to our understanding of both the dignity of the person and rights surpassed his Dominican colleagues.

Las Casas was perhaps the first to insist that absolutely all people were fundamentally equal and to root the claim in God without the slightest toleration for qualification or ambiguity. Although respectful of philosophical sources, he did not hesitate to discard even the authority of Aristotle if it compromised revealed truth. Las Casas' approach is well revealed in his treatment of Aristotle's discussion of "barbarians" and "natural slaves." The first definition of barbarian is a "cruel, inhumane, savage, pitiless human being who has withdrawn from reason." Las Casas notes that the Greeks, Romans, and even the Spaniards would fit this definition at times! A second rendering of the term refers to those who do not know Scripture or speak a different language. But even cultured nations have not known the Gospel or been familiar with the language of other nations. Hence, Greeks and Romans referred to one another as barbarians. Surely these understandings of barbarianism were insufficient to deny people their rights. Finally, there were Aristotle's "natural slaves," who are incapable of self-government and need to be ruled by others. Las Casas insists that such a category cannot be applied to the Indians in any general way. Beyond that, Las Casas simply rejects Aristotle's claim that such people could be hunted like beasts, saying, "Too bad for Aristotle," who was "ignorant of Christian truth and charity." The Indians, he writes, "have been created in the image of God" and are therefore capable of "entering the Kingdom of Christ . . . as they are our siblings . . . redeemed by the most precious blood of Christ." For Las Casas, they are the poor of the Gospel, the least of Christ's brethren, and therefore have a special place in God's eyes and in the eyes of all true Christians. The image of God is within them and this is the evangelical basis of all human rights.[100]

What is unique in Las Casas is the direct way he roots rights in two specifically theological claims: (a) Christians are obligated to love all people, and (b) all people are images of God in whom Christ dwells. Moreover, he insisted that the Indians' civil status conform to their theological one! The Christological basis of his approach is perhaps most clearly revealed in this famous passage from *History of the Indies:*

> Supposing, Sir, that you were to see Our Lord Jesus Christ abused—someone laying hands on him, afflicting him, and insulting him with all manner of vituperation—would you not beg with the greatest urgency and with all your strength that he be handed over to you . . .? Indeed, Sir, I have but acted in that very manner. *For I leave, in the Indies, Jesus Christ, our God, scourged and afflicted, and buffeted and crucified, not once but millions of times,* on the part of Spaniards who ruin and destroy these people . . . depriving them of life before their time. . . .[101]

It would not be an exaggeration to say that the radical Christocentrism of Las Casas' perspective opened up a deeper dimension of morality that distanced the friar from most of his countrymen. One area where Las Casas staked out new ground concerned liberty of conscience. It was already well established in his time that the faith could only be accepted freely. The debate was over the extent to which force might be used to remove obstacles to the faith. Las Casas considered the acknowledgment of the rights of a people to their own way of life and to their own conscience in matters of religion a requirement of his own faith. Hence, what seems to many as the paradox that Las Casas labored his whole life to convert the Indians to Christianity, yet so ardently defended their right to maintain their own practices. The reason is that Las Casas thought the faith itself granted the right to choose religious beliefs, even if they be mistaken. Hence, the other pillar of Las Casas' approach to the Indians was that all attempts to convert them should be nonviolent. Concerning the issue of removing obstacles to the faith, Las Casas claimed that the real obstacle to the faith was the counterwitness of the Spaniards' own behavior.[102]

A second principle enunciated by Las Casas was consent of the governed, articulated here over a hundred years before the fuller doctrine of popular sovereignty had been expounded by the Jesuits. Las Casas originally argued that the freedom of the person simply excluded domination and oppression. However, he continued to develop the implications of this freedom to embrace a doctrine well ahead of its time. In *De regia potestate,* he had stated in the abstract the principle of the consent of the governed. This was not novel; it was implied by Aquinas centuries before. However, he began to apply it quite literally to the case of the Indians in relation to the Spaniards, meaning that Spanish rule was completely subject to Indian approval. Consent was the "natural foundation and efficient cause" of any valid transfer of sovereignty away from the Indians themselves. Moreover, the transfer of sovereignty could not simply take the form of some ruler giving away the peoples' rights, nor would even a decision by a majority suffice; in the latter case, such action would be against liberty and could not therefore prejudice those who chose to remain free.[103]

In the sixteenth century, Francisco Suárez developed the link between natural law and natural rights. Although it is the case that Saint Thomas did not develop a theory of subjective rights, there is a logical link between the two concepts. For example, in Saint Thomas' natural law theory, it is morally legitimate to defend oneself from attack. Moreover, he affirms that it is acceptable for people to possess goods as their own. Do these assertions entail that there exists a right of self-defense and a right to own private property? Saint Thomas did not proceed to make the step, but the logical connection between the claims is clear. In the sixteenth century, when totalitarian theories of divine rights were being advanced, Suárez made the connection explicit. Beginning with the traditional sense of *ius* as what is fair and in harmony with justice, he proceeded to claim that *ius* refers as well to a moral capacity residing in the person by which, as in the case of private property duly held or wages duly earned, one could be said to have a right to the property and the wages.[104] The moral power of *ius* is truly an object of justice itself.[105] The objective sense of *ius* as law and its subjective sense as a right are here united. Later, Suárez will make of liberty itself an article of the natural law "since nature itself confers upon man the true dominion of his liberty."[106]

Modern Catholic social teaching has embraced the proposition that people have subjective rights, in accord with the developments outlined above. In *Pacem in Terris,* John XXIII refers to a rather extensive list of "natural rights": to live, to be respected, to receive an education and the benefits of culture, to worship God in accord with his conscience, to have a family, to work and to engage in other economic initiatives, to own property, to form associations with others, to migrate, to participate in public life, and to receive legal protection for one's rights.[107] He emphasizes that these rights have corresponding duties, including: to preserve one's life, to respect the rights of others, and to collaborate with others to build up the civic order.[108]

> The natural rights of which we have so far been speaking are inextricably bound up with as many duties, all applying to one and the same person. These rights and duties derive their origin, their sustenance, and their indestructibility from the natural law, which in conferring the one imposes the other. . . . Every basic human right draws its authori-

tative force from the natural law, which confers it and attaches to it its respective duty.[109]

Conclusions emerge on two levels when we consider the origins of rights in Western political thought. First, rights claims on behalf of the person emerged as a conclusion from ongoing reflection on the nature and dignity of the person as an image and likeness of God. This remains politically and legally significant, because the origin of the person in God is the ground of the person's transcendence, the only ultimately reliable source of rights. Moreover, this theological context irrevocably links respect for the rights of the person with respect for the entire gift-character of existence. We respect people by recognizing rights within them, and we understand that this respect is a special case of the broader claims made on us by our character as creatures. To respect the rights of others is a necessary but insufficient requirement of the deeper commandment to love them, even those who are our enemies. This deeper context of the imperative to love is the only way to insure that rights do not become overly abstract and ultimately separate from the concrete character of people as creatures of mind, body, and spirit. Moreover, that it is a person who is the subject of rights means that the dimension of autonomy conferred by rights can never be separated from the pole of solidarity. Second, it is important to maintain the connection between the subjective and objective senses of *ius*. It is natural law which confers liberty on the person and opens up spaces for him to exercise it. The subjective sense of *ius* must operate within the objective sense of *ius* as law.

In our own time, it is precisely the separation of the philosophy of rights from its original grounding in the person as discussed here, in its full theological-philosophical context, which undermines authentic rights, renders rights theory increasingly incoherent, and ultimately contributes to undermining the dignity of the person altogether. Alasdair MacIntyre describes well the philosophical and moral roots of the problem.[110] Prior to the Enlightenment, at the time the theory of rights was developed, the language of morality was set in a framework consisting of three parts. First, there was an objective sense, rooted in philosophy and theology, of human nature in its mature state as realizing the ends and purposes to which the person is directed by nature, or natural finalities. Included among them would be the traditional mandates of the natural law. Second, there was a corresponding sense of human nature in its current, existing condition, a state of imperfection. Third, there was the language of morality, the identification of certain actions as good or evil. In this context, MacIntyre notes, the classification of actions as good or evil is to say that such actions either contribute to the person's goal of realizing his telos—in the case of good actions—or prevent him from realizing the same—in the case of bad actions. In other words, the coherence of moral theory and moral language is ultimately contingent upon our knowledge of the telos of the person. The problem came with the acceptance of the Enlightenment claim that the ends and purposes of the person are not knowable. Such a claim renders moral claims incoherent and ultimately unintelligible, the ends which served as the basis for making moral evaluations no longer held to be a legitimate object of our knowledge. If there are no ends to which I am ordered by nature, then how could the realization or the failure to attain any end be objectively identified as good or evil? MacIntyre notes that the Enlightenment attempted to reconstruct morality on other bases, the first of which was utilitarianism, which attempted to avoid the issue of the telos altogether by identifying the good with the useful. The problem is that in the final analysis what is useful is so only in reference to some end, and thus we are back to asserting a telos, only this time a telos which in terms of the theory has no objective basis.

The other attempt has been to compensate for the lack of an objective morality in terms of rights. This, too, is impossible, because the assertion of rights in the absence of an objective morality splits the two meanings of *ius* and thereby removes the basis for asserting a right in the first place. A right was and is a right because it is morally right to permit the action allowed by the right. The removal of the moral underpinning ultimately makes rights indistinguishable from mere subjective desires. To make matters worse, natural rights outside of natural law can only root rights ultimately in an autonomous "individual." This creation of the modern Western imagination is the doppelganger of the older concept of person, stripped of the latter's grounding in God, transcendence, the gift-character of existence, and solidarity with others; in short, everything which could make him real. We are left with autonomous individuals with an endless series of desires they now term "rights," and nothing other than raw political power to determine which of these various claims will be recognized.

This last point is worthy of separate attention. One of the political consequences of grounding natural rights in natural law was to provide rights with their firmest guarantees. Recall that natural law served as the foundation in Western thought of limited government. Government is limited because there is a law which stands above it and which it cannot violate. Rights guaranteed by natural law have then the most secure of all foundations. When rights are asserted in the context of the denial of natural law, they have no secure basis and are indistinguishable from desires or wants. Ultimately, the variety of rights claims are intrinsically incompatible, and the state is left to decide among them with no firm philosophical foundation upon which to do so. It is inevitable in such a context that decisions will be arbitrary and determined by raw exercises of political power. Curiously, the ahistorical and irrational claim that rights are best preserved in the absence of objective morality has gained popularity in intellectual circles. John Paul II understands the development well:

> Authentic democracy is possible only in a state ruled by law and on the basis of a correct conception of the human person. . . . Nowadays there is a tendency to claim that agnosticism and skeptical relativism are the philosophy and the basic attitude which correspond to democratic forms of political life. Those who are convinced that they know the truth and firmly adhere to it are considered unreliable from a demo-

cratic point of view, since they do not accept that truth is determined by the majority or that it is subject to variation according to different political trends. It must be observed in this regard that if there is no ultimate truth to guide and direct political activity, then ideas and convictions can be easily manipulated for reasons of power. As history demonstrates, a democracy without values easily turns into open or disguised totalitarianism.[111]

Modern rights theory offers further reason for reducing democracy to force in that it removes any firm foundation for obedience to the state. Having denied that society rests on any objective moral basis, why should anyone obey a law that violates their chosen moral sense? Vukan Kuic demonstrates the problems with theorists such as John Rawls and Sanford Levinson, both of whom espouse individualistic, morally relativist theories of democracy.[112] Rawls and Levinson claim that in a democracy each citizen forever retains the right to interpret for himself the principles of justice, there being no morally binding interpretation of these same principles. True, as stated above, democracy does not transmit all of its powers, but this was never intended to mean that laws were not binding in conscience under normal conditions, to assert a perpetual right for the individual to opt out of the laws. As Kuic notes, even the notion of civil disobedience is rooted in the supposition that laws are morally binding under normal circumstances. The theories of Rawls and Levinson, however, provide no basis for being morally bound by the law. If democracy cannot produce morally binding laws, then it, too, has no legitimate authority. The larger point, however, is that modern rights theories, grounded in the individual, tend to delegitimize authority in principle, pitting a false conception of freedom against an equally false conception of authority. Only in the recovery of the person can either concept be restored to its proper place.

## Notes

1. Joseph Ratzinger, *Church, Ecumenism and Politics* (New York: Crossroads, 1988), 147-148.

2. The following summary is drawn from Austen Ivereigh, *Catholicism and Politics in Argentina: 1810-1960* (New York: St. Martin's Press, 1996), 3-11.

3. Christopher Dawson, *The Dynamics of World History,* ed. John Mulloy (New York: Sheed and Ward, 1962), 203-208.

4. Austen Ivereigh, *Catholicism and Politics in Argentina,* 6.

5. Thomas Aquinas, quoted in Paul Sigmund, ed., *St. Thomas Aquinas on Politics and Ethics* (New York and London: W.W. Norton and Co., 1988), 48, 46.

6. Thomas Aquinas, *Summa Theologiae,* I-II, 93, 4.

7. Thomas Aquinas, *Summa Theologiae,* I-II, 91, 2.

8. Thomas Aquinas, quoted in Paul Sigmund, ed., *St. Thomas Aquinas on Politics and Ethics,* 45.

9. J. Neville Figgis, *From Gerson to Grotius* (Cambridge: Cambridge University Press, 1923), 61.

10. J. Neville Figgis, *The Theory of Divine Right of Kings* (Cambridge: Cambridge University Press, 1896), 5.

11. I draw upon the following for the exposition of the doctrines taught by Suárez and Bellarmine: John Clement Rager, *The Political Philosophy of St. Robert Bellarmine*, 2nd ed. (Spokane: Apostolate of Our Lady of Siluva, 1995); and James Scott Brown, ed., *The Classics of International Law* (London: Clarendon Press, 1949). The specific work is *De Legibus, Ac Deo Legislatore*. Hereafter the work will be referred to as *De Legibus*.

12. Francisco Suárez, *De Legibus*, 364-365.

13. Francisco Suárez, *De Legibus*, 366-367. Bellarmine's view corresponds exactly. See Rager, *The Political Philosophy of Robert Bellarmine*, 27.

14. Francisco Suárez, *De Legibus*, 48-49.

15. Thomas Aquinas, *Summa Theologiae*, I-II, 90, 3.

16. Francisco Suárez, *De Legibus*, 90, 113.

17. Thomas Aquinas argued that human law derived from the natural law in two ways: by way of conclusion from the principles of natural law, or by way of application from the natural law's general formulations. For an example of the former, the human law against killing derives from the natural law principle which forbids harming another. An example of the latter would be tax codes which are an attempt to apply the general principle that all members of the community should contribute to the common good. What Suárez is saying is that human or civil laws which derive their validity directly from the natural law itself merit similar respect from lawmakers.

18. Francisco Suárez, quoted in Yves R. Simon, *Philosophy of Democratic Government* (Notre Dame: University of Notre Dame Press, 1993), 171.

19. John Clement Rager, *The Political Philosophy of Robert Bellarmine*, 27-29.

20. Francisco Suárez, quoted in Yves R. Simon, *Democratic Government*, 172.

21. Francisco Suárez, *De Legibus*, 375-376.

22. The following summary of Bellarmine's theory of popular sovereignty is taken from John Clement Rager, *The Political Philosophy of Robert Bellarmine*, 29-33.

23. John Clement Rager, *The Political Philosophy of Robert Bellarmine*, 30.

24. The following historical discussion of popular sovereignty and alternatives to it draws on Austen Ivereigh, *Catholicism and Politics in Argentina*, 10-13.

25. Jean-Jacques Rousseau, *On the Social Contract*, quoted in David Wootton, ed., *Modern Political Thought: Readings from Machiavelli to Nietzsche* (Indianapolis and Cambridge: Hackett Publishing, Inc., 1996), 467.

26. Jean-Jacques Rousseau, in Wootton, ed., *Modern Political Thought*, 470.

27. Jean-Jacques Rousseau, in Wootton, ed., *Modern Political Thought*, 470.

28. Jean-Jacques Rousseau, in Wootton, ed., *Modern Political Thought*, 472.

29. Jean-Jacques Rousseau, in Wootton, ed., *Modern Political Thought*, 477.

30. Austen Ivereigh, *Catholicism and Politics in Argentina*, 13.

31. Hans Urs Von Balthasar, "On the Concept of Person," *Communio* 13 (Spring 1986): 24-25.

32. John XXIII, *Pacem in Terris*, no. 46.

33. Yves R. Simon, *A General Theory of Authority* (Notre Dame: University of Notre Dame Press, 1980), 13-22.

34. Yves R. Simon, *General Theory*, 29.

35. The following summary of Simon's explanation of the common good is taken from my previous book, Thomas R. Rourke, *A Conscience as Large as the World* (Lanham and London: Rowman & Littlefield, 1997), 92-94.

36. Yves R. Simon, *Democratic Government,* 64. As an example of a partnership, Simon cites the relationship between a handicraftsman and a moneylender in which the handicraftsman does all the work and the moneylender provides all of the financing. Although both benefit from their partnership, their efforts are relative to individual goods only, as none of the effects of their work are traceable to the partnership itself.

37. Yves R. Simon, *Democratic Government,* 65. The point seems particularly poignant at the present time, when available evidence shows that anxiety and depression afflict tens of millions of people in the United States. Curiously, the connection between the epidemic spread of such afflictions and the loss of the sense of solidarity in our society is generally bypassed.

38. Yves R. Simon, *Democratic Government,* 65-66.

39. Yves R. Simon, *The Tradition of Natural Law* (New York: Fordham University Press, 1992), 91.

40. Yves R. Simon, *Natural Law,* 91-92.

41. Thomas Aquinas, *Summa Theologiae,* I-II, 19, 10.

42. Thomas Aquinas, *Summa Theologiae,* I-II, 19, 10.

43. Yves R. Simon, *Democratic Government,* 41.

44. Yves R. Simon, *Democratic Government,* 41. Emphasis in original.

45. Yves R. Simon, *Democratic Government,* 55.

46. Yves R. Simon, *General Theory,* 57. Emphasis in original.

47. Yves R. Simon, *General Theory,* 158.

48. Pius XI, *Quadragesimo Anno,* nos. 79-80.

49. Joseph Komonchok, "Subsidiarity in the Church: The State of the Question," *The Jurist* 48 (1988): 298-300.

50. John Paul II, *Centesimus Annus,* no. 49.

51. Yves R. Simon, *General Theory,* 158.

52. *Gaudium et Spes,* no. 75.

53. John Paul II, *Centesimus Annus,* no. 48.

54. John Paul II, *Centesimus Annus,* no. 48.

55. John Paul II, *Centesimus Annus,* no. 49.

56. As discussed in the first section of this chapter, the limitations would be those imposed by divine and natural law; laws should always intend the common good. Moreover, authority is obligated to serve the society, which implies respecting its moral and cultural inheritance.

57. Thomas Aquinas, *Summa Theologiae,* I-II, 90, 3.

58. Thomas Aquinas, *Summa Theologiae,* I-II, 105, 1.

59. Thomas Aquinas, *Summa Theologiae,* I-II, 105, 1.

60. Bellarmine's views concerning the best form of regime are from Rager, *The Political Philosophy of Robert Bellarmine,* 18-24.

61. Francisco Suárez, quoted in Simon, *Democratic Government,* 173. The original source is not cited therein.

62. Yves R. Simon, *Democratic Government,* 184.

63. Yves R. Simon, *Democratic Government,* 190-192. Simon makes the point that there is a perpetual danger here in that, when carried too far, the legitimate consulting role of the people can extend into an insincere transmission of authority. This occurs in cam-

paigns of opinion in which the people take on the disposition that their elected officials should obey them. The people may legitimately do this only under grave circumstances.

64. Yves R. Simon, *Democratic Government,* 184-190.

65. Yves R. Simon, *Democratic Government,* 217.

66. E.E. Schattschneider, *The Semi-Sovereign People* (Glenview, Ill.: Holt, Rinehart and Winston, 1959), 35. This will be discussed further below and in chapter four.

67. Yves R. Simon, *Democratic Government,* 221.

68. Yves R. Simon, *Democratic Government,* 222.

69. Yves R. Simon, *Democratic Government,* 150.

70. Thomas Jefferson, in *Jefferson: Writings,* ed. Merrill D. Peterson (New York: Library of America, 1984), 1381.

71. Thomas Jefferson, quoted in Gary Hart, *Restoration of the Republic: The Jeffersonian Ideal in 21st-Century America* (Oxford: Oxford University Press, 2002), 82-83.

72. Thomas Jefferson, in Peterson, ed., *Writings,* 1380.

73. Thomas Jefferson, in Peterson, ed., *Writings,* 1399.

74. Hart explicitly denies that Jefferson's theory of ward republics is an example of subsidiarity. This is because he defines subsidiarity as "the delegation of responsibility to associations . . . for the purpose of undertaking functions that, in a republic, would be matters of public, common concern to all citizens" (Hart, *Restoration of the Republic,* 19). But this is not the understanding of subsidiarity advanced here. Hart is further concerned that subsidiarity might in such a case become an excuse for avoiding government responsibility or an argument for privatization. Here Hart misunderstands both subsidiarity and the relationship between the government and the common good. Subsidiarity authentically understood is about preserving the subjectivity of society and personal initiative. It does not deny to political authority its role of promoting the common good materially considered. However, as we have seen, it matters for the common good that a variety of particular goods be pursued, and that associations other than the state pursue various components of the common good. It is not the role of the state to stifle such life, rather to encourage it, coordinate it when necessary, resolve conflicts when they become destructive, and realize dimensions of the common good not otherwise realized. Hart's formulation does not explicitly state that all dimensions of the common good are to be directly under the control of government, but it does not deny it either. It is important not to collapse all common life into the state, for we then run the danger of an authoritarian state. That Jefferson's own thinking ultimately supports subsidiarity as presented here is certainly questionable. The claim made here is that the ward republic approach can be understood in a way compatible with subsidiarity, Jefferson himself not having addressed the issue per se.

75. Gary Hart, *Restoration of the Republic,* 85.

76. Gary Hart, *Restoration of the Republic.*

77. Gary Hart, *Restoration of the Republic,* 175-218.

78. Gary Hart, *Restoration of the Republic,* 210.

79. Gary Hart, *Restoration of the Republic,* 166.

80. Richard Dagger, *Civic Virtues: Rights, Citizenship, and Republican Liberalism* (Oxford: Oxford University Press, 1997), 159.

81. Gary Hart, *Restoration of the Republic,* 167.

82. The previous discussion of the trends in regulation is from William Greider, *Who Will Tell the People? The Betrayal of American Democracy* (New York: Simon and Schuster, 1992).

83. Norman G. Kurland and Dawn K. Brohawn, "Beyond Privatization: An Egyptian

Model for Democratizing Capital Credit for Workers," in John H. Miller, ed., *Curing World Poverty* (St. Louis: Social Justice Review, 1994), 247-268.

84. Jim Hightower, *If the Gods Had Meant Us to Vote, They Would Have Given Us Candidates* (New York: Harper Collins, 2001), 248-249.

85. Quoted in Hart, *Restoration of the Republic*, 29.

86. The preceding examples of challenges to national sovereignty are from Jim Hightower, *If the Gods Had Meant Us to Vote*, 355-60, 360-61, 362-367.

87. One of the reasons for this is the fact that these nations have so much external debt and must satisfy creditors. However, the accumulation of the debt was to a significant degree the result of the decisions made by the banks and these international institutions, so moral responsibility should be diffused. Moreover, the fact of the national debt does not morally justify placing intolerable economic burdens on people who had nothing to do with borrowing the money and did not benefit from it.

88. The preceding discussion of power and responsibility draws on Romano Guardini, *Power and Responsibility* (New York: Sheed and Ward, 1957). Of course, the above is not intended to suggest that no one is responsible for the exercise of power. Ultimately, it is people in various positions of authority who decide to develop and use technologies, to place market values above other moral concerns, to reduce democracy to a variety of procedures, and to rely on expert opinions. What is being claimed is that there is a real sense that the power is diffused in political and economic processes such that no one seems ultimately to be in control.

89. Romano Guardini, *Power and Responsibility*, 14-15.

90. Quotations are from Romano Guardini, *Power and Responsibility*, 7-8.

91. Quoted material from Hans Urs Von Balthasar, *Theo-Drama: Theological Dramatic Theory*, Vol. IV, *The Action* (San Francisco: Ignatius Press, 1994), 65, 159; J. Schwartlander, quoted in same, 159. Emphasis mine.

92. The subject of the relationship between the medieval theory of natural law and the development of subjective rights has been much disputed. The debate is whether or not there is a continuity or discontinuity between the two, whether natural rights developed logically out of natural law theory, or whether natural law, concerned with the objective rectitude of actions, is incompatible with a doctrine of subjective rights. The respective positions are outlined by Brian Tierney, *The Idea of Natural Rights* (Atlanta: Scholars Press, 1997) stressing the continuity; and Ernest Fortin, *Classical Christianity and the Political Order*, ed. Brian Benestad (Lanham: Rowman & Littlefield, 1996), stressing the essential disjuncture. Fortin does not deny Tierney's claim that traces of subjective rights are to be found in the Middle Ages. He insists, however, that they were never conceived as natural. Other scholars supporting the thesis that natural law and subjective rights are irreducibly different and incompatible are C.B. MacPherson and Leo Strauss. Jacques Maritain, John Finnis, and James Tully see rights as a legitimate development of natural law. It is worth noting that the modern Catholic social teaching explicitly asserts that rights are inherent to human nature. For example, John XXIII writes that "each individual man is truly a person. . . . [with] a nature . . . endowed with intelligence and free will. As such he has rights and duties" (*Pacem in Terris*, no. 9). It is not germane to the argument here to address the dispute. The point here is simply that rights developed as a consequence of the dignity of the person and are explicitly the result of Christian theology.

93. Francisco Vitoria, *De justitia*, 2.2ae, 62.1, 64, quoted in Brian Tierney, *The Idea of Natural Rights*, 259.

94. The foregoing interpretation of Vitoria is from Brian Tierney, *The Idea of Natural*

*Rights,* 259-260.

95. Francisco Vitoria, *De indis,* in Anthony Paden and Jeremy Lawrance, eds., *Francisco Vitoria: Political Writings* (Cambridge: Cambridge University Press, 1991), 233-292.

96. Francisco Vitoria, in Paden and Lawrance, eds., *Political Writings,* 240-41, 243-244, 250-251.

97. Francisco Vitoria, in Padan and Lawrance, eds., *Political Writings,* 249, 247, 248.

98. Brian Tierney, *The Idea of Natural Rights,* 268.

99. Francisco Vitoria, *De indis,* in Padan and Lawrance, eds., *Political Writings,* 239, 251.

100. Bartolomé de Las Casas, quoted in Gustavo Gutiérrez, *Las Casas: In Search of the Poor of Jesus Christ* (Maryknoll: Orbis Books, 1993), 295-297.

101. Bartolomé de Las Casas, quoted in Gutiérrez, *Las Casas,* 62.

102. Gustavo Gutiérrez, *Las Casas,* 155-189.

103. Gustavo Gutiérrez, *Las Casas,* 382-390; Brian Tierney, *Doctrine of Natural Rights,* 279-286.

104. Francisco Suárez, *De Legibus,* 30.

105. Francisco Suárez, *De Legibus,* 31.

106. Francisco Suárez, *De Legibus,* 278.

107. John XXIII, *Pacem in Terris,* nos. 11-27.

108. John XXIII, *Pacem in Terris,* nos. 28-35.

109. John XXIII, *Pacem in Terris,* nos. 28, 30.

110. Alasdair MacIntyre, *After Virtue: A Study in Moral Theory* (Notre Dame: University of Notre Dame Press, 1981).

111. John Paul II, *Centesimus Annus,* no. 46.

112. John Rawls, *A Theory of Justice* (Cambridge: Harvard University Press, 1971); and Sanford Levinson, *Constitutional Faith* (Princeton: Princeton University Press, 1988). The following discussion is based on Vukan Kuic, *Yves R. Simon: Real Democracy* (Lanham: Rowman & Littlefield, 1999), 78-80.

# 4

# The Person and Political Economy

A personalist society must have an economic organization grounded in, subject to, and in service of the person. What this means and does not mean is the subject of this chapter. Broadly considered, a personalist economic order must be characterized by the fullest participation possible in the production, distribution, and enjoyment of goods and services. At all levels, the person must retain sovereignty over the means of production as well as the organization and direction of the work. The economy is for the sovereign people, not the people for the economy. As in the political order, the economic system must promote solidarity as well as autonomy, in accord with the ontological makeup of the person. Solidarity must be present not only among the workers as workers, but as citizens. The economy must foster the communities closest to the person, such as the family and the local community. These communities should be relatively self-sufficient. For those engaged in wage labor, a personalist economy must promote living wages. It must, moreover, assure justice in exchanges between (a) workers and owners, and (b) sellers and consumers. Finally, personalism demands that the generation of wealth and economic power never be allowed to compromise the integrity of the political order. The economy is a part of the common good; therefore, it remains the province of political authority to set the limits beyond which the pursuit of wealth would compromise the broader good of the civil society.

## Economic Globalization: The Depersonalization of Contemporary Capitalism

The clear hegemony of neoclassical economic theory in public policy, the mass media, and in the academic study of economics has marginalized the critique of globalization. In an unproductive development, this critique is typically presented as a creature of the left side of the political spectrum. This is somewhat justified when the proposals offered to resolve the problems of globalization are simply to centralize more and more power within the state. However, the case against globalization is an intellectually solid one. Globalization in action defies many of the soundest themes of political economy. Ironically, the globalized political economy is particularly opposed to the political and intellectual traditions of the nation which has most promoted it, the United States of America; no nation's heritage emphasizes more the importance of the widespread distribution of ownership, the need to preserve popular sovereignty, and the need to maintain the national Constitution as the supreme law of the land. As we will see, globalization is discarding these quintessential values.

From a personalist perspective, the first area of concern is the removal of economic power from the level of the person and transferring it to an increasingly oligarchic concentration of ownership. The evidence supporting the contention is overwhelming. Of the world's top hundred economies, fifty are corporations. The sales of just the ten largest multinationals exceed the gross domestic product (GDP) of the hundred poorest nations added together. Two hundred corporations control almost 30 percent of global economic output. Excluding financial institutions, the top three hundred multinationals own 25 percent of the world's productive assets. Sixty percent of the world's productive capital is in the hands of the largest fifty financial institutions. In a number of industries, we are looking at the real possibility of a handful of companies dominating the market within the next couple of decades.[1] The clear and ongoing tendency toward more mergers among the largest firms makes it unlikely that the trend toward greater concentration of ownership will be reversed. Mergers are seen as a way of managing the potentially destructive competition and to accumulate capital needed to fuel increasingly expensive investments. Even in the absence of mergers, the same factors increasingly prompt strategic alliances which only further the phenomenon of concentration.[2] Moreover, power within these companies is similarly being concentrated. Finance, marketing, and proprietary technology functions are being consolidated within corporate headquarters, while other functions are being farmed out to low-wage nations.

Globalization also contributes to the concentration of ownership of land on a global basis. Large agribusinesses can produce larger volumes of food products at lower prices than smaller producers. Moreover, the ongoing mechanization of agriculture favors the larger companies who have the capital to purchase the machinery. Similar purchases by smaller producers have generated debt, bankruptcy, and loss of land. The situation is worse, as always, for the poorest of the small landowners in the developing world. As the Pontifical Commission on Justice and Peace reports, the concentration of land ownership in the developing world is one of the major sources of the social injustice therein. Industrialization is pursued at the expense of agriculture. Measures adopted include: protectionism for industrial, but not agricultural, products; manipulation of exchange rates for national currencies in ways prejudicial to agriculture; price controls for agricultural products; and worsening conditions for the marketing of produce. National governments manifest favoritism for multinational agribusinesses and lack of consideration for traditional forms of agriculture. In many cases, the desire to expand exports, as a way of offsetting chronic balance of payments problems, prompts regimes to favor the concentration of land ownership in the hands of those who work with international agribusinesses. Policies penalize small producers who serve the domestic market while rewarding those who produce for export. The creation of infrastructure and services openly favor large landowners. Fiscal policies are similarly prejudicial, avoiding progressive taxation while allowing large landowners to amortize their debts in reduced time periods. Small landowners cannot get the credit they need, nor can they produce products for the global market, as they are unable to meet the new export standards.[3] All too often, the lands of the poor are appropriated to produce crops for export. The displaced people migrate to urban slums to eke out a living in sweatshops similarly linked to production for the external market.

The destruction of small, local communities is one of the most depersonalizing consequences of the centralizing tendencies of globalization. Some of the destruction is measurable, such as the alarming spread of malnutrition in Latin America, precisely in nations that have most enthusiastically embraced the globalization agenda: Argentina, Mexico, and Brazil. Beyond that, there is the deeper destruction of the personal ties which define community. The economic and cultural cannot realistically be separated; a community of people needs an economic base. The destruction of the latter causes the death of the former. Speaking of his home town, Port Royal, Kentucky, agrarian author Wendell Berry notes that eighty years ago his town had eighteen businesses, all of which served the local community. Now, excluding the post office, there are only three. There is no market for produce within forty miles, no garage or repair shop, no doctor and no school. Like countless others, his community is dying.

> For a long time, the news from everywhere in rural America has been almost unrelievedly bad: bankruptcy, foreclosure, depression, suicide, the departure of the young, the loneliness of the old, soil loss, soil degradation, chemical pollution, the loss of genetic and specific diversity . . . the depletion of aquifers, stream degradation, the loss of wilderness, strip mining, clear-cutting, population loss, the loss of supporting economies, the deaths of towns.[4]

The standard response is to invoke the "efficiency" of mechanized agriculture and large-scale enterprise in general. With this shibboleth as the standard-bearer, the people have been separated from the land, replaced by machines and toxic chemicals, the ultimate effects of which destroy topsoil and deplete the land's natural fertility. Efficiency is really the name for producing massive quantities at the cheapest possible price. As Berry aptly notes, globalization is a process which asks us to sacrifice every value other than cash value, and to count as nothing everything that is lost in the process.

Real efficiency is something entirely different. It is neither cheap (in skill or labor) nor fast. Real efficiency is long-term efficiency. It is to be found in means that are keeping with and preserving of their ends, in methods of production that preserve the sources of production, in workmanship that is durable and of high quality. In this age of consumerism, planned obsolescence, frivolous horsepower and surplus manpower [in short, the age of globalization], those salesmen and politicians who talk about efficiency are, in reality, talking about spiritual and biological death.[5]

The destruction of communities and the destruction of the environment frequently go hand in hand; witness the impacts of the mining and timber industries in the Philippines. There, the indigenous Igorot people traditionally engaged in small-scale "pocket mining" of gold veins on their ancestral lands. Today, the lands are dominated by the Benguet Corporation, which engages in export-oriented open-pit mining, tearing away trees, destroying topsoil, and dumping waste in the riverbeds. Moreover, the company uses chemicals that have poisoned the water and killed cattle. The mining has ruined rice farming and fishing. Similar devastation accompanies large-scale clear-cutting by timber companies. Agriculture declines as rivers become muddier and shallower. Flooding is far more frequent in some areas; creeks have dried up in others. Rats, formerly kept in check by forest predators, now ravage farmers.[6]

Wage arbitrage is clearly another constituent component of globalizing firms. Simply put, wage arbitrage is the transference of jobs from high-wage to low-wage areas. Driven by the cost-cutting imperatives of global competition, producers hope to increase profits. In the process, jobs are frequently destroyed, and entire communities devastated by the loss of their economic base. The boom town goes bust very quickly. On the other side of the coin, there is a growing global market of low-wage laborers, increasingly women and children working long hours without benefits. Those in the United States wishing to understand globalization need only cross the border into Mexico where more than 2,000 *maquiladora* factories have been set up, employing the practices thought by many to have disappeared a century ago: wages under $4.00 per day, absence of social obligations, unhealthy working conditions, environmental destruction, and the exploitation of adolescent labor. As Mexican professor Gueramina Valdés-Villalva explains, "We have begun to see more fourteen-year-olds in the plants. . . . Workers do not age in this industry—they leave. Because of the intensive work it details, there is constant burnout. If they've been there three or four years, workers lose efficiency. They begin to have problems with eyesight. They begin to have allergies and skin problems."[7] The exploitation of women and children is on the increase, one component in what is euphemistically termed "flexible-production" practices, which include short-term contract labor often done at home. Women and children cut rubber, punch data, weave carpets, stitch or sew clothes, all without benefits or guarantees of future employment. Of course, such "flexible" labor practices only make it more difficult for adult men to find regular employment.[8]

The treatment of workers is so bad that it is rightfully associated with a rebirth of slavery. As Kevin Bales, the world's foremost researcher on the subject, explains it, slavery is formally illegal everywhere, yet it abounds. The key is to have control over people without formal ownership. In a sense, it mimics the globalizing economy by shifting away from ownership and fixed assets to the control and use of resources. By not asserting actual ownership, the new slavery avoids the costs of maintaining unproductive workers, particularly when they are either too old or too young to work. Bales explains:

> Transnational corporations today do what European empires did in the last century—exploit natural resources and take advantage of low-wage labor—but without needing to take responsibility for their survival. Similarly, the new slavery appropriates the economic value of individuals while keeping them under complete coercive control—but without asserting ownership or accepting responsibility for their survival. . . . Seasonal tasks are met with seasonal enslavement, as in the case of Haitian sugarcane cutters. In the new slavery the slave is a consumable item, added to the production process when needed, but no longer carrying a high capital cost.[9]

Contemporary slavery is hidden behind a facade of fraudulent labor contracts which serve both to entrap and to conceal. A typical pattern is that a recruiter goes to a rural area in a Third World nation and promises work at good wages and under good conditions. Once the "guest workers" are taken far enough away, they are coerced and treated arbitrarily. This is compounded by the fact that on many occasions the enslaved are brought to another country.

Americans are shocked to learn that such things actually occur in places controlled by U.S. law, as in the case of Saipan, which became a U.S. commonwealth in 1976. Clothing companies such as Brooks Brothers, Gap, Abercrombie and Fitch, J.C. Penney, and Levi Strauss import a billion dollars worth of clothing per year from there, taking advantage of the effective enslavement of thousands of young people on the island. These companies contract with Chinese, Taiwanese, and Korean entrepreneurs to produce clothing very cheaply. The key to the low costs is their recruitment of labor from China, Bangladesh, the Philippines, Sri Lanka, and other Asian nations. Promising high wages, they sign the unsuspecting youth to indentured labor on Saipan. The "guest workers" usually have to borrow two to seven thousand dollars for the privilege. When they arrive for their work experience under American law, their passports are seized, and they are forced to sign "shadow contracts" waiving basic human rights. This effectively coerces them into staying for their contracted term. They work twelve to sixteen hours a day, often seven days a week, and are frequently unpaid. They are regularly beaten and harassed. The factories are sweatshops with unsafe conditions. They live in barracks resembling a prison, complete with inward-pointing wire fences topped by razor wire. Workers are charged for the unsanitary food and clothing they are given. They sleep eight to a room. Aside from the confiscated passports, the workers are obliged to earn enough to repay what they borrowed to pay the recruiters. The clothes produced are legally marketed with the emblem "Made in the USA."[10] Kevin Bales reminds us of the disquieting result of these forms of slavery:

> Slaves in Pakistan may have made the shoes you are wearing and the carpet you stand on. Slaves in the Caribbean may have put sugar in your kitchen and toys in the hands of your children. In India they may have sewn the shirt on your back and polished the ring on your finger. They are paid nothing. . . . They made the bricks for the factory that made the TV you watch. In Brazil slaves made the charcoal that tempered the steel that made the springs in your car and the blade on your lawnmower. Slaves grew the rice that fed the woman that wove the lovely cloth you've put up as curtains. Your investment portfolio and your mutual fund pension own stock in companies using slave labor in the developed world. Slaves keep your costs low and returns on your investments high.[11]

On the other end of the spectrum, workers in the developed world face the ongoing threat of future job cuts. Sixty-six thousand workers in the United States lost jobs in the 1990s producing the same products made in Saipan. The relationship between concentration of ownership and job cuts is well established; mergers are followed by job cuts. The corporate strategy is part of a process by which global corporations are transforming themselves to become more competitive through internal reorganization. One part of this process, as we have seen, is contracting out much of the actual manufacturing to low-wage nations. The other part has been downsizing personnel in the developed nations. Mergers only encourage this, as they inevitably produce "redundancies," that is, people who do the same job. The discharging of workers is followed by the expectation that stocks will go up in value. The other part of the process is that cost-cutting engendered by the job cuts inspires speculators to invest in the stock of the downsizing corporations. Concentrations of investor money in huge mutual funds like CREF give the latter significant influence over corporate behavior. Investors in the stock market are concerned with the value of the stock, not jobs.

The displacement of workers and increasingly difficult conditions for those still employed are difficult problems to ignore, even in the developed nations. If it were not for the low-paying service sector, unemployment would be devastatingly high in the United States. The willingness of the United States to adopt more "flexible" labor systems, hiring more temporary workers with low wages and no benefits, keeps unemployment from attaining the double-digit figures common in Europe. By the mid-1990s, global unemployment had reached its highest level since the Great Depression. Due to downward pressure on wages occasioned by the off-loading of manufacturing to the developing world, average wages in the United States began to stagnate three decades ago, and the phenomenon continues. American consumers are told that they are better off, but any price benefits delivered by the marketplace have been offset by the decline in real wages. People felt this way because their real wages were declining; their purchasing capacity was not keeping up with prices.[12]

Technology is clearly contributing to job instability, official rhetoric to the contrary. As governments have no control over the process by which manufacturing jobs are off-loaded to the developing world, they tell their own citizens that the technology that replaces their jobs is truly their friend, that it creates jobs. The more accurate claim is that technology both creates and destroys jobs. Jeremy Rifkin says that in the past it was the case that new technologies displaced workers in one sector while new sectors emerged. Given, however, that cost-cutting is the principle motivation behind job cuts, and that technology is spreading to every sector of the economy, the troubling question is if job creation will keep up with job displacement. Today, technological displacement negatively impacts employment in manufacturing, agriculture, and even the service sector. Even if Rifkin's dire prediction that "sophisticated software technologies are going to bring civilization ever closer to a near-workerless world" is exaggerated, the evidence is clear that computer technology is eliminating layers of management and compressing job categories.[13] The corporate goal is to reduce workers to a minimum, as in AT&T's plans to replace thousands of telephone operators by computerized voice-recognition systems.[14] The auto industry illustrates the problem as well. Workers are being replaced by new, high-tech assembly systems. The Toyota Lexus LS 400 is manufactured with a scant 18.4 hours of human labor. Chrysler, GM, and Ford average under thirty hours of labor per car produced.[15] Clearly, technology is not creating jobs in auto assembly.

The official response to the job problem and stagnating wages is to leave the free market alone and to promote education as the solution. In a way, the proposal implicitly criticizes workers, suggesting that workers who formerly earned living wages were really overpaid, and therefore rightly replaced by their counterparts in the developing world. The solution, therefore, is for workers to make themselves worth more through education. The logic of the argument is faulty in that it implies that jobs are somehow generated as a response to the development of worker skills, carefully sidestepping the actual dynamic by which jobs are lost. Nevertheless, the Clinton administration pinned its hopes on retraining workers. Less than 20 percent of those who were retrained under federal programs were able to find employment at 80 percent of their former salary. Nor should there be any surprise in that, given that job skills are not an independent factor leading to the creation of corresponding employment. Yet, the argument has its appeal. If workers can increase their productivity through skill acquisition, then they should get correspondingly higher wages. If there were no global overabundance of labor, the argument might hold, but the abundance of labor of all kinds outside of the developed world is the underlying factor driving the process. Originally, it was low-skill workers who felt the crunch, but now it impacts workers increasingly in all areas requiring scientific or technological skill. Therefore, the assumption that job training is going to solve the problem ignores its underlying cause. There is even a presumed sense of cultural superiority implicit in the argument, that educational opportunities will endlessly confirm the superiority of American workers. At any rate, the empirical evidence does not confirm that job training and resultant increases in productivity lead to higher wages. As one study concludes:

> Investment in training programs is based on an unproved leap of faith and a shaky assumption. First . . . the training solution is grounded on the assumption that employers will change the way they organize production when the skill level of workers improves, and that skilled labor creates a demand for itself. There is little empirical evidence to support this view.[16]

Ongoing employment patterns clearly disconfirm the proposition that the loss of low-skill manufacturing jobs will be replaced by high-paying technology jobs, official rhetoric notwithstanding. The real job market is low-tech. President Clinton's own Bureau of Labor Statistics predicted that of the thirty job categories most likely to grow the fastest up to 2006, only seven require a bachelor's degree. Most are in the service sector, as in cashiers, salespersons, teacher aides, receptionists, child-care workers, clerical supervisors, maintenance workers, restaurant employees, packers, guards, and clerks.[17]

None of this is to suggest that technology is inherently bad; merely that, when the sense of the person as the end to be served in economic organization is lost, technology can contribute to the depersonalization of society. This occurs, as John Paul II writes, "when the mechanization of work 'supplants' [people], . . . when it deprives many workers of their previous employment, or when, through exalting the machine, it reduces man to the status of a slave."[18] Technology has today become tied to the ruthless global competition that propels globalization, compelling firms to produce more with less, and thereby cut costs. Existing plants are closed, workers are discarded by the thousands, and newer, more technologically sophisticated plants are opened in other areas. Workers in the United States have been familiar with the process for three decades, as manufacturing industries, most notably automobiles and steel, have lost jobs numbering in the hundreds of thousands. In addition to job loss, the technology-driven competition has encouraged the wave of mergers we continue to see.

Far from being aberrations, all of the aforementioned practices are directly linked to cost-cutting, and this imperative drives the globalization process. Corporations failing to cut costs will be undercut by those who do. We can see, therefore, how woefully inadequate is any argument that would claim that the problem occurs primarily at the level of the individual firm, and can be resolved by an appeal to the moral principles of individual managers and firms. To argue in this way is to miss the systemic nature of the problem, and it is surely not an argument that managers of global corporations would make. Even the very largest firms, such as General Motors, IBM, and Eastman Kodak, have experienced the merciless nature of the global competition. To fail to reduce costs entails the loss of investor confidence, followed by ousted managements, and thousands of lost jobs. The situation is even worse for workers, who now must face the fact that job cuts are alternately both indicators of corporate failure and a sign of good management practice. Globalization, as a manifestation of economic liberalism, is in fact a system governed by the rule of competition. Firms that fail to cut costs will be undersold by those that do. Owners of capital are generally not willing to risk extinction by paying their workers living wages or refusing to introduce cost-cutting technologies.

Again, what is at issue is not primarily the morals of individual managers or firms, but a system governed by the pursuit of profit and that disciplines and eliminates firms that fail. A common refrain is that the profit motive is constitutive of any sound economic order. The claim is not entirely false, but it misses the point. A personalist economic order will have profits as part of the system, but it is precisely here that the personalist approach and contemporary globalization diverge radically. In *Centesimus Annus,* John Paul II clearly affirms the legitimacy of profit, but only in the context of a broader understanding that "the purpose of a business firm is not simply to make a profit, but it is to be found in its very existence as a community of persons who in various ways are endeavoring to satisfy their basic needs and who form a particular group at the service of the whole of society." This implies the commitment on the part of other goals, such as "a sufficient wage for the support of the family, social insurance for old age and unemployment, and adequate protection for the conditions of employment."[19] No serious analyst of globalization in the last three decades would want to argue that globalization does anything other than to render all of these personalist commitments optional.

Jack Welch, former General Electric CEO, warned prior to his retirement that American firms face a "hurricane" wherein "shakeouts will be more brutal." The technological revolution, associated with the ever-present competition to cut costs, forces firms to remain competitive in order to adapt to the market pressures. The same technology which cuts costs increases the capacity to produce, a development accelerated by the desire to produce in new, developing markets. The problem is that there are too few buyers to purchase all of the new capacity. It is this imbalance between an ever-growing productive capacity and an effective demand curtailed by job losses and stagnating wages which will cause the "shakeouts" to which Welch refers. As William Greider points out, the overcapacity problem seems to be growing:

> The productive overcapacity is neither temporary nor diminishing.
> Autos are the leading example of the dilemma . . . but the same trend
> is visible in steel, aircraft, chemicals, computers, consumer electron-

ics, drugs, tires and some others. The particulars vary from sector to sector, but the overriding fact is gross oversupply of capacity, despite the many years of plant closings. . . . At a minimum, the growing imbalance between supply and demand guarantees that the storm of dislocations and shakeouts must continue.[20]

It sheds considerable light on what might otherwise appear to be a complicated web of interactions comprehensible only to economists to consider that the essentials of the competitive and disruptive process were in many ways well explicated sixty-seven years ago by an agrarian economist, decades before even the rumblings of the present process were heard. T.J. Cauley, in 1936, warned of the impacts of "technocracy" to be wrought by ongoing changes in the ways of production, that it would "occasion a considerable economic and social disturbance." Changes in manufacturing inevitably discard those employed under the older technology. Some of the displaced will get jobs in the new production, but many "never will find employment again." Even those who find jobs will most likely have to relocate, as the centers of new industry need not coincide with the old. Under such a process, Cauley writes that "there can be no real stability of community life, and there can be very little, if any, true family life." The entire process is "one of ceaseless change and turmoil." Cauley also perceived the limits of the much ballyhooed claim that the labor-saving propensity of mass production will continually cut prices. As components of the final price, there are charges for interest, dealers' commissions, raw materials, machinery, and advertising, none of which are reduced by mass production. Actual factory costs of producing an automobile Cauley estimated at less than 10 percent of the final price. The only viable solution, Cauley proposed, was to diffuse property ownership, to disperse control over the sources of wealth production.[21]

What is usually called "free trade" is another much misunderstood feature of globalization that causes further dislocation. It is appealed to most frequently by corporations and the governments that represent them. It is rare to see teams of workers rallying on its behalf. The justifications, typically, are couched in terms of the efficiency and increases in net production which result from increased competition. Competition, however, is merely a polite term for warfare, and so global competition means warfare among producers. From a personalist perspective, the first casualty is usually smaller and local producers who cannot compete with the global firms. Critics have long emphasized that free trade agreements simply encourage producers in the United States to relocate in low-wage areas. An examination of the NAFTA agreement bears this out, as well as serving as a perfect example of the destructive impacts of globalization. Prior to the implementation of NAFTA, Mexico pursued a dangerous policy of borrowing enormous amounts of money to service its foreign debt and cover the costs of consumer debt and capital flight. Mexico attracted seventy billion dollars in foreign investments by offering high-interest bonds and selling public corporations. Mexican stocks also enjoyed the impact of the speculative bubble that developed.

No more than 10 percent of the foreign investment represented the creation of actual investments in capital goods. Shortly after the passage of NAFTA, the speculative bubble burst, as foreign investors rushed to take their money out. The resulting financial crisis caused a devaluation of 40 percent for the Mexican peso. This destroyed what was supposed to be the job-creating impacts of NAFTA; Mexicans could not afford to buy the U.S. products now 40 percent more expensive. As the critics had predicted, Mexico became a low-wage export zone for goods entering the United States. Mexico hardly benefited either. The devaluation, combined with high interest rates, caused an internal debt crisis of epic proportions, as most borrowing in Mexico was done on variable interest rates. In addition to the epic level of insolvency, austerity measures cost Mexico 750,000 jobs. Wall Street investors in Mexican bonds prevailed upon the Clinton administration to administer a fifty billion dollar taxpayer bailout, but the real crisis in Mexico—both small and large businesses unable to cope with their new debt burdens, major bank failures, unpaid and unemployed workers—was ignored.[22]

Economist Adrian Wood has done an extensive study to show that job losses in the developed nations resulting from trade are ten times as large than generally recognized.[23] The problem is that the labor-intensive components of manufactured goods produced in the United States have vanished as the production of labor-intensive goods has been replaced by imports. Changes in trade with the underdeveloped nations to the south reduced the demand for unskilled relative to skilled labor in the north by approximately 20 percent. In addition, this process has negatively impacted equality of incomes, contributing to declining wages. Moreover, Wood sees the scope for expanding the skilled labor supply by government action limited.

The free trade banner is in fact a shibboleth which consistently hides three realities poorly understood: (a) It is pursued for the benefit of the multinationals and most definitely not for the good of small producers; (b) the majority of world trade is massaged by political negotiations between multinationals and nation-states; and (c) a large percentage of "trade" is actually intrafirm transactions. We will consider these briefly in order. Concerning (a), free trade often prevails in the political forum because to negate it would seem to deny the right of a producer to procure an overseas market for his product. The reality is actually something quite different. In the minds of the CEOs of multinational firms, free trade means their right to monopolize markets globally, acquire universal access to resources, and nullify any attempts to regulate their behavior on the part of local, state, and even national governments. Indeed these are the principle motivations behind the formation of the World Trade Organization and the NAFTA tribunal. As previously discussed, these institutions are being used to strip the people of political sovereignty and establish a global regime of corporate libertarianism. Concerning (b), the flow of investments and the subsequent flow of goods have little to do with the comparative advantages of free trade theory. A far better analogy is what Greider calls "the global jobs auction," in which governments, in order to attract jobs, promise a variety of tax breaks, subsidies, and agreements to nullify a wide range of regulatory laws, negatively impacting the environment, workplace safety, and basic worker rights. Formerly considered an example of the weakness of Third World regimes, such practices are increasingly common on the part of government in the developed world. To take one example, the State of Alabama pledged to Mercedes-Benz over $300 million in tax breaks and subsidies, an additional $60 million to finance worker training, and agreements to purchase $75 million worth of vehicles, all to create a mere 1,500 jobs. Having secured the initial investment, it is increasingly a common practice for companies to shake down state and local governments for additional benefits as time goes on, in a process euphemistically referred to as "corporate retention." Finally, concerning (c), an increasing percentage of "world trade" is merely intrafirm transactions, companies moving their own products from one subsidiary to another. Under such circumstances, the expansion of free trade is surely to expand the profits of the multinationals, but it is no victory for smaller producers or workers.[24] Greider sums it up:

> In sum, despite the reigning pieties, the global system could not properly be called a free-trade regime. When all of the contradictions, exceptions, and purposeful evasions were taken into account, most of the world's trade was not a free exchange based on market prices. One way or the other, trade was massaged and regulated, managed explicitly by governments or internally by the multinational corporations or often by both in discreet collaboration.[25]

The principles of globalization—maximizing growth, allowing free reign to the multinationals, and hollowing out the substance of government—prevail because the methods of calculating costs and benefits are rigged in their favor. First, there is an ongoing exclusion of nonmonetary values from public policy making. Proponents of globalization are everywhere politically ascendant largely because of their success in determining the universe of discourse. For example, consider the content of public debates on economic liberalization generally or free-trade agreements specifically. Those arguing that liberalization will mean an increase in the net production of wealth and downward pressure on the prices of consumer goods generally carry the day, precisely because they have been able to convince people that these are the variables which should be counted. However, as Wendell Berry asks, "What is the cost of a destroyed local community?"[26] There are economic costs, as people in the community must travel more to purchase goods and services, sources of work are destroyed, the number of owners is reduced, and care of the land declines. Above and beyond these measurable losses (which nonetheless never seem to be adequately accounted for in official calculations), there are clearly losses of immense moral and cultural significance which apparently do not count at all. I refer here to everything associated with the loss of a community, such as the loss of the experience of solidarity, the loss of the opportunity for children to follow in a way of life passed down from their parents, the loss of a reasonable sense of security about the future, and the loss of entire families done in by the economic and psychological pressures of job loss. No approach to the economy worthy of the name personalism can put these important values on the back burner or pretend they are not relevant.

Over and above the exclusion of nonmonetary values, economic globalization as it exists today contains a strong bias in favor of growth as measured in monetary terms as the overarching goal of economic policy, particularly for the developing nations. In many ways, the highly touted economic growth is an illusion brought about by converting more and more goods and services into commodities to be bought and sold on a market at a measurable price. Increasingly, this includes elements as diverse as the production of food, clothing, and shelter; childcare, health care, and care for the elderly; housekeeping; security; and entertainment. The conversion of these into the money economy makes people more and more dependent on access to money, a serious liability for the majority of poor people. To take a hypothetical example, consider a rural community that was largely self-sufficient in food production and child care. Wealthy they are not, but they have sufficient goods to sustain their life, and they have a stable culture passed on reliably from generation to generation via strong families. Under the pressures of the global market, convert that same community to one where subsistence is eliminated and child care is largely taken over by paid agents of public or for-profit agencies. There is widespread hunger, the majority unable to earn sufficient wages to purchase food in the new economy. People begin to move away in large numbers in search for work. Those who find employment can no longer take time to rear their children, so they have to pay for this to be done. The economist would come along and pronounce that all of this is "growth," there being far more measurable economic activity than before. The community, however, has been destroyed, along with its economy, and most people suffer for it at all levels. Of such changes does "economic growth" consist. Similarly, the depletion of natural resources, even when their maintenance is central to the economic viability of a community, counts as growth. For example, consider clear-cutting by the lumber industry, the practice of cutting down an entire forest area without provision for the long term. The local lumber economy is destroyed, but current sales will count unilaterally as "growth." This is true of the depletion of many other natural resources as well. Moreover, costs associated with contending with the consequences of this "growth" also show up in the assets or income column. Disposal of toxic wastes in rural communities and in Third World nations, cleaning up industrial waste, health care for the victims of environmental toxins, money spent on social services associated with the community-destroying impacts of globalization—all of these count as growth in an unqualified manner. Consider the absurdity that the damage caused by the Exxon-Valdez oil spill itself does not count against economic growth, yet all of the money spent to clean it up contributes positively! Finally, the transfer of ownership of land away from small owners engaged in life-sustaining activities such as food production, harvesting timber, small industries, and fishing, to corporate-dominated, profit-producing export industries, shows up unequivocally as growth, the destruction of communities and the declining numbers of owners notwithstanding. Given these distorted ways of calculating gains and benefits, wherein many evils count as contributions to growth and entire categories of losses show up not at all, globalization will likely to continue to dominate the agendas of the corporations and the governments sponsoring them.

Global economic integration is shifting the very nature of government in morally troubling ways. We have already seen examples of this in our discussion of the irregular favors granted to corporations as part of the "global jobs auction," and the serious threats to sovereignty implied in the globalist corporate agenda. Public policy increasingly becomes the servant of market demands, with little or no regard for other values. Moreover, it is now widely recognized that the influence of wealthy, private interests—most notably corporations—plays a discomforting role in the formulation of policy. Calls for the reform of financing campaigns are only the tip of the iceberg.

The deeper issue is the sundering of the moral connection between political authority and the common good of the people whom the former is supposed to serve. Nowhere is this more evident than in the breakdown of morally defensible policies concerning taxation and tax collection. In addition to the outright tax breaks and subsidies they receive, corporations are allowed to skirt billions of dollars in taxes around the world by gaming the tax codes of the various nations in which they operate. This is by now fully recognized, acknowledged by official agencies of the U.S. government. One method is called "transfer pricing," a practice which takes advantage of the fact that so much of what is called "trade" is really intrafirm transaction. Prices are manipulated as they cross national boundaries to the end of declaring profits where taxes are either the lowest or the most poorly collected. This sets up a dynamic similar to the search for low wages; nations that refuse to grant "tax holidays" or that challenge the existing practices will not attract the new investments upon which economic and political success depend.

Nowhere has the transformation of the role of government from service of the common good to service of the monied interest been more striking than in the Third World. For the last two decades, in what can only be called a wholesale loss of popular sovereignty, public policy (including public spending, taxation, wages, valuation of currency, education, public health, and programs for literacy and nutrition) has become increasingly subject to the demands of foreign creditors and the recommendations of foreign economists who serve them. After eighteen years of following the neoliberal prescriptions imposed by the banks and the International Monetary Fund, the total stock of Latin American debt went from $257 billion to approximately $700 billion. The percentage of GDP devoted to servicing the debt remains at a crippling 36 percent. The policies pursued to keep Latin America solvent include debt-equity swaps by which foreign creditors purchase more and more Latin American resources. As a result, it is increasingly the case that most of the largest businesses in Latin America are disproportionately owned and controlled by multinationals based in Europe or the United States. The result is an unprecedented political and economic polarization in which the governments increasingly speak for and speak to an elite which grows ever richer and powerful and distanced from the strictly local economy, while the vast majority sink into an unspeakable poverty. The presidents of Argentina, Brazil, Mexico, and Chile have all announced that their respective nations have entered the First World. Although the rhetoric is clearly inflated, it is surely true of the elite. James Petras summarizes the situation well:

> Today, 15-20 percent of Latin Americans share a "First World" lifestyle; they send their kids to private schools; belong to private country clubs . . . ; get facelifts at private clinics; travel in luxury cars on private toll roads; and communicate via computer, fax and private courier service. They live in gated communities, protected by private police. They frequently vacation and shop in New York, Miami, London or Paris. Their children attend overseas universities. They enjoy easy access to influential politicians, media moguls, celebrities and business consultants. They are usually fluent in English and have most of their savings in overseas accounts or in dollar-denominated local paper. . . . They are the audience to which presidents address their grandiloquent First World discourse of a new wave of global prosperity. . . . The rest of the population lives in a totally different world. Cuts in social spending and the elimination of basic food subsidies have pushed peasants towards malnutrition and hunger. Large-scale redundancy of factory workers and their entry into the "informal sector" means a subsistence existence and reliance on the "extended family," [and] community-based charities . . . for survival. Slashed public health and education budgets result in increasing payments and deteriorating services. Cuts in funds for maintenance of water, sewage, and other public services have resulted in a resurgence of infectious diseases. Declining living standards measured in income and living conditions is the reality for two-thirds or more of the population. There has been a decline from Third World welfarism to Fourth World immiseration.[27]

At the risk of some oversimplification, it can be said that globalization is a process by which the principle of subsidiarity is being subverted. As previously discussed, subsidiarity declares it an injustice to assign to a higher association functions that lower associations, closer to the people to be served, can perform. It is often understood by Catholics as a reason for objecting to the expansion of the power of the state when there are reasons to believe that private associations can perform the same function. While concurring with this interpretation, I wish to assert a broader role for the principle of subsidiarity as applying within the private sector as well. I see nothing inherent in the definition of subsidiarity which would preclude my reading. As the central purpose of subsidiarity is to preserve the priority of the person as the origin and purpose of society, there is no basis for assuming that private associations cannot become sufficiently large and powerful to compromise it. I submit that *a solid argument can be made in terms of subsidiarity against the destruction of small, local businesses and farms brought about by corporations and agribusiness.* Small landholdings have suffered the most with the least amount of attention, but many more people are beginning to question the wisdom of permitting huge conglomerates like Wal-Mart to come into a community and undermine all of the local enterprises. Proponents of globalization will protest this claim on the basis of an alleged superiority of the corporate oligopolies in terms of "efficiency," but the principle of subsidiarity itself suggests an alternative account of efficiency that challenges the narrow, materialistic, and utilitarian understanding of the term as used by economists. Given the reading of subsidiarity advanced here, the principle cannot be misused by the proponents of globalization as an a priori argument against state intervention into the global market.

Even if my reading of subsidiarity were wrong, the principle does not simplistically support economic liberalism, since the mandate of nonintervention only holds so long as the lower level of association is adequate to the task. When this latter condition fails to hold, intervention is required. For example, John Paul II states that globalization requires "effective international agencies which will oversee and direct the economy to the common good."[28] Moreover, Third World nations relying most strictly on economic liberalization have clearly fared the worst in ameliorating conditions for their poor. Nations achieving success in this regard, such as Taiwan and South Korea, have had highly interventionist states.[29]

## The Person and Political Economy I: Principles of Justice

Economic globalization under liberal principles removes from the people and the communities closest to them the capacity to make decisions on the most important economic matters, such as investment and employment. As we saw in the preceding section, the resultant centralization of power creates a host of other aberrations. In the remaining sections of this chapter, we will explore how to reorient the economy back to the service of all the people. This can only be accomplished when the economy is based on sound, personalist ethical principles. We will consider first the ethical precepts governing production, social justice, and owner-worker relations, and the meaning of work.

The deepest meaning of the economy is to produce goods and services to meet basic human needs. Personalism demands intense concern with the entire human and ethical components involved in production, beginning with the motivations within people for engaging in production in the first place. At first, the answer may seem too obvious to warrant the question; the motivation for production is the production of wealth. But wealth must always be considered a means, not an end. When we consider various forms of wealth, such as property, homes, cars, or money (a means to these other means), we must recall that they are all ultimately for the good of the person, the ultimate measure of what is good or bad in the economic order. Therefore, when we say that wealth is what is intended by production, we must qualify our understanding of wealth to include, in addition to the wealth itself, its human use; it is the latter that, strictly speaking, is the end of both work and wealth. This derives ultimately from what John Paul II calls "the first principle of this order, namely the universal destination of goods and the right to common use of them."[30]

As modern capitalism has fallen increasingly under the sway of materialism, utilitarianism, and centralization, the direct association between production and use is increasingly obscured by production for exchange. Whenever this occurs, profit becomes separated from the service of work. When the distance between service and profit of work is small, there is a subordination of profit to service. Consider the small businessman who serves his local community, rendering services to customers who are pleased with his work and with whom he maintains a broader relationship as a member of the same community. Here profit is subordinated to service, and human needs are clearly met to the benefit of all. Problems emerge when the distance between service and profit increases as it does in the contemporary global economy, where profit-making emerges as the primary motivation independent of serviceability to the real needs of people. Of course, some kind of service is usually performed, except in the cases of outright fraud. Nevertheless, the connection between profit and service is increasingly tenuous, and in many cases the service is largely fictitious.[31]

Concerning illusory services, neoclassical economics rejects the concept. Nevertheless, the failure on the part of economists to integrate it into their work does not thereby render the phenomenon nonexistent. The most obvious example is the accepted activity of government to prevent the sale of harmful products and to criminalize or permit civil liability in cases of fraud. Aside from such examples, we can consider the example of salesman and telemarketers who clearly attempt to persuade people to buy things for which they have no need. Producers walk away with profits, but consumers end up with products that are grossly out of proportion to their income and their needs. As I write here in the summer of 2003, the news is of record numbers of home foreclosures and personal bankruptcy. Surely the work of advertisers and marketers of many kinds contributes mightily to the phenomenon of the highly indebted household, something which is clearly not a good for either the family or the broader society.

To deny the existence of the prevalence of illusory services in the contemporary economy is an obvious negation of practical knowledge; everyone knows it is true. This brings us to the point that economists choose to ignore when they make the market the beginning and end of their inquiry. At issue here is the very meaning of economics as a science related to the human good. Economics claims to be a discipline characterized by ethical neutrality. However, as Yves R. Simon argues, there is no need to accept the claim of ethical neutrality on the part of any science dealing with the human good, and clearly economics is that. When we consider the absurdity of compensation rendered for service which is not humanly genuine, and when we notice that such activities are clearly on the increase, and we recognize further the immense harm caused by such activities, it is impossible to accept the belief that the common sense principle of genuine service of work is irrelevant in economics, whatever difficulties might be involved in attempting to quantify its violation.[32]

Another related problem occasioned by the separation of profit from service is what Simon refers to as "one-way exchanges," which show up in the relationship between certain kinds of merchants and society. Simon speaks of commercial activity in the sense used by Aristotle and Saint Thomas; that is, operations in which profit is obtained by a change in the price of a product. The wealth accumulated by such people represents wealth lost by the members of society who do business with them. In commercial transactions so defined, there is no real exchange of values; all the wealth goes one way. In order to avoid a profitless and irrelevant discussion, it will be conceded that many merchants do produce real use value. The issue is not to find the platonic form of such activities, or to find them in complete isolation from the actual generation of real value; the point is that such activities do exist. There is compensation granted corresponding to no service, generated simply by fortuitous (from the standpoint of the profiting merchant) changes in prices.

What Simon referred to decades ago as "one-way exchanges" are by any honest estimation a much larger component of contemporary activity than ever before, and a matter of serious ethical concern. What David Korten calls "extractive investments" correspond precisely to what Simon calls "one-way exchanges." Extractive investments occur when an investor acquires control of a genuinely productive asset, then discards it for profit. Such sales are one-way exchanges, as the investor has extracted value while creating none. In the worst cases, the common wealth of the society declines. Speculative economic activities are perhaps the worst example. These occur when an investor is simply gambling on the rise or fall of prices. Speculative profits capture wealth created by others, and occur when global operators take advantage of temporary price differences, purchasing where the product is cheaper and selling where it is higher. It takes place in entire markets for commodities, currency exchanges, and financial instruments such as stocks and bonds. Many of the speculative markets did not even exist prior to the 1970s. There are "derivatives contracts" that involve speculation on stock prices, currency prices, interest rates, and "hedge funds" that specialize in high-risk, short-term speculation. The amounts of money involved are truly staggering. The daily transaction in currencies is over $800 billion a day, no more than 10 percent of which corresponds to actual exchanges of goods and services. The total value of outstanding derivatives contracts alone is approaching the world's total stock of productive fixed capital investments, that is, $20 trillion.[33] Such activity can and does harm entire nations. Losses in the value of stocks or currencies occasioned by speculation undermine the savings and retirement funds of millions of people. Profits derived are simply extracting wealth from those who actually produce it. In light of the explosion of global speculation, the need to reconsider the moral imperative to link production and profit to the service of genuine human needs is ever more pressing.

Speculative economic activities have existed in all democratic societies. The issue is not simply to eliminate them, but to stem this clearly pathological development wherein speculative activity rivals and in some cases surpasses the actual production of goods and services! The U.S. economy was the world's strongest prior to the creation of futures markets, derivatives markets, and hedge funds. There is, therefore, no essential relationship between proliferating speculation on the one hand and economic liberty and wealth production on the other. Given the harm it causes, siphoning away billions of dollars from what could be healthy economic activity and placing it in the hands of essentially parasitic agents, there is no reason why such activity could not be greatly reduced by regulation.

The problem of unequal exchange in modern capitalism, so lamentably ignored by economists, is also relevant to the market for labor. Modern globalized capitalism legally acknowledges that the modern wage earner is equal to the employer, but this equality is often merely formal and lacking in substance, so often evidenced today. Exploitation exists under the wage system whenever compensation is below the value of the service rendered. It is increasingly the case around the world that workers must simply accept the wage offered, regardless of the relationship between the wage and the cost of living. Such relationships are a form of servitude. Personalism demands that a worker never be treated as a mere commodity or factor of production, subject to the impersonal laws of supply and demand. Forty years ago, Yves R. Simon insisted that this issue was the most pressing ethical concern for modern democracies. Given the obvious growth in the exploitation of labor in the era of globalization, his point needs to be underlined today. Despite the proliferation of the free market it remains the case that *"alienation through unequal exchange is the thing that democracy, in the second phase of its revolutionary development, has to deal with, just as alienation through institutional bondage was the thing that democracy had to deal with in its first revolutionary phase."*[34]

The global market economy undermines the sense of solidarity among workers. Workers from various nations are simply pitted against one another as part of the global jobs auction. The organizations which they form to represent them have been greatly weakened, their effectiveness reduced by the same processes which place downward pressure on wages; unions are aware that corporations can simply ignore them and relocate somewhere else. Moreover, in an environment wherein there is a disjuncture between service and profit, production for profit causes work to lose its character of genuine social fruitfulness. Workers inevitably assume the same attitude as producers; that is, they adopt profit as the principle motivation for work. The primacy of the profit motive within the hearts and minds of the workers corrodes their sense of community, and greatly reduces the lived experience of work as a common good. The sense of communion in desire, knowing and wanting that others produce the goods as a result of their common effort, declines under the primacy of the profit motive. This explains much of the loneliness and alienation workers experience today. In the absence of communion, workers often experience a heavy sense of boredom and lack of human purpose in their work.[35]

Economic organization needs to be revised so as to make it accountable to the people. In subsequent sections, we will focus on reversing the tendency toward concentration of ownership as the key to a personalist economy. Nonetheless, even if that should be accomplished, there will still be a need to define the relationship between workers and owners, and government and the economic order. Actual policies will need to be sensitive to specific circumstances, but the following six principles would seem to have a universal character.

1. The value of the market is that, under the right circumstances, it greatly aids the implementation of the principle of subsidiarity, allowing for personal economic initiative and freedom. Moreover, it serves as a necessary bar to the perennial tendency for the heavy arm of the state to assume more and more control over the lives of people. On a related matter, there is today the growing influence of rationalist, antipersonal tendencies which insist that society evolve according to schema designed by men, which only encourages the centralizing tendencies of the state. Nonetheless, the market is for the person, not the person for the market. Free-marketers are fundamentally wrong when they measure economic progress by anything other than the actual condition and lives of people. Market reforms must be subjected to the test of actual results. Is the principle of the universal destination of goods being realized? Is poverty reduced? Is the overall role of the person expanded? No authentic personalist can ever fail to put these questions in the forefront of the economic discussion; to define implementation of market reforms as the ultimate criterion of progress is contrary to personalism.

2. While never denying the potential contributions of the market to promoting a better distribution of goods and services, John Paul II reminds us that "there are many human needs which find no place on the market." Moreover, "it is a strict duty of justice and truth not to allow fundamental human needs to remain unsatisfied and not to allow those burdened by such needs to perish."[36] In addition, even with reference to goods and services which might under some circumstances be adequately distributed by the market, they are not in many cases so distributed due to market imperfections. Markets can and do decline into recessions and depressions, and remain imperfect distributors. For this reason, there must be mechanisms of distribution according to needs and "free distribution."[37] Nonmarket distribution according to needs is recognized in policies such as granting tax deductions to those who have spouses and children to support. Simon refers to a policy in France whereby all employers contributed to a fund based upon the size of their enterprise and the number of employees. The money in the fund was distributed to workers as a supplemental family allowance according to the size of their respective families. Such policies clearly allow for distribution according to need over and above market results. Concerning free distribution, the emphasis on the market method discourages the needed discussion of this issue. More-

over, it conjures up absurd images of people handing out dollar bills on street corners. Nonetheless, such mechanisms have always existed. We tend today to think in terms of mechanisms of direct distribution by the state, but history provides many other examples. In the Middle Ages and the Renaissance, many laws and customs allowed for free distribution of many goods, such as free access to common resources such as land, forests, and water.[38] What a boon it was to be able to use a nearby forest to build a home and heat it! That is why it is simplistic to insist that the commodification of all resources is necessarily a victory for justice. Most desirable would be to promote such mechanisms in a way that is both regular and dependable, hence institutionalized, yet avoid whenever possible handing over such institutionalization to government control. Whenever the state gets directly involved, it encourages the decline of the creativity and willingness to take personal responsibility upon which authentic economic personalism depends.

3. Consumer cooperatives are an excellent way of maintaining justice in prices because they return profits to their members. Unfortunately, the momentum of the movement seems to have stalled, the initiative of people forestalled by overreliance on wage mechanisms for income, an unfortunate byproduct of contemporary capitalism. Opportunities abound not only to expand cooperatives but to apply the principle to all regulated utilities (telephone, gas, electricity, cablevision, water) and mass-transit systems, potentially involving almost all people. The mechanism is called a Consumer Stock Ownership Plan (CSOP), and works as follows. Existing utilities would be allowed to expand by receiving low-interest credit from commercial lenders, repayable by future profits. Consumers would be sold shares in the new investment on credit, to be repaid by future profits on their investment. Each regular user would have a separate account. After the initial investment is paid off, consumers would receive shares of ownership which would fund their use of the utility or mass-transit system.[39]

4. Prices and wages must ultimately be linked to a morally adequate assessment of human needs. This can never be perfect, and the market price can serve as a just price under conditions in which participants are reasonably equal and free, *conditions which generally do not prevail in the global marketplace today,* for reasons outlined in the previous section; given the existing concentrations of wealth and power, the market favors corporations over workers. Of what, then, should a fair price consist? Surely, the basis for the price must be the cost of production. However, as Simon correctly argues, even under the most ideal conditions, the cost price would not be the just price. If we wish to avoid the perils of socialism, then we must allow people to take initiative in two important areas: capitalization to fund future investments and nonmarket distributions; that is, distribution according to needs and free distribution. Concerning compensation for work, much iniquity creeps into both the market system and our thinking about it. Those who receive a living wage prefer to pay low prices even though these prices prevent other workers from making an adequate living. When we insist on relating compensation to needs, we can see the injustice involved when an eighteen-year-old who has never worked in his life and has no one to support, receives

a contract for ninety million dollars from Nike Corporation to advertise the latter's sneakers; the contract may involve no more than the equivalent of a few weeks of work, with a sum greater than that of all the workers who manufacture the shoes in a given plant, many of whom live in subhuman conditions. Simon makes the point that there is no legitimate dimension of the common good that demands that someone be paid an income a hundred times greater than his needs,[40] while millions of full-time workers lack necessities. As absurd levels of compensation are today repeatedly doled out to athletes, entertainers, and those involved in speculative enterprises, while workers go hungry and farmers lose their land, we can see how inadequate the market today is even for reaching a modicum of justice concerning prices and wages.

5. The primary purpose of a firm lies in its constitution as a community of persons working in solidarity to satisfy their own needs and those of other citizens. Profit is a practical necessity, but the purpose of the firm cannot be reduced to it. This is necessary so as to preserve the sense of solidarity in the workplace. At the same time, it must be recognized that, in the absence of changes in the broader economic and cultural environment, along lines suggested in this chapter, it is practically impossible to expect any real shift in this direction.

6. It must be recognized that various degrees of state intervention have served to promote alleviation from exploitation. Just as one cannot in justice proclaim a priori that market reforms guarantee more justice, so one cannot claim a priori that state intervention is unjust. The principle of subsidiarity is always valid, but it is not a simplistic argument against regulation, for when the moral ends to be attained are not and probably cannot be realized at the lower level of social organization, then intervention may be required. Moreover, *intervention may strengthen the autonomy of institutions.* To protect family farms, small businesses, viable labor unions; to facilitate broader ownership of productive resources; and to protect people from arbitrary behavior on the part of mammoth enterprises and financial oligarchies—these remain legitimate goals on the part of a state.

The issue of state intervention is unfortunately obscured in our time by the unfruitful ideological debate between, on the one hand, so-called conservatives who endlessly cite the considerable evidence of shortcomings and abject failures of government regulation, and, on the other, contemporary liberals who endlessly cite the considerable evidence of the improvements wrought by government action. This debate has long outlived its usefulness, especially in that it is now cast simply as being either in favor of "big government" or opposed to it. This is an utter misconception in that justice cannot be served by simply embracing one or the other; one should not choose to be for or against state action independent of assessing the extent to which the intervention is or is not likely to promote appropriate moral ends, based on all of the available evidence. For example, those who oppose national regulation of health care simply as a matter of principle, without considering the benefits of universal coverage and with disregard for people who suffer without it, are wrong to do so. Similarly wrong are those who oppose in principle integrating private agencies into the delivery of social services and oppose school vouchers independent of any improvements that might result therefrom. Ideology in both cases is a poor substitute for justice.

A final point concerning state regulation of corporations is necessary because of the now considerable historical confusion surrounding the issue. The point was made palpable to me a few years ago when teaching a class in American Political Thought. When discussing liberal and left arguments against corporations, one student, flustered, argued that the activities of the modern business corporation were simply "the American way." Subsequent discussion confirmed that the majority of students more or less concurred in the judgment. History, however, confirms that the contemporary corporate-state relationship stands in opposition to an older American tradition that should be revived. As Jane Anne Morris has written, people like Jefferson, Adams, and Paine were unabashedly anticorporate. Abraham Lincoln expressed serious disquiet about the growing role of corporations at the end of the Civil War, going so far as to worry about the future of the nation. The traditional, common-sense thinking about corporations was precisely that they were a potential threat to be regulated. It was obvious to people a century ago that to allow corporations to grow and become unaccountable was destructive in a democratic republic. Consider, for example, the following examples of state regulation of corporations in the state of Wisconsin:

- Corporations had to have a clearly stated public purpose in order to be chartered in the first place. The state could ask for evidence that this purpose was not being fulfilled by any other set of institutions. A charter could be revoked for going beyond this purpose.
- Management and stockholders could be held liable for corporate acts.
- Directors of the corporation had to be chosen from the stockholders.
- Corporations could not own other corporations.
- Corporations could make no political contributions.
- Corporations were limited in terms of the amount of capital they could amass.
- Corporations could only incorporate in the state where they did their business.
- Charters were granted for a specific period of time, not in perpetuity.[41]

Economic personalism should not simplistically argue for the reimplementation of all of these provisions without qualification, but in their tenor they are by no means out of date. Surely, as corporations may validly operate today on a national level, some level of national-level regulation is needed. Nonetheless, the older approach of implementing regulation at the point of incorporation remains valid and admirably in accord with subsidiarity. In any case, the intent behind such provisions is in each case clear: In recognition of the tendency for corporations to avoid accountability, laws were passed to encourage it. These regulations were also designed to insure that corporate behavior would be linked to both the people who comprised them and those they were established to serve. Economic personalism does demand the revitalization of these connections, as today work-

ers are isolated from owners, and owners are isolated from everyone via nonac-
countable ownership. As Wendell Berry notes, the modern business corporation
is set up to avoid accountability to any community, a situation in which "the buck
never stops." Responsibility is characteristically passed up the ladder of corporate
management and then finally diffused among owners who are customarily too
diffused and unaware to exercise real accountability.[42] Economic personalism also
demands that the tenor of these regulations be revisited so as to limit corporate
size and power, no aspect of the common good being served by their present mag-
nitude.

Another needed change is in the legal area. The definition of the modern
business corporation as a "person" under the law should be reconsidered. Persons
are legally responsible for their behavior, but the corporation makes itself
accountable to nothing but profits. Increasingly, they are accountable to no community of human beings anywhere on this planet. Under their legal status as persons, corporations are almost never closed down, no matter how egregious their
violations of the public trust. They can use their vast financial resources to lobby
against and even resist laws passed by due process. They can challenge governments at all levels, even sue communities at all levels who interfere with their preferred autonomy. To define such entities as "persons" before the law is a ghastly
moral development, rendering the needed regulation of their behavior increasingly difficult. Moreover, their legal status as persons suggests that society should
be organized so as to serve them, not the other way around. Corporations should
be conceived not as persons but as organizations which popular sovereignty permits under conditions established by law, along the lines of traditional American
thinking.

## Social Justice

Economic organization must be implemented in accord with principles of
social justice. Admittedly, social justice has been and remains the source of a
great deal of confusion and muddled meanings. Those of a conservative bent have
often been in the foreground here, denying that the content of social justice is
knowable, and/or denying that it can be defined as a virtue. Michael Novak goes
to the extreme and claims that "the use of the term social justice is moral imperialism by the imposition of abstraction."[43] This is usually a prelude to the false
assertion and abandonment of moral responsibility involved in advancing the
claim that what needs to be done is simply to implement free-market methods of
economic organization. I have gone over this ground elsewhere.[44] Here I would
like to review salient dimensions of the concept of social justice.[45]

It is worthwhile to begin by recalling the principle of solidarity enunciated
so eloquently by economist Heinrich Pesch. This is of great importance to personalism because it so explicitly links solidarity to the ontology of the person previously outlined. Solidarity is grounded in the person as an image and likeness of
the Trinity:

God gave to each one of us a soul made in His own image.... But God did not simply manifest in each soul the fullness of His infinite existence. The unity of souls which society represents also contains no less clearly the impact of His divine character. Human society, with the all-embracing bonds of a life led in community with others and in interdependence, is merely a reflection of that divine community where the three Divine Persons dwell in the consummate unity of their infinite being. Among human beings there is everywhere the condition of solidarity, i.e., that forward and backward flowing movement of life, and that mutual permeation of one by all and all by one, by which all members of society . . . mutually determine their own destiny, and because of which nothing that affects the whole, remains a matter of indifference to the individuals.[46]

The meaning of justice can only be properly understood when rooted in the person so conceived. Prior to the specifically Christian influence, the notion of social justice was truncated precisely by the absence of this sense of solidarity at the core of the person. Reviewing the history of the concept, William Ferree claims that Thomas Aquinas was the first to understand social justice as *a special virtue which has the Common Good as its special object.*[47] As we have already seen in our exposition of the common good, the latter is all-encompassing and embraces every act of virtue. Echoing Saint Thomas, Pesch asserts further:

> Social justice . . . requires the fulfillment of all obligations as well as the realization of all claims which have the well-being of society as their object. Now if we take social justice in its broadest sense, as the kind of justice which ought to apply *within* a well-ordered society, then it would naturally include legal, and distributive, and commutative justice all together.[48]

What Saint Thomas left unanswered, according to Ferree, is whether or not there were specific acts that directly had social justice as their object. Ferree contends that Pius XI's landmark encyclical, *Quadragesimo Anno,* clarified the issue. What social justice demands is something properly social. For example, Pius XI states that every effort should be made to guarantee that the head of a household garner a wage sufficient to support his family. However, if for some reason this cannot be done, "social justice demands that changes be introduced as soon as possible whereby such a wage will be assured to every adult workingman."[49] In another encyclical, *Divini Redemptoris,* the same point is underlined:

> It happens all too frequently, under the salary system, that individual employers are helpless to insure justice, unless, with a view to its practice, they organize institutions whose object is to prevent competition

incompatible with fair treatment of the workers. Where this is true, it is the duty of contractors and employers to support such necessary organizations as normal instruments enabling them to fulfill their obligations of justice. . . . Social Justice demands that wages and salaries *be so managed, through agreement of purposes and wills* . . . so as to offer to the greatest possible number the opportunity of getting work and obtaining suitable means of livelihood.[50]

In the above citations, two points emerge clearly. First, social justice is acting in concert with others to organize society so as to make it just. Second, there are two levels of justice: an interpersonal level, and a broader, social level. The distinction is clear in the example given concerning wages. Pius XI concedes that, under certain systems of economic organization, it may not be possible for an employer to pay a just wage. This would be a violation of commutative justice, or justice in the exchange between worker and employer. But that is not the end of the story. Pius XI clearly acknowledges that the violation of commutative justice may be due to an injustice at the level of social organization, or social injustice. The individual employer may be helpless to do anything about the low wage he pays, and for that reason may not be culpable for the objective injustice. In such a case, Pius XI makes clear, social justice demands that employers, in conjunction with the rest of society, work together to reorganize the system. It is in this kind of action in concert at the social level that we find the virtue of social justice. The distinction between the two levels is again evident in the following passage:

> So as to avoid the reefs of individualism and collectivism, the two-fold character, that is individual and social, both of capital and ownership, and of work or labour must be given due and rightful weight. Relations of one to the other must be made to conform to the laws of strictest justice. . . . Free competition, kept within definite and due limits, and still more economic dictatorship, must be effectively brought under public authority. . . . The public institutions themselves, of peoples, moreover, ought to make all human society conform to the needs of the common good; that is, to the norm of social justice.[51]

Commenting on the above, Ferree underlines a point frequently ignored. When an employer cannot afford to pay a just wage, commutative justice still demands that it be paid. The employer who cannot afford to pay is not culpable for the violation, and need not pay it. Social justice does not demand that the just wage be paid anyway; what it demands is the effort on the part of employers to work together to reorganize the economic order so that just wages become possible to pay. Moreover, Ferree remarks that "the power to make all human society conform to the norms of Social Justice is vested in *institutions,* in *organizations of men,* not in men as isolated individuals. Social Justice is something *social."*[52]

Similarly, it is essential to recognize the social character of work itself. Pius XI enunciates:

> It is obvious that . . . in the case of work . . . there is a social aspect also to be considered in addition to the personal or individual aspect. For man's productive effort cannot yield its fruit unless a truly social and organic body exists, unless a social and juridical order watches over the exercise of work, unless the various occupations . . . cooperate with and mutually complete one another . . . unless mind, material things, and work combine and form as it were a single whole.[53]

Based on this conception of social justice, Ferree formulates seven laws of social justice, three of which will be mentioned here. First, the unity of society cannot be founded on competition, but cooperation.[54] It is a social observation of profound significance, and well-recognized in all dimensions of social life with the exception of the economy. No one argues that competition is the best way to promote the good of the family, nor the common good of any group, be it a team of workers, a sports team, an army, or a nation. This is because recognition of the point is commonplace, almost self-evident. Yet, when it comes to the economic common good, we are told that it is reached by competition, of workers against one another around the world, of enterprises against one another, of nations against one another, of cities against rural areas, of global producers against local ones. We have seen earlier how the gerrymandering of calculations of benefits and losses stacks the deck in favor of globalization. Here we get to the deeper root of the problem: the social good is in the final analysis the result of cooperation, not competition.

The second law is that all citizens are responsible for building up the common good and promoting social justice.[55] Of course, this does not negate the special function of authority to reconcile particular goods with the common good and various dimensions of the common good with one another. Most people contribute to social justice through their pursuit of particular goods and their own attempts to improve the lower institutions of which they are part. The moral commitment is to the improvement of the institutions in which one participates, as opposed simply to looking out for one's particular interest. In this way, common effort promotes social justice throughout all levels and institutions in society. For example, consumers and farmers working together to form local produce markets; the formation of local cooperatives; organizing to enforce or promote new laws to preserve the health of our land, water, and air; establishing soup kitchens in solidarity with the poor—all of these would be examples of the pursuit of social justice. The point is that it is incumbent on all to be involved in this great effort.

The third law is that all vital interests should be organized.[56] As with the previous point, it is up to the people themselves who are directly involved in each interest to take responsibility for their organization; organization in a personalist perspective must always be from the bottom up. It is worth noting that the failure of people to take responsibility for organizing the institutions of which they are part does not mean that such institutions will be disorganized; it means that they will be organized badly. If people do not organize for the common good, then some set of interests will inevitably impose an order which is not for the common good. This is precisely what has happened to the U.S. economy. It is as well-organized as any set of institutions can be, but the organization has been progressively removed from the people and institutions accountable to them and of which they are part.

## Work

We have finally to consider the meaning of work and its relation to ownership and the role of the state. Here, a theory of personalism benefits greatly by what is undoubtedly one of the most profound statements of economic personalism, *Laborem Exercens*. In this landmark document, John Paul II begins by recalling the biblical foundation, in the mandate of the Book of Genesis: "Fill the earth and subdue it." He sees in this command the deepest anthropological dimension of work. He writes, "Man is the image of God partly through the mandate received from his creator to subdue, to dominate, the earth. In carrying out this mandate, man, every human being, reflects the very action of the creator of the universe."[57] Because of the great dignity of the person as an image and likeness of God, John Paul II contends that "man is therefore the subject of work. As a person he works, he performs various actions [which] must all serve to realize his humanity, to fulfill the calling to be a person. . . ."[58] Man's exercise of dominion in his work must be genuine, such that "throughout the process [of work] man manifests himself and confirms himself as the one who 'dominates.' " Here John Paul II distinguishes two dimensions of work: (a) the objective, which concerns man in his relationship to external objects, including what he produces, and (b) the subjective, the inner dimension of work as the result of the free exercise of man's will and intellect. Dominion, he insists, actually refers more to the subjective dimension, for this "conditions the very ethical nature of work. In fact there is no doubt that human work has an ethical value of its own, which clearly and directly remains linked to the fact that the one who carries it out is a person . . . a subject that decides about himself."[59] Moreover, the Gospel portrays the Son of God Himself as one who spent most of His life working. John Paul II sees in this a revelation a "gospel of work, showing that the basis for determining the value of human work is not primarily the kind of work being done, but the fact that the one doing it is a person. The sources of the dignity of work are to be sought primarily in the subjective dimension, not in the objective one."[60]

John Paul II is careful to contrast this Christian version of work with the various "materialistic and economistic" trends in economic thought which dominate in the modern world. He defines economism as the error of "considering labor solely according to its economic purpose," for to do so "includes a conviction of the primacy and superiority of the material, and directly or indirectly places the spiritual and the personal . . . in a position of subordination to material reality."[61] This error is clearly present in both purely market approaches as well as socialistic approaches to the economy, in which work is understood as a factor of production to be bought and sold on the market or to be used by the state as it sees fit. Although more human ways of considering work have evolved, "the danger of treating work as a special kind of 'merchandise' or as an impersonal 'force' needed for production (the expression, 'work-force,' is in fact in common use) always exists. . . ."[62] In fact, the contemporary development of "a one-sidedly materialistic civilization" tends to overemphasize the objective dimension of work and reduce the subjective to a "secondary level." Considering the cost-cutting and labor-saving motivations behind contemporary globalization, the Pope's concerns about economism seem particularly apropos.

There are three levels of essential human values which are related to work. First, there is work in its personal dimension, as something good for man, corresponding to his dignity, by which he transforms nature and achieves fulfillment as a person. The second sphere of values is found in family life, for which work serves as a foundation. Work not only makes the family possible, but makes it possible for the family to achieve its purposes, the most important of which is the education of children. The third sphere is the larger society to which the person belongs, for society is the result of the work of many generations. "All of this," John Paul II writes, "brings it about that man combines his deepest human identity with membership of a nation and intends his work also to increase the common good developed with his compatriots, thus realizing that in this way work serves to add to the heritage of the whole human family, of all the people living in the world."[63] It is worth noting here how profoundly personalist John Paul II's vision is, respecting each of the constituent dimensions of the ontology of the person: his (a) autonomy, (b) freedom, (c) rationality, and (d) intrinsic solidarity with others.

The foregoing view of the person has profound implications for the understanding of capital. Labor has priority over capital. More specifically, labor is always "a primary efficient cause" of production, while capital is "a mere instrument or instrumental cause." In order to make the relationship between labor and capital clear, he goes back to the biblical theme that man is called to subdue the earth. All production reduces to people working in conjunction with nature, prompting him to write, "At the beginning of man's work is the mystery of creation." The reintroduction of this theme is to prepare the way for clarifying the role of capital, which he sees as, in addition to natural resources, "the whole collection of means by which man appropriates natural resources and transforms them in accordance with his needs." All these means, including the most modern and technological, are the result of human labor. No matter how sophisticated these instruments, they remain just that, instruments subordinate to the person who remains the center and end of the entire economic process.

The organization of work must reflect these anthropological foundations. Unfortunately, the same materialistic and economistic trends which depersonalize labor also distort the role of capital. The Pope insists that the opposition between capital and labor must be overcome, and this can only be accomplished when the priority of labor over capital is recognized. It can be so when we realize that the existing level of technological development and capital goods are no more than "the inheritance of what is given to the whole of humanity in the resources of nature and the inheritance of what others have already developed on the basis of those resources . . . by producing a whole collection of increasingly perfect instruments for work." Correctly understood, capital may condition man's work, but it is never a "subject" putting man in a position of dependence in relation to it. To treat man as an instrument of production amounts to a reversal of the moral order and the order of creation.[64] In a strongly worded passage, he writes:

> Isolating these means [of production] as a separate property in order to set it up in the form of 'capital' in opposition to 'labour'. . . is contrary to the very nature of these means and their possession. They cannot be possessed against labour, they cannot even be possessed for possession's sake, because the only legitimate title to their possession . . . is that they should serve labour and thus by serving labour that they should make possible the achievement of the first principle of this order, namely, the universal destination of goods and the right to common use of them.[65]

By way of conclusion, John Paul II reasserts that the position of "rigid" capitalism, as well as that of socialism, remains unacceptable. In and of itself, this might seem commonplace, but what has not been noticed sufficiently is the grounds upon which the Pope makes the claim. What is to be rejected specifically is the principle "that defends the exclusive right to private ownership of the means of production as an untouchable 'dogma' of economic life," a right in need of "constructive revision both in theory and practice."[66]

Essential to any such revision is a full understanding of the rights of workers. Here John Paul II asserts the following five points at the basis of any just economic order:

- Workers' rights must flow from the correct understanding of work as part of man's essential calling, his duty to "work out of regard for others, especially his own family, but also for the society he belongs to . . . since he is the heir to the work of generations and . . . a sharer in building the future of those who will come after him. . . ."[67]
- Solidarity is a virtue to be encouraged in the organization of work.[68] This refers both to solidarity between workers and owners, and among the workers. In all cases, workers' rights should preserve the subjective experience of solidarity as a participation in the common good.
- As a means of promoting solidarity, it must be recognized that issues related to work are never simply the province of the actual, or direct, employer. A broad

range of people and institutions, such as the state and associations of workers and producers, comprise "indirect employers" who are also responsible for insuring a just labor policy.

- It is the role of the state to enforce a just labor policy, in conjunction with indirect employers. In the formulation of labor policy, the right to work must be considered fundamental. Hence, unemployment itself must be viewed as an evil to be avoided. This calls for a just and rational coordination of work. The state has special responsibilities here, but these do not include any centralization in violation of subsidiarity. The state cannot directly insure a right to work without violating subsidiarity.
- The common use of goods is the first principle of the social order. In order to insure its realization, workers are entitled to either living wages or some combination of wages and other sources of income sufficient to sustain a family. They are entitled to access to affordable health care and a pension. Workers' rights to free association must always be recognized, although labor unions should not be partisan.[69]

### Principles of Political Economy II: Small Property, Decentralization, and Popular Sovereignty

Globalization is undermining popular sovereignty in both the political and economic orders. As economic and political power is increasingly concentrated, the substance of popular sovereignty is progressively hollowed out. It is obvious at this point that, under existing conditions, simply turning matters over to the free market will simply encourage this process of centralization. In the unfair competition among unequals, the large concentrations of capital will inevitably win, accumulate more capital, and continue to translate that into more influence over the state. This connection between ownership and democracy is by no means a new insight. The prevalence of free-market propaganda has made this commonplace insight into the nature of true democracy sound like an argument from the left, but it is in fact as old as Aristotle, a principle of the American foundation, and recognized by thinkers as diverse as Protestants, Catholics, and Muslims.

The thesis that popular government is based on an economy dominated by small, independent owners of land was first cogently argued by Aristotle. Aristotle studied the constitutions of city-states in ancient Greece, and concluded:

> The principal differences of democracies result . . . from the different qualities of the people that enter into their composition[;] . . . the best kind of democracy and likewise the most ancient on record, is that in which the people subsist by agriculture; because the best class of working people are those employed in the rural labors of agriculture and pasturage, especially in the former; and the manners and habits of husbandmen are also the best adapted to counteract the evil tendency

of democratic institutions.[70]

In this kind of democracy, all citizens would be treated alike, and all would equally participate in government. It would be a constitutional government based on laws of universal applicability.

The connection between the democratic form of government and the way of life of the small landowners was direct and necessary. Elaborating on the characteristics of the people best qualified to implement and reap the fruits of democratic government, Aristotle writes that such people:

> subsisting chiefly by agriculture, and possessed, as is usual with such a people, of very moderate fortunes, naturally arrange themselves into a legal and well-constituted democracy. They may subsist comfortably by labour, they would soon be ruined by idleness; they contrive a government, therefore, which requires as little expense of time as possible; and employ on all occasions, when it is practicable, the great machine of law to save the labor of man. . . . Among such a people, government is carried on without salaries, without revenues, and without taxes. The affairs of the community, therefore, are left to assume this natural order; since men have no undue motive to engage them to abandon their own profitable concerns, in order to employ themselves in matters which will be much better managed without their unreasonable interference.[71]

*There is nothing dated in Aristotle's identification of a healthy democracy with the characteristics of a society of small landowners.* Indeed, one could catalog many of the contemporary problems with democracy by reference to the absence of what a society of small landowners contributes to this system of government. Five features are noteworthy. First, Aristotle saw that democracy flourished in a society of citizens with moderate fortunes. The very wealthy, he noted, are used to giving orders and being obeyed, having the means to arrange their lives in such a fashion. They dislike obeying others. They inevitably tend to carry such attitudes over to the political arena, and tend to believe society would be best if people of their kind made the rules. Aristotle recognized that such attitudes were inimical to the principle of self-government, for in such a system, people would have to make laws for themselves, take all into account, and be obedient to the laws created. On the other hand, the poor are overly accustomed to obeying and being subservient to others, lacking experience in managing their own affairs. As such, they are not well fit for governing the affairs of their community. The ideal democratic citizen, in Aristotle's view, is the one of moderate fortune, who has a lived experience of managing his own affairs, accustomed both to governing and being governed. Such people are both competent to make fair laws and willing to obey them. Second, democracy is best supported by citizens of a character to work and take real responsibility. A proliferation of the idle will undermine responsible self-government. A society of small landowners, by its very nature, will be one of working and responsible people. Third, in such a society, there is no desire to finance a governing class looking for things to do. Such people inevitably attempt to create activities for themselves and give themselves power in the process. Fourth, government in such a society is no drain on society through salaried personnel and taxation. Under such circumstances, government is most likely to do only what is really needed for the common good. Fifth, small landowners desire to live under laws which protect their ownership, their economic activity, and their families. They are motivated both to create such laws and to obey them. In other words, the small landowner is most likely to exercise his sovereignty with moderation.

It is informative to consider as well what Aristotle learned about the constituent features of failed democracies. As Douglass Adair put it, "It was the Hellenic city-dwelling artisan whose misuse of popular sovereignty had cast a dark shadow over the term democracy down through the ages."[72] The worst kind of democracy was the one dominated by the multitudes living in the cities. In an urban democracy, he noted, citizens cannot afford to participate in the functions of government without being paid. The state must collect revenues to pay people to participate, and this leads to the abuse of public funds being used by the multitude to give themselves a life of leisure. The outvoted rich stop participating in the assemblies. Society ceases to be governed by settled laws, and rather by the random decrees of a people who make themselves into a tyranny. Like a tyrant, the multitude punishes virtue and rewards vice, influenced as they are by demagogues.[73]

Victor Hanson explains that Aristotle's association between democracy and a society of small landowners, as well as his disquiet over the subsequent development of urban-based democracy, are well grounded in the historical development of ancient Greece. Western democracy, even Western culture itself, arose out of agrarianism, when communities of small landowners formed, governing themselves by their own laws, providing for their own defense, each citizen an owner of land on which he was free to manage for himself and his family. Prior to the formation of this civilization, the city-state, there were no free citizens. According to Hanson, the very word "citizen" had no equivalent in the non-Greek world surrounding it. The success of the agrarian-based democracy, however, created problems, with the proliferation of cities and commerce. Those who benefited from the wealth produced on the land transformed the original equality of the countryside, an equality based on a common commitment to hard work and responsibility, into an urban democracy increasingly based less upon hard work and the sense of civic duty and more upon taxation and deriving income therefrom. The democracy that began in an agrarian society characterized by hard work, virtuous self-restraint, and the sense of duty tended to devolve into an urban society based on self-centeredness and overindulgence, and using an increasingly expensive government to promote both.[74]

In the modern period, Thomas Jefferson echoed many of the same themes as he proposed a political economy for the budding American democracy. For Jefferson, farming, education, and democratic liberty were inextricably intertwined.[75] One of his greatest convictions, which he expressed in a letter in the last weeks of his life, was "that the mass of mankind has not been born with saddles on their backs, nor a favored few booted and spurred, ready to ride them legitimately, by the grace of God."[76] In order for the person to be free and realize his potential, Jefferson believed that he had to own land and other property. By ownership, Jefferson meant real control over the capacity to use one's property. Ownership provided the basis for independence and authentic citizenship. Having traveled extensively in Europe, Jefferson was aware of the landless peasantries in Europe, where the unequal division of property caused an economic, political, and social marginalization, a "wretchedness" that deeply troubled him. The legislators, he contended, must be ever solicitous to come up with new ways to subdivide property, insuring that these divisions are in accord with man's natural inclinations; by the latter he meant that property should, upon the death of the owner, pass equally to all children or other relations. Moreover, taxation should be eliminated for landholdings below a certain level, then progressively levied according to the size of the holding. In all situations where there were uncultivated lands and idle poor, Jefferson believed that property rights had extended beyond natural right. Going back to the common Christian belief that the earth was given for the sustenance of all, Jefferson believed that, in the case of unemployment, the worker could call upon the fundamental right to work the land to provide for his family's sustenance. Therefore, he believed that government should strive to maximize the number of citizens who are actually landowners.[77] "Cultivators of the earth," he argued, "are the most valuable citizens. They are the most vigorous, the most independent, the most virtuous, and they are tied to their country, and wedded to its liberty and interests by the most lasting bonds."[78] They were the true foundation of freedom. Jefferson took great pride that beggars were seldom encountered in the United States, a nation where it was not hard to gain a subsistence.

Alongside Jefferson's conviction that a democratic republic must be rooted in small landowners were three concerns. First, although not opposed to manufacturing or industry, he was concerned that its domination would create "artificers" who would undermine the liberties of the people. Second, he feared that urbanization would strip the citizenry of the independence and security he valued so. Finally, when Jefferson spoke of ownership, he did not mean acquiring stocks and bonds. Even in the eighteenth century, small stockholders had no real voice in managing a business. To depend on property over which one exercised no control was no firm basis for a free and independent citizenry. Real wealth was identified with virtue and work. Paper wealth was prone to the manipulation of financial values by the few. Its growth had no intrinsic relation with virtue. For this reason, Jefferson held paper wealth in contempt.[79]

Although the wealth-producing capacities of the Industrial Revolution had a deadening impact on the instinct for ownership as the centerpiece of freedom and a democratic political order, the distributist movement in England emerged in the late nineteenth and twentieth centuries as a reaction against the centralizing tendencies in both socialism and capitalism. The most well-known authors associated with it were the English Catholics, Hilaire Belloc and G.K. Chesterton.[80] Both emphasized that the capitalist state was one where fewer people were owners of the means of production and the great majority were dispossessed. Although they were formally free and would protest insistently should anyone deny that they were so, the truth was that the many were dependent on the smaller number who did own, and had to enter into a contract with them in order to secure a livelihood. Such relations were inherently unequal, the workers having no real option other than to accept the wage offered. Here is where Belloc and Chesterton saw an essential similarity between socialism and capitalism: Both stripped most people of political and economic power and transferred it to a governing elite. Keeping people in dependence on wages was similarly vital to both systems as a way of insuring that the people would be malleable. Chesterton contended that the implementation of particular policies could help to reverse the trend to concentration. These were: to tax contracts so as to discourage the sale of small properties to large owners and to encourage the fragmentation of extended properties; to terminate primogeniture; to establish free law for the poor that would protect and preserve small property; and to protect by law, including taxes, new experiments in small property.[81]

It is worth recalling that the social teaching of the Church does support the principle of expanding ownership along personalist lines. Consider the following from *Gaudium et Spes:*

> Since property and other forms of private ownership of external goods contribute to the expression of the personality . . . and furnish one an occasion to exercise his function in society . . . it is very important that . . . ownership . . . be fostered. Private property . . . confers on everyone a sphere wholly necessary for the autonomy of the person and the family, and it should be regarded as an extension of human freedom. Lastly, since it adds incentives for carrying on one's function and duty, it constitutes one of the conditions for civil liberties.[82]

More specifically, John Paul II has insisted on the importance of revitalizing agrarian life, as has the Pontifical Commission on Justice and Peace. The Pope laments that agricultural work is not properly appreciated by society, and that former owners pushed off the land are exploited by larger ones, particularly in developing countries. The Pope urges immediate and radical changes to restore agriculture to "its just value as the basis for a healthy economy."[83] In its 1997 document *For a Better Distribution of the Earth*, the Pontifical Commission on Justice and Peace repeats the argument from *Gaudium et Spes* quoted above specifically in the context of agrarian reform. The commission explicitly links the following proposals as ways of bringing about needed reform in the agrarian sector:

(a) At the juridical level, there should be laws that maintain and guarantee the effective diffusion of private property; (b) the widest possible distribution of private property, specifically, small agrarian properties and tools and equipment necessary for such owners, should be facilitated; and (c) tax policies which will insure the continuity of the property in the ambit of the family should be adopted.[84]

Although one can find some sympathy for an argument in favor of increasing small businesses, when it is made clear that this includes making every effort to increase the number of small farms, it is very difficult to get any political traction whatsoever. This is ironic in that the argument in favor of small business is historically but an offshoot of the agrarian argument. Unfortunately, farmers have no means of making their case in the current political system. Neither political party supports them. They are not assembled as an interest group that carries any weight. Therefore, despite the impressive pedigree of great minds that have stressed their importance for democracy, from Aristotle to Jefferson to the agrarians of the twentieth century to the Catholic Church, arguments in favor of them are generally dismissed without the benefit of serious argument. Nevertheless, in light of the fact that great minds from different cultures, religions, and time periods have all insisted on the connection among healthy agrarian life, widespread ownership of productive property, and democracy, it is worthwhile to make the case again, keeping in mind the circumstances of today.

It is timely and important to assert again the connections among small properties, local community, and democracy, for several reasons. First, along the lines stated by Aristotle, the small property owners engaged in managing their own economic units have the kind of experience essential to democratic citizenry. In their exercise of management, they have a daily experience of self-government. The management of a farm or a small business requires hard work and self-discipline; there is a minimal waste of resources. Successful operations require honesty with self and others and the maintenance of relationships with the surrounding community characterized by accountability and trust. These experiences and the virtues which correspond to them are just as important for self-government at the levels of both the local community and the nation. Moreover, the community characterized by nearly universal property ownership, with many farms, is ideal for the direct democracy which, as we have seen, is the archetype of democratic government. Moreover, democracy at the level of the large unit is contingent upon the existence of democracy at the lower level. If modern democracy is to recover its authentic meaning of substantive self-government, then it can only do so if there is an intense experience of democracy at the level closest to the person, in which people can fully participate in actual self-government. Finally, authentic democracy at the local level is the only way to reverse one of contemporary democracy's worst features; that is, turning over the substance of democratic decision-making to unelected and increasingly unaccountable experts who inevitably aggrandize themselves and downplay the significance of actual participation for the health of democracy.[85]

Second, small ownership of productive property, and rural life especially, reinforce the sense of personal autonomy at the basis of personalist democracy. This is undercut today principally by the large-scale organization which finds in technology its raison d'être and its governing ethos. Technological imperatives inevitably reduce people to replaceable and interchangeable factors of production, conditions particularly unfavorable to preserving any sense of the uniqueness and rightful autonomy of the person. Technology and its concomitant, the division of labor, fatally erode the link between the uniqueness of the person and the personal imprint of his personhood in his work; it makes no difference who does the work because the latter has the quality of sameness. As a result, there is steadily less room for the particularity of a person in work, resulting in the loss of work-related skills. For example, we are already facing a critical level in the number of Americans who even have the knowledge of how to run a farm. These developments leave us with a population increasingly bereft of any genuine sense of their own uniqueness and autonomy. Moreover, they have not even the means for acquiring such a sense. Owning no capital and performing standardized tasks, they experience nothing but an increasingly heavy sense of their replaceability. On a small farm and in small handicraft shops, such conditions do not prevail. There, the sense of uniqueness and autonomy is grounded first of all by the fact of owning productive resources. It is reinforced and buttressed over time by the accumulation of specific knowledge and skills tied to unique personalities. There can be no question that the sense of being unique and autonomous is greatly aided by the proliferation of agriculture and crafts in the context of small ownership.

Third, the predominance of technology in economic organization undermines the reality of community, which necessarily diminishes the persons who comprise them; when people lack needed experiences of solidarity, their personalities wither. We have already discussed one of the principle mechanisms which causes this in the contemporary capitalist economy; that is, the increasing disjuncture between the experience of genuine service of others and the profit of work. Workers lose the sense of solidarity in the workplace and assume the attitudes of the owners: They embrace the primacy of the profit motive. Second, technological society erodes community because it so heightens the experience of fluidity and change that these increasingly take on the role as the governing exemplars for all areas of social life. Technology promotes job losses and job changes, then career changes, changes of location for both work and home, and changes in the organization of society. As every other structure falls in the face of technological imperatives, *so eventually does the moral.* Technology suggests that all organization is contingent upon a specific set of circumstances which the existing technology permits. When technology advances, organization changes. In such an environment, it becomes increasingly difficult to speak in terms of timeless values, even those which support the family. The pressure is ultimately to enforce any and all mandates arising from technological imperatives and to make optional any other rules, including moral ones. Families and communities revolve around a pole of stability over time which is in tension with the high-technology economic organization of our time. Third, technology increasingly transforms the sense of time, reducing the sense of connection among past, present, and future. Technological displacement greatly expands the quantity of things believed to belong to the past and not the present, and does so at an increasingly faster rate. As I learned through embarrassing personal experience, by the mid-1990s, many adolescents had no experience of listening to music on recorded albums placed on turntables. This dominant experience of fluidity impacts popular thinking about morality as well. Traditional sexual morality, in particular, seems to many to simply belong to a former age of stable families and communities which no longer exists. The other side of this is the corresponding loss of any personal sense of preserving civilization as a sense of mores for future generations. There can be no question that modern technological civilization contributes enormously to the weakening of family and community life. Moreover, as Simon writes, "In so far as men deprived of community life and delivered to loneliness are ready material for antidemocratic movements, it must be confessed that technology, by creating circumstances unfavorable to the family community, prepared material for [such movements]."[86]

Fourth, rural life especially serves democracy by serving as a check on the lust for power that technological society generates. Again, technology serves here as exemplar. It centralizes power in fewer and fewer hands, and generates a fascination with controlling it for different ends. Moreover, the centralization of power, a disturbing component of contemporary globalization, generates a deeper sense that power needs to be controlled. Moreover, if one faction does not engage in the competition for it, they fear that others will. In such an environment, society becomes dominated by the desire for power, such sentiments becoming the norms in political and economic spheres. Fewer and fewer seem to realize that such attitudes are dangerous and ultimately destructive of the foundations of democracy grounded in the person. Rural life revolves around the principles of communion with nature and the pursuit of happiness. Without idealizing agrarian life, it most certainly keeps alive the need to work in accord with nature and to value communion with the natural world and to find happiness in such communion and other activities unrelated to the acquisition of power. Without such activities, as people lose the sense of the intrinsic value of simple, natural joys and pleasures, societies will increasingly be devastated by struggles for power. "All that is necessary," Simon writes, "is awareness of a link between farm life and the preservation and promotion of things that can never become indifferent to men—communion with universal nature, the conquest of time through everlasting faithfulness, temperance, dignity in [simplicity], holy leisure, contemplation."[87]

One of the most significant contributions of rural life to any genuinely personalist democracy is that it preserves the person, man himself, as the very principle of integration; man himself is the measure of everything else. On a family-sized farm, production is directly for personal use. What is produced and in what quantities are directly related to the real human need and the real proportions of what is needed. There is no alienated work for the purpose of producing frivolous goods or goods out of proportion to human needs. There is no tendency to create or stimulate artificial needs. Labor is oriented to the full range of needs to be met, division of labor being kept to a minimum. Thus, farm work and farm life has a character of wholeness and integration not generally found elsewhere.[88] No one concerned for the well-being of the person can possibly be indifferent to the loss of such an institution.

The last contribution of rural life to democracy is ironically and surprisingly in its impact on the world of ideas in democratic societies, and particularly so in our own time. As the contemporary world abandons traditional wisdom in its political, economic, and educational life, there is a pressing need to preserve it. Moreover, as our intellectual life is overrun by materialists, technocratic barbarians, moral relativists, postmodernist sophists, and nihilists (and a large number of others who have lost the sense of freedom and courage to fight these), there is an equally pressing need for people possessed of genuine independence of mind. There is precious little of it in academia today, which has become a stifling environment of superficiality and conformity. The only hope for preserving any personalist sense of democracy is to decrease the influence of the predominant intellectual trends on the larger society. This will not be easy to do, but it shows the need for vibrant rural life. As Victor Davis Hanson bluntly notes, the academic needs independently minded people to resist him, now more than ever.

> It is impossible to [preserve a democratic republic] without the agrarian prerequisite . . . because a reservoir . . . of tough, unpleasant, and independent people . . . is always needed in a democracy to ensure against the tyranny of an urbanized and uniform majority, to provide a pristine reminder of the original plan when others have forgotten or rejected it. The metropolitan . . . always loses a pragmatic view of nature and man's effort to master it and so ultimately finds comfort in, not unease with, the daily replication of thought, action, and comportment among like kind, comfort in a bland sameness and stasis which finally is so lethal to the idea of participatory democracy. And in America democracy and capitalism . . . will ultimately bury us all . . . if there not be a body of independent thought and action outside our reach. And that counterpoint and corrective to the evolution of American culture . . . is not to be found in the corporation, the government, or the university. . . . Even our abstract thinkers . . . ignore the farmer. . . . They write essays on liberty and responsibility, on the moral and ethical sense, on God and man . . . without any notion . . . that all man's thought—as Pericles and Socrates saw—must be balanced by the physical, that the farmer and his soil—as Euripedes and Aristophanes believed—grow the first good citizen.[89]

### Principles of Political Economy III: Expanding Worker Ownership

A personalist economy is one which greatly values the most widespread distribution of the ownership of property, and, more broadly, the productive resources commonly referred to as capital. The corporate form of ownership is problematic, tending to promote the concentration of ownership, and, ultimately, an economic centralization that effectively removes control over land and capital from the hands of the vast majority. Nevertheless, the corporate form of ownership is with us and is likely to remain so. In this section, we will explore ways of promoting equity expansion and economic democracy within the corporate framework. These proposals should all be interpreted, however, within the broader, personalist framework for ownership that is directly related to control, as in small enterprise and family-size farms.

Although Catholic social thought has emphasized the living wage, decent working conditions and working hours, the need for a day of rest, and retirement benefits, the theme of ownership has not been ignored. Pope Leo XIII wrote:

> It is easy to see that anyone who does anything of any kind for pay does it primarily to get something of his own, something that belongs to him and no one else. . . . If, therefore, a man spends less on consumption and uses what he saves to buy a farm, *that farm is his wage in another form,* as much at his disposal as was the wage itself. It is precisely in this power of disposal that ownership consists, whether the property be in real estate or in movable goods.[90]

Moreover, the Pope insisted, "the law should support this right and do what it can to enable as many as possible of the people to choose to exercise it."[91]

Pope John XXIII explicitly addressed the theme of workers as owners not simply of property broadly considered, but owners of the properties where they work. In the subsection of the encyclical *Mater et Magistra* entitled "Shared Ownership," the Pope insists that it is good for workers to become owners of wealth-producing property. "It is especially desirable today," the Pope states, "that workers gradually come to share in the ownership of their company, by ways and in the manner that seem most suitable."[92] In *Laborem Exercens,* Pope John Paul II strongly emphasizes the unity of labor and capital. To break down the unjust division between ownership of the means of production and labor, the Pope again suggests "proposals for joint ownership." Labor should be associated with the ownership of capital "as far as possible."[93]

In what remains, I would like to sketch an alternative approach to political economy, applicable to both the developed and underdeveloped worlds, which is consistent with Catholic social thought and charts a new course, different in kind from what I claim are the failed models of Marxist socialism and capitalism. This model, originally developed by Louis Kelso, and first articulated by Kelso and Mortimer Adler, is remarkably consonant with Catholic principles.[94] More recently, Norman Kurland of the Center for Economic and Social Justice has tirelessly promoted these ideas in Washington.

Louis Kelso is best known for being the intellectual force behind the ESOP, or employee stock ownership plan. Kelso was motivated to provide this new financing technique based upon the insight, shared by many others, that advances in technology have the long-term effect of concentrating higher levels of productivity into fewer workers. One of the fundamental contradictions of contemporary capitalism, Kelso observed decades ago, was that the purpose of technological innovations was to reduce the labor content of production by substituting an increased productiveness of capital. The logic is inescapable. Clearly, technological innovation was for the purpose of long-term cost-cutting. Obviously, the initial investments in the new technology would only increase costs. Therefore, the hope was that, in the long run, the net increase in costs engendered by the new investments in technology would be more than offset by the net decrease in labor costs.

It is important to be precise about the claim being made here. The argument is not that technology always and necessarily eliminates jobs. The claim is that, "as capital productiveness replaces and supplements labor productiveness, labor's aggregate percentage market claim on aggregate production must *decrease*." Robert Ashford argues that this occurs even though:

1. Sometimes more labor work may be created than eliminated;
2. Wages for some workers may increase; and
3. Average wages (of those still working) may increase. Nonetheless, in the long run, only some—and never enough—people will benefit from the higher productivity. The rest will earn less and will become increasingly dependent on redistribution and the earnings of others to make ends meet.[95]

Kelso's theory has often been too quickly ignored based on data which demonstrate that labor claims up to 75 percent of national income. The problem is that these statistics embody the very conceptual prejudice which Kelso challenged. Kelso's argument is that, as labor productiveness declines relative to the productiveness of capital, massive redistribution schemes have been implemented to redress the problem. The increased productiveness of capital has been defined conventionally as the increased productivity of the worker, and used to justify high levels of taxation on capital, inflated wages, padded jobs, and a host of redistribution measures to divert income from capital to workers and the unemployed. All of this, however well-intentioned, fails to confront the underlying problem of the increased productiveness of capital through technological innovation and the corresponding decline in the productiveness of labor.

The root problem of capitalism today is the highly unequal distribution of ownership of wealth-producing assets, and the perpetuation of that system through traditional methods of finance. To finance new investments, large corporations rely heavily on borrowing money. The existing credit system, however, is based on the principle of collateral: One must be an owner of capital in order to pay back the loan in the event that the investment goes bad. As a result, the owners of the new investment are those who were already owners. It is precisely this limited access to credit which, according to Kelso, explains why capitalism generates inequities generation after generation; most people do not have the collateral for capital acquisition loans.

That the collateral principle is completely unnecessary has been proven beyond reasonable doubt by one of the world's most interesting banks, the Grameen Bank in Bangladesh. This bank is 100 percent owned by formerly propertyless people who became borrowers and are now part owners, not only of the productive assets they purchased on credit, but of the bank itself. Without going into all of the details of this fascinating institution, whose principles are now being employed in the United States as well, let it suffice to point out that the bank started out and grew *based on the complete rejection of the collateral principle.* The founder of the bank, Dr. Mohammed Yunus, began by giving small loans to destitute women, not for the purpose of consumption, but precisely to purchase a productive resource, be it a cow, or the tools and equipment necessary to start very small microenterprises such as making bamboo stools. Borrowers were organized into groups. Each borrower is required to keep up on her payment as a condition for any of the members of the group to receive new loans. The sense of mutual responsibility thus engendered effectively replaced the collateral principle. Dr. Yunus' theory, embodied in the Grameen Bank, served as one of the linchpins for the microcredit movement; that is, loans for the establishment of small businesses.[96] The approach has the following advantages: (a) The loans are small and therefore not a threat to the global financial system; (b) it avoids centralizing power in the state, which promotes subsidiarity; and (c) it avoids the obvious failures of the macrocredit approaches of the International Monetary Fund and the World Bank, which appear in the long run only to increase debt and strip debtor nations of their sovereignty.

Kelso's solution to the problem was the ESOP, or employee stock ownership plan. Kelso overcame the collateral problem by creating a trust —the ESOP—that would borrow in the name of the worker. Let us say, for example, that a ten-million-dollar firm with one hundred workers wishes to double its plant capacity and hire one hundred additional workers. Management would set up an ESOP to cover all 200 employees. The ESOP borrows the ten million dollars, then purchases a corresponding ten million dollars worth of stock in the name of the workers. The firm guarantees the ESOP's credit by agreeing to pay out of future projected earnings sufficient funds to service the ESOP's debt. The stock is either pledged as collateral or held in an unallocated account. As the ESOP debt is paid off, blocks of stock are allocated to individual workers. The average employee will earn about $50,000 in new equity and the right to future dividend checks to supplement his wages and retirement benefits.[97] Moreover, there is *no redistribution involved*. The original owners lose none of their equity in their original holdings.

The system creates new owners without confiscating the assets of others.

Beyond being a new method of corporate finance, the ESOP method illustrates a broader principle of social justice, one which our ideologically driven capitalist society is still a long way from accepting, and that is the principle of acknowledging capital credit as a fundamental right of citizenship. In other words, access to credit should be democratized. Resistance to this principle is drawn from the beliefs that (a) we should strive to be "virtuous savers" instead of borrowers, and that (b) credit is a privilege instead of a right. Both of these beliefs fail to distinguish between two kinds of credit. The first is consumer credit, the kind most Americans are already familiar with to the tune of thousands of dollars per household. Consumer credit, as those who use it know all too well, creates debt. On the other hand, capital credit is self-liquidating, which is to say that it is used to purchase something which will in time pay for itself. Self-liquidating credit is granted all the time in the contemporary capitalist world. The methodology of the ESOP, as William Greider points out, is no different from the leveraged buyouts that became a topic of wide discussion in the 1980s, when corporate executives bought ownership of their own companies by borrowing millions and pledging assets and the future profits of the companies. The ESOP merely extends the practice so that the workers can buy ownership as well.[98]

A move in the right direction is well stated in the *Universal Declaration on the Sovereignty of the Human Person Under God*, approved on August 22, 1997 at the Second Annual Conference of the Scholars for Social Justice. One of the most salient features of this document is that it states clearly the inherent connection between the promotion of a culture of life with the need for a new economic paradigm, one that "transcends the power-concentrating defects of both traditional capitalism and traditional socialism." The new paradigm, the document asserts, must include "expanded capital ownership." Therefore, "access to the means of acquiring property" must be seen "as a fundamental human right." The document also endorses the "democratization of capital credit as the key to widespread ownership."[99]

What is needed today can be likened to the Homestead Act of the nineteenth century. At that point in time, the most productive asset was land. Essentially, the government extended credit so that people could purchase productive assets. In return, people had to be good stewards of the land and make it productive. If they did, the land became theirs. Today, there is a new frontier of technology, and it is of even greater extent than the terrestrial frontier of the nineteenth century. In 1982, Norman Kurland, a longtime associate of Louis Kelso, articulated a new framework to adapt the Homestead Act to our own time, calling it "The Industrial Homestead Act." Like its counterpart of 1860, the new Homestead Act would widely disseminate the ownership of the most productive asset, capital, through access to capital credit.[100]

If there is to be a democratization of the credit system, what would become of bad loans? Kelso proposed a system of commercially insured capital credit. Kelso argued that most casualty insurers would come to underwrite commercial capital credit insurance. However, to accelerate the process, Kelso proposed the establishment of a Capital Diffusion Reinsurance Corporation "to reinsure any portion of any two-factor financing risk assessed as reasonable and insurable but not already insured by the commercial capital credit insurance underwriters."[101] Through the system of capital credit insurance, banks and other lenders would be insured against the loss on acquisition loans to the ownership trusts. In other words, the risk of business failure would be competitively priced and included in the cost of the capital. Thus, the government's role in the process would be quite secondary, primarily spreading the risk among insurers by pooling risk premiums. The government's liability would be strictly limited by the premiums flowing into the existing insurance pool. Taxpayers would not be liable for losses.

Although Kelso is most well known for the ESOP mechanism, he always insisted that the mere creation of the mechanism was insufficient for the kind of transformation to an economy based on universal ownership. Kelso's most profound proposal was to return the Federal Reserve Bank to its originally stated purpose of providing for the credit needs of an expanding private economy. Norman Kurland has made the following specific proposal:

> The discount mechanism of the Federal Reserve (Section 13 of the Federal Reserve Act of 1913) should be reactivated with appropriate modifications and safeguards, to allow commercial banks which are members of the Fed to discount "eligible" industrial, commercial and agricultural paper, representing member bank loans to leveraged ESOPs, IRAs and similar approved ownership-expanding mechanisms of securing access to capital credit for employees and other citizens.[102]

Where is all of this finance capital to come from? One of the more challenging conceptual barriers to understanding the Kelsonian proposals is the deeply embedded yet incorrect assumption that credit must be generated out of past savings. If this were indeed the case, then it would be necessary to redistribute the savings of capital owners to those who are not owners. It looks like a new welfare system which redistributes savings instead of income. But it is not the case that credit must be generated out of past savings. Harold Moulton, former president of the Brookings Institution, demonstrated the fallacy over sixty years ago. Moulton argued:

> The traditional theory that an expansion of capital construction and consumptive output occur *alternately*—that the process of capital formation necessarily involves the curtailment of consumption and the transfer of labor and materials from the production of consumption goods to the creation of capital goods—finds no support whatever in the facts of our industrial history. . . . Funds with which to finance new capital formation may be procured from the expansion of commercial

bank loans and investments. In fact, new flotations of securities are not uncommonly financed . . . by means of an expansion of commercial bank credit.[103]

What Moulton refers to is what Kelso would come to call "pure credit." This is credit which is made available without taking away the wealth of existing holders. Although this may seem impossible, we can understand the proposal once we recall that credit is a social creation; it is not a resource like oil or iron ore. Pure credit is a social creation, which is to say that it is an agreement to pay off a debt incurred today by future income. The savings required to pay off the loan are generated in the future instead of the past.[104]

The next logical concern is whether this manner of generating credit might be inflationary, as it seems to inject millions of dollars into the overall supply of money. The truth of the matter seems to be that this approach is not only noninflationary, but would actually represent an improvement over the way the Federal Reserve Bank actually works now. Currently, and contrary to its originally stated purpose, the Federal Reserve does not generally monetize capital credit. Rather, the Federal Reserve Bank currently extends credit to the government. Through the working of the Open Markets Committee, the Fed buys and sells U.S. Treasury paper, permitting the huge budget deficits which have become a widely recognized problem. Although the Federal Reserve has worked diligently to keep inflation down, it does so by keeping levels of growth far below their potential. In a letter to Mississippi Representative Bennie Thompson, Federal Reserve Chairman Alan Greenspan wrote that a growth rate between 2 and 2.5 percent per year is the reasonable estimate of the level of growth the U.S. economy can manage without inflation. He concedes that this level of growth leaves many people unemployed, and failed to mention the millions more confined to part-time work, those who have given up looking for work, college-educated students delivering pizzas, and older white-collar workers displaced by corporate restructuring.[105]

The Kelsonian approach would encourage higher levels of growth occasioned by new investments. Moreover, the credit extended to the private sector would not be inflationary. The dangers of any long-term, accelerating inflation are greatly reduced by the Kelsonian ideas, because the credit, unlike credit given for government spending, is actually backed by assets and newly created wealth. Thus, a new discipline would be introduced into the system. The Kelsonian approach would forbid offering "pure credit" to the government, and discourage the state from borrowing to meet budget deficits. As Norman Kurland has proposed, "All newly created Fed money and bank credit would be asset-backed."[106]

Kelso's proposals have nothing whatsoever to do with any kind of government control of the allocation of credit. As Kurland has clarified, all credit allocations would be handled exclusively by member commercial banks, subject to market competition, with special safeguards to prevent government allocations of credit or the use of such funds for speculative purposes or public sector investments. Moreover, as economist Norman Bailey observes, the Fed in its own way "allocates" credit every day. In a commentary on Chairman Greenspan's letter to Representative Thompson, in which Greenspan claimed that the Federal Reserve does not allocate credit, Bailey writes:

> As to the inadvisability of the Federal Reserve System "allocating" credit, it does that everyday—the allocation is 100% to the government and 0% to the economy. A simple way to demonstrate that fact is to imagine the federal debt magically disappearing. The Federal Reserve system would have no assets (other than some gold artificially valued well below market) and thus would be unable to issue any liabilities (Federal Reserve notes and credits). There would be no money supply—an absurdity.[107]

One of the most hopeful features of Kelso's approach is the hope it holds out for stimulating a noninflationary economic growth. Once the infrastructure for expansion of capital credit is in place, there is every reason to believe that rates of growth would be higher than they currently are. When the poor and middle classes acquire stock representing the capital requirements of firms, they have a new source of income. After the loan is paid off and they begin to receive income from their ownership, they will most likely generate more consumer demand. Note again that this is not an artificially created demand, but one which is based on the actual ownership of assets. *Kelso creates a necessary link between the expansion of supply via expanded ownership and a corresponding property-based increase in demand.* Robert Ashford summarizes the point neatly:

> Because of the increasing productiveness of capital, production cannot be financed so that it distributes on market principles the consumer income necessary to purchase the consumer goods produced (and necessary to achieve sustainable economic growth) unless capital is acquired on market principles by the people expected to consume what it produces. . . . By financing the ownership of new productive capacity into people with substantial unsatisfied needs and wants (essentially the people who presently derive little or no income from capital ownership), the new system would establish a long-term, self-sustaining basis for growth. . . .[108]

It is important to keep in mind that the Kelsonian proposals can be applied to both developed and underdeveloped economies. In some senses, many of the Third World economies, particularly those in Latin America, are very ripe for the kinds of approaches Kelso championed. Privatization is the wave of today. Unfortunately, the net impact of the privatizations is more often than not to concentrate more and more wealth into fewer and fewer hands. The tragedy of the Latin American privatization process is usually missed because of the conventional assumption that it makes no difference who owns the wealth so long as it is "privatized."

If privatizations in nations such as Argentina had been done according to Kelsonian principles, then the outlook for millions of workers might be quite different. Instead, privatization was simply an opportunity for those already owners of wealth to become fabulously rich. No new income flows were generated through the creation of new owners, and as a result Argentina is in what should be called a depression[109] (because unemployment rates are over 20 percent in some provinces).

In conclusion, the proposals originally put forth by Louis Kelso are in accord with economic personalism and make genuine economic sense. Kelso's approach is the only one this author is familiar with that generally avoids the pitfalls of both liberal capitalism—and its variant, the interventionist Keynesian state—and socialism. Both systems are flawed in that they concentrate too much power in the hands of the few. Socialism's flaws are in many respects more fundamental in their disregard for the genuine autonomy of the person. However, capitalism continues to disregard its central problem, the concentration of ownership. Mainstream economics still proceeds as though it makes no difference who owns. Kelso's proposals are an excellent corrective which have the added benefits of promoting both the principle of subsidiarity and the right of economic initiative. His works deserve the serious attention of all who seek a truly personalist economic order.[110]

## Notes

1. David C. Korten, *When Corporations Rule the World*, 2nd ed. (San Francisco: Kumarian Press and Berrett-Kohler Publishers, Inc., 2001), 210.

2. William Greider, *One World: Ready or Not* (New York: Simon and Schuster, 1998), 171.

3. Pontifical Commission on Justice and Peace, *Para una mejor distribución de la tierra: el reto de la reforma agraria*, (Buenos Aires: Paulinas, 1998), 6, 13-17. Translations are ours.

4. Wendell Berry, *Sex, Economy, Freedom and Community* (New York and San Francisco: Pantheon Books, 1993), 5.

5. Wendell Berry, *A Continuous Harmony: Essays Cultural and Agricultural* (New York: Harcourt, Brace, Jovanovich, 1972), 94-95.

6. Robin Broad and John Cavanagh, *Plundering Paradise* (Berkeley: University of California Press, 1993) 24-31; 61-72.

7. G. Valdés-Villalva, quoted in William Greider, *Who Will Tell the People? The Betrayal of American Democracy* (New York: Simon and Schuster, 1992), 383.

8. Richard Barnet and John Cavanagh, *Global Dreams: Imperial Corporations and the New World Order* (New York: Simon and Schuster, 1994), 294-296.

9. Kevin Bales, *Disposable People: New Slavery in the Global Economy* (Berkeley: University of California Press, 1999), 25.

10. The account of Saipan is from Jim Hightower, *If the Gods Had Meant Us to Vote, They Would Have Given Us Candidates* (New York: Perennial, 2001), 330-344.

11. Kevin Bales, *Disposable People*, 3-4.

12. William Greider, *One World,* 119.

13. Jeremy Rifkin, *The End of Work: Decline of the Global Labor Force and the Dawn of the Post-Market Era* (New York: G.P. Putnam's Sons, 1995), xv.

14. David Korten, *When Corporations Rule the World,* 212.

15. William Greider, *One World,* 106, 110.

16. Katherine McFate, Roger Lawson, and William Wilson, *Poverty, Inequality, and the Future of Social Policy* (New York: Russell Sage Foundation, 1995), 645.

17. Statistics from Bureau of Labor Statistics, published in Jim Hightower, *If the Gods Had Meant Us to Vote,* 232-233.

18. John Paul II, *Laborem Exercens,* no. 5.

19. John Paul II, *Centesimus Annus,* nos. 34-35.

20. William Greider, *One World,* 21, 104.

21. T.J. Cauley, "The Illusion of the Leisure State," in Herbert Agar and Allen Tate, eds. *Who Owns America? A New Declaration of Independence,* 2nd ed. (Wilmington: ISI Press, 1999), 365-380.

22. William Greider, *One World,* 259-273.

23. Adrian Wood, *North-South Trade, Employment and Inequality* (Oxford: Clarendon Press, 1994).

24. William Greider, *One World,* 93-94, 101, 22.

25. William Greider, *One World,* 137.

26. Wendell Berry, *Sex, Economy, Freedom and Community,* 7.

27. James Petras and Henry Veltmeyer, *Globalization Unmasked* (London: Zed Books, 2001), 88-89.

28. John Paul II, *Centesimus Annus,* no. 58.

29. This rather obvious point is frequently ignored by economic liberals who continue to quote examples such as these as evidence of the benefits of liberalization. The truth is that the nations following what leaders in the United States pretentiously call "the Washington consensus" are the Latin American nations where two-thirds or more remain mired in the poverty described above. Asian nations look more to the Japanese model characterized by significant state involvement and state-business cooperation. As obvious as this is, it generally has little impact on policy discussions in the United States. This is a tribute to the domination within the United States by corporate leaders and neoclassical economists.

30. John Paul II, *Centesimus Annus,* no. 14.

31. Yves R. Simon, *Work, Society and Culture* (New York: Fordham University Press, 1971), 121-122.

32. Yves R. Simon, *Work, Society and Culture,* 126.

33. David Korten, *When Corporations Rule the World,* 187-192.

34. Yves R. Simon, *Philosophy of Democratic Government* (Notre Dame: University of Notre Dame Press, 1993), 248.

35. Yves R. Simon, *Democratic Government,* 65.

36. John Paul II, *Centesimus Annus,* no. 34.

37. Yves R. Simon, *Work, Society and Culture,* 133-142. The term "free distribution" is Simon's.

38. Yves R. Simon, *Work, Society and Culture,* 141.

39. Norman G. Kurland, "Beyond ESOP: Steps Toward Tax Justice," in John H. Miller, ed., *Curing World Poverty,* (St. Louis: Social Justice Review, 1994), 165-166. For a

fuller discussion of the principles of expanding equity, see the last subsection of this chapter.

40. Yves R. Simon, *Democratic Government,* 250.

41. Jane Anne Morris' work is cited in Jim Hightower, *If the Gods Had Meant Us to Vote,* 392-395.

42. Wendell Berry, *Another Turn of the Crank* (Washington, D.C.: Counterpoint Press, 1999), 12.

43. Michael Novak, *The Catholic Ethic and the Spirit of Capitalism* (New York: Free Press, 1993), 76-77.

44. Novak's false claim, in diametric opposition to the Catholic tradition Novak claims to represent, is critiqued in my previous work, Thomas R. Rourke, *A Conscience as Large as the World* (Lanham and London: Rowman & Littlefield, 1997), 53-61.

45. I will rely considerably here on a remarkable little volume originally written in 1948: Rev. William J. Ferree, *Introduction to Social Justice,* ed. Michael D. Greaney (Arlington: Center for Economic and Social Justice, 1997). This volume underlines the crucial but most frequently ignored contribution of Pope Pius XI's *Quadragesimo Anno.*

46. Rupert J. Ederer, ed., *Heinrich Pesch on Solidarist Economics* (Lanham: University Press of America, Inc., 1998), 47.

47. William Ferree, *Social Justice,* 5.

48. Rupert J. Ederer, ed., *Heinrich Pesch on Solidarist Economics,* 176. Legal justice, defined originally by Aristotle in the Fifth Book of his *Nicomachean Ethics,* simply meant all acts of virtue insofar as these were mandated by law. Distributive justice is the justice owed to the various parts of society by society itself. Commutative justice is justice in individual exchanges.

49. Pius XI, *Quadragesimo Anno,* no. 71.

50. Pius XI, *Divini Redemptoris,* nos. 53, 74. Emphasis mine.

51. Pius XI, *Quadragesimo Anno,* no. 110.

52. William Ferree, *Social Justice,* 17-18. Emphasis in original.

53. Pius XI, *Quadragesimo Anno,* no. 69.

54. William Ferree, *Social Justice,* 36. Four other principles Ferree mentions are: (1) the common good be inviolate; (2) one's particular good is one's own place in the common good; (3) higher institutions must never displace lower ones; and (4) freedom of association should be preserved.

55. William Ferree, *Social Justice,* 38.

56. William Ferree, *Social Justice,* 41.

57. John Paul II, *Laborem Exercens,* no. 4.

58. John Paul II, *Laborem Exercens,* no. 6.

59. John Paul II, *Laborem Exercens,* no. 6.

60. John Paul II, *Laborem Exercens,* no. 6.

61. John Paul II, *Laborem Exercens,* no. 13.

62. John Paul II, *Laborem Exercens,* no. 7.

63. John Paul II, *Laborem Exercens,* nos. 9-10.

64. John Paul II, *Laborem Exercens,* nos. 13, 7.

65. John Paul II, *Laborem Exercens,* no. 14.

66. John Paul II, *Laborem Exercens,* no. 14. We will take up the specific proposals in the last subsection of this chapter.

67. John Paul II, *Laborem Exercens,* no. 16.

68. John Paul II, *Sollicitudo Rei Socialis,* no. 40. The specific interpretation of soli-

darity is my own, but in accord with both what John Paul II writes concerning solidarity and the theory being advanced here.

69. John Paul II, *Laborem Exercens,* nos. 16-20.

70. All quotations from Aristotle in this section are from Douglass G. Adair, *The Intellectual Origins of Jeffersonian Democracy,* ed. Mark E. Yellin (Lanham, Boulder, New York, Oxford: Lexington Books, 2000). The cited passage is on page 39.

71. Douglass G. Adair, *The Intellectual Origins of Jeffersonian Democracy,* 45.

72. Douglass G. Adair, *The Intellectual Origins of Jeffersonian Democracy,* 43.

73. Douglass G. Adair, *The Intellectual Origins of Jeffersonian Democracy,* 44.

74. Victor Davis Hanson, *The Land Was Everything: Letters of an American Farmer* (New York: Free Press, 2000), 138-139. See also Victor Davis Hanson, *Fields Without Dreams: Defending the Agrarian Ideal* (New York: Free Press, 1996).

75. Wendell Berry, *The Unsettling of America: Culture and Agriculture* (San Francisco: Sierra Club Books, 1977), 143.

76. Thomas Jefferson, quoted in Wendell Berry, *The Unsettling of America,* 143.

77. Thomas Jefferson, in Merrill D. Peterson, ed., *Thomas Jefferson: Writings,* 841-842, 1400, 259.

78. Thomas Jefferson, quoted in Wendell Berry, *The Unsettling of America,* 143.

79. Gary Hart, *Restoration of the Republic,* 111.

80. For examples of their writings on economics, see Hilaire Belloc, *Economics for Helen* (London: Arrowsmith, 1924); and G.K. Chesterton, *Collected Works,* Vol. V., eds. George Marlin, Richard Rabatin, and John Swan (San Francisco: Ignatius Press, 1987).

81. G.K. Chesterton, *Collected Works,* Vol. V., 98.

82. *Gaudium et Spes,* no. 71.

83. John Paul II, *Laborem Exercens,* no. 21.

84. Pontifical Commission on Justice and Peace, *Para una mejor distribucion de la tierra,* no. 37. Translation ours.

85. Yves R. Simon, *Democratic Government,* 307.

86. Yves R. Simon, *Democratic Government,* 316.

87. Yves R. Simon, *Democratic Government,* 295-296, 322.

88. Yves R. Simon, *Democratic Government,* 300-301.

89. Victor Davis Hanson, *Fields Without Dreams,* 270-271. Emphasis mine.

90. Leo XIII, *Rerum Novarum,* no. 4.

91. Leo XIII, *Rerum Novarum,* no. 34.

92. John XXIII, *Mater et Magistra,* no. 77.

93. John Paul II, *Laborem Exercens,* no. 14.

94. The original proposals were put forth in Louis Kelso and Mortimer Adler, *The Capitalist Manifesto* (New York: Random House, 1958).

95. Robert Ashford, "Louis Kelso's Binary Economy," *The Journal of Socio-Economics,* Vol. 25, #1 (1996): 15.

96. The foregoing summary of the Grameen Bank and the microcredit movement is based on discussions with those involved in the organization Working Capital. The latter is an attempt to use the same principles formulated by Dr. Yanus in the context of the urban United States. Some of the leaders in Working Capital traveled to Bangladesh to study the Grameen Bank organization. As a faculty member at Florida International University, I invited representatives to come to the university to speak to my classes. Unfortunately, I cannot presently recall their names.

97. The preceding example is taken from Norman Kurland, "Beyond ESOP: Steps

Toward Tax Justice," in John Miller, ed., *Curing World Poverty,* 161-162.

98. William Greider, *One World,* 419.

99. "Universal Declaration on the Sovereignty of the Human Person Under God," approved on August 22, 1997, at the Second Annual Conference of the Scholars for Social Justice, held in the Pallotine Renewal center, St. Louis, Missouri. Among the initial signers were Judie Brown, President of the American Life League; Rev. Matthew Habiger, President of Human Life International; and Norman Kurland, Center for Economic and Social Justice.

100. Norman G. Kurland and Michael D. Greaney, "The Third Way: America's True Legacy to the New Republics," in John H. Miller, ed., *Curing World Poverty,* 269-280.

101. Louis Kelso and Patricia Hetter Kelso, *Democracy and Economic Power* (Cambridge, Mass.: Ballinger Publishing, 1986), 109.

102. Norman Kurland, "The Federal Reserve Discount Window: An Untapped Off-Federal Budget Source of Expanded Bank Credit for Accelerating Private Sector Growth, New ESOPs and Genuine Economic Empowerment for All." (Arlington: Center for Economic and Social Justice, 1995), 3-4.

103. Harold Moulton, *The Formation of Capital* (Washington, D.C.: The Brookings Institution, 1935), 47-48, 104.

104. Norman Kurland, "Federal Reserve Discount Window," 7.

105. Chairman Greenspan's views were obtained from a copy of a letter he wrote to Congressman Thompson, dated April 7, 1995.

106. Norman Kurland, "Federal Reserve Discount Window," 4.

107. Norman Bailey, letter to Norman Kurland, May 5, 1995.

108. Robert Ashford, "Louis Kelso's Binary Economy," 13, 20.

109. Technically, Argentina is not in a depression because the overall rates of growth have only declined modestly and are increasing again. This reveals the biased way in which economies are evaluated. Regardless of the proliferation of unemployment and misery, so long as there is overall economic expansion, there is no depression, merely "growing pains" associated with "structural adjustment."

110. There is a tension between the Kelsonian approach and the living wage proposals of the Church. Kelso did not see the imperative for raising wages. Moreover, a Kelsonian today would undoubtedly argue that, as capital is replacing labor as the wealth-producing factor, the approach of raising wages fails to reflect the actual decline in labor's participation in the production of wealth. In fact, wage increases are artificial and inflationary, as they do not correspond to the actual production of wealth. The debate is clearly by no means an academic one. However, the goal in each case is indeed to expand the income of those who are now workers. One wants to raise wages; the other, transform workers into owners and generate two flows of income. The successful implementation of Kelso's proposals would likely create a situation where worker-owners would cease to demand higher wages as they themselves would profit via their ownership. At any rate, to break down the distinction between capital and labor is the goal of both Kelso and John Paul II.

# 5

# The Person and Culture

As personalism is a call for society to be organized around the person, a claim that society itself arises as a concrete expression of the wills and intellects of the people who comprise it, personalist philosophy is inseparable from a particular kind of morality and culture to undergird it. Indeed, so important is the moral-cultural component of the personalist movement that Mounier, the early personalists, and Dorothy Day and the Catholic Worker movement all resisted institutionalization. This was to emphasize the primacy of personal commitment and actions designed to re-establish a civilization in which love personally expressed would replace the impersonal "processes" and "isms" which increasingly govern the world. Indeed, all of the reforms suggested in the previous two chapters, designed to make our political and economic systems more accountable to the person, mean absolutely nothing in the absence of a culture of personalism. If societies are to become more personalist, the culture must change first, and it is to the explication of what this means that the present chapter is directed.

## Christian Personalism and Diversity

At the core of current cultural debates is a variety of claims about the meaning and relative value of the universal and the particular. Within the context of a nation, or even at a global level, is there any legitimate sense in which we can posit a dominant culture? Should cultures other than the dominant be encouraged to assimilate into the latter, or should the converse be upheld? Should each culture rather resist assimilation and hold fast to its particularities? Such questions cannot be answered without reference to a general account of the relationship between the one and the many as it relates to moral values. That account is to be found in the person of Christ. As we have already seen, it was precisely reflection on the personhood of Christ that brought the phenomenon of person into full view for the Western mind. We turn now to see how the correct understanding of the person of Christ resolves the conundrum of the one and the many and provides the basis for a culture of personalism.

We owe it to Hans Urs Von Balthasar for demonstrating how the philosophical problem of the one and the many is only really resolved by the theological doctrine of the Incarnation.[1] In philosophy, the issue is best seen in the conflict between empiricism, which emphasizes the particular and the concrete, and rationalism, which emphasizes the universal and the abstract. Neither approach has an adequate account of what it leaves out. Empiricism in its extreme reduces to positivism and the loss of the universal. Rationalism in its extreme is seen in Hegel, for whom the genuinely particular is eliminated by the development of the Absolute. Theological approaches are similarly wanting. The many is absorbed into the one, as in Eastern mysticism, or the one is diffused into the many, as in polytheism, pantheism, or animism. Short of God Himself entering into history in the way indicated by the Incarnation, it is not possible that any particular revelation could ever be held to have universal significance. For no matter what revelation a Buddha or Mohammed might bring, there are only two possibilities with respect to its universality: (a) The revelation is particular to those who receive it, thus lacking in universality, or (b) the revelation is truly universal. If the latter, the character of universality can only be derived from something itself universal, and hence transcending the particularity of Buddha or Mohammed or any other human person. Therefore, the particularity of Buddha or Mohammed lacks universal significance.

Only Christianity solves this dilemma. In Von Balthasar's words, Jesus Christ is the "concrete universal." That He is so is the implication of the doctrine of the Incarnation. Jesus is a Divine Person, hence possessing the absolute universality of truth and goodness. Yet, by taking on flesh, He is as particular with respect to time and place as any other human being. In Him, the universal is concrete and particular, and the particular is the universal. By possessing the divine nature, Jesus is no less human, as the Council of Chalcedon made clear. He is immersed in history, in a particular place and time, yet all historical norms are forever to be judged by Him. He includes within Himself all that is true, good, and human, and is the concrete and universal norm by which truth, goodness, and humanity are determined in all times and places.

Two conclusions emerge from this theological premise that are at the core of any attempt to formulate a political, economic, and social philosophy along personalist lines. These are that (a) the particular has the capacity to embody the universal, and (b) the universal is encountered only through the particular. Where this is first seen is in the Christian community. Each local community, gathered around the Eucharist, belongs to the universal church precisely through membership in the local. Members of the local community deepen their participation in the universality of the church precisely through their depth of commitment to the local church. The particularity of the local community is no obstacle to attaining the fullness of Christian life in all its dimensions. In fact, it is the only way to attain universality.

In addition to revealing the capacity of the particular to embody the universal, the Incarnation also reveals the dignity of the human person as one having the capacity to receive the fullness of divine life. So far elevated above the material world and every institution composed by man, the human person, in light of the Incarnation, can be nothing less than the principle of integration for all social organization; the political, economic, and social order must be recast with the person at the center. Indeed, that has been the core of the proposals in the preceding chapters. In this reorganization, the guiding principle is not that the person should detach himself from the local and the particular so as to become the best person and citizen. Rather, it is only when the person unites with other particular persons, in politically, economically, and socially viable local communities, that the common good of a nation or indeed the world can be attained. Only in concrete, local practices can persons realize the common good at the broadest levels. It is through attachment to the particular that universal values such as social justice become real. The challenge is to establish local institutions—political, economic, and cultural—through which the universality of the person can be expressed.

The life of Christ reveals yet another component of personhood which must be at the core of personalist culture. The form of the Incarnation is the *kenosis* of God so beautifully revealed in the Letter to the Philippians:

> Let each of you look not only to his own interests, but also to the interests of others. Have this mind among yourselves, which is yours in Christ Jesus, who, though he was in the form of God, did not deem equality with God something to be grasped at, but emptied himself, taking the form of a servant, being born in the likeness of men. And being found in human form he humbled himself and became obedient unto death, even death on a cross (Philippians 2:4-8).

Revealed here is that persons fulfill themselves, paradoxically, by self-giving. A personalist culture will at its core be one of mutual giving and receiving. It is most assuredly not a culture of consumerism, for the latter is based on the false anthropological assumption that happiness is to be found in self-centered materialism.

The strength of the perspective which views the social order in light of the Incarnation is that it accounts for the capacity of the particular to reflect the universal, and avoids the pitfalls of seeking the universal abstracted from or in the absence of the particular. Affirming the reality of universal values such as truth, rights, and justice, it similarly avoids exalting the particular at the expense of the universal. In the absence of this incarnational perspective, one of two tendencies will prevail. First, in the case where the universal is emphasized, the value of the particular, the local, and the singular person is likely to be obscured. This results in the centralization of political, economic, or cultural power. At its worst, it can issue in severe authoritarianism or even totalitarianism. These latter conditions can take place under either secularist or religious conditions. Thus, for example, what was characterized as an overly centralized global economy is of a piece with the Islamic authoritarian state under Ayatollah Khomeini. Both tend to reduce the person to an object to be controlled by centralized authority. The other error would be the glorification of the particular at the expense of the universal. At its extreme, this would deny the very existence or at least the value of universals. Ultimately, from such a point of view, difference itself becomes glorified as the overarching value. Such tendencies tend to undermine any assertion of authority, being hyperlibertarian or anarchic in orientation.

It must be conceded, and indeed it has been throughout, that to base a society's culture on the person is to acknowledge Christian influence, personhood and Christianity being linked both conceptually and historically. In the present time, this will inevitably be met, at a minimum, by the charge of violating the separation of religion and politics. At the maximum, the proposals will be likened to the former Taliban regime in Afghanistan. Such hysteria aside, the influence of religion on culture is frequently misunderstood in our time; the entire subject is distorted by ahistorical presuppositions negating the demonstrable connection between Christian thought and the now widely recognized human values the faith introduced, such as constitutional government and rights. Prominent scholars such as John Rawls and Richard Rorty insist that the nature of democracy is the absence of a commonly held morality believed to be binding for objective reasons.[2] Such claims are in stark contrast with the historical roots of both democracy and rights. Brian Tierney has aptly demonstrated the medieval roots of both; the culture out of which arose Western notions of freedom, rights, and constitutional government was one which adhered to the Christian faith and the objective sense of morality intrinsically connected to it.[3] Natural law is the foundation for Western democracy in that it established the existence of a law higher than the state and to which the state itself is bound. This was the foundation of limited government upon which the entire edifice of democracy was built. In the absence of natural law, restraints on government are left to the vagaries of the passing winds of political power. Indeed, political outcomes themselves become the result of power, not principle. The loss of the objective sense of values in fact is the cultural basis of totalitarianism. This truth has never been lost on tyrants who have always rejected the existence of any set of values independent of their own judgments.

In addition to limiting the aggrandizing tendencies of the state, it must be noted further the degree to which Christianity has provided Western civilization with a broader set of human values. Its capacity to do so is rooted in the relationship between faith and reason explored in chapter two. Rather than undermining reason, faith respects its legitimate autonomy and in fact preserves its integrity by insisting that reason respect its own limits and refuse to absolutize itself arbitrarily. That is why philosophy prospered under Christian aegis, as did all of the profound human values discovered by pre-Christian societies, particularly education, the love of learning, family, and the arts. The logic of the Incarnation mandates precisely this. All that is authentically natural, and particularly what is human, is not only valued, but given greater dignity as coming from the hand of the transcendent Creator. Moving to specifics, we have already mentioned that Western notions of democracy and rights were in many ways the by-products of the specifically Christian understanding of personhood; no one today complains that in promoting democracy and human rights we are implicitly advancing dimensions of Christian thought, as these are now part of our universal human heritage. And surely there are more values that are now broadly recognized as human despite their Christian origins. Christianity mandates love of neighbor and the relief of human suffering without regard to religious distinctions, based on the belief that to succor the suffering is to aid the least of Christ's brethren. These notions, too, have become part of what came to be called and is now widely promoted as social justice. All of these notions are, as a matter of historical fact, rooted in the special dignity of the person revealed by Christianity.

Special attention must be given to the entire area of freedom of conscience, rightly emphasized today. More elaborate discussions of freedom are found in chapter two and below. For the moment, let us simply concede that insofar as freedom of conscience implies freedom of action, no society has nor will any society permit unlimited freedom. In the practical order, freedom always coexists with some notion and practice of social order which excludes behaviors antithetical to it. There being no such thing as a state governed by moral neutrality, we can simply dispense with any arguments contrary to personalism coming from this quarter.[4] Aside from impossible claims of freedom without limit, it should nonetheless be asserted that freedom of conscience is a constituent dimension of personalism. It is the very nature of a person as free to seek the truth, including the truth about God. Respect for the person demands that this search be respected. Moreover, it is the nature of the person to adhere to the truth when found, to order his life around it. Authentic religion can only be a free response to God rooted in the intellect and will of a person. In order to realize his dignity and pursue his vocation as a person, one must be immune from external coercion. This was unambiguously stated in Vatican II, and has been rigorously upheld since. The Council Fathers, referring to religious freedom, wrote, "This freedom means that all [people] are to be immune from coercion on the part of individuals and of social groups and of any human power, in such wise that no one is to be forced to act in a manner contrary to his own beliefs, whether privately or publicly, whether alone or in association with others, within due limits."[5]

It bears emphasis that we are not simply talking about a private right to hold a belief, but the right to adhere to the belief, act on it, and bring it into the public square. This means the right to practice one's faith and to bring the human values derived from it into public life. As John Paul II explains, to act in accord with one's conscience and to discharge that conscience publicly are rights of citizenship which cannot be taken away without doing grave violence to the human person. Religious people have the same rights of citizenship as any other citizen, and under no pretext can they be relegated to second-class status.[6]

The orientation of personalism to build the most profound human solidarity mandates dialog among religions. I choose the word "mandates" advisedly, for dialog is an absolute necessity. Recall that personalism asserts the absolute unity of human personhood. This unity will never be anything more than an abstraction or a pipe dream unless profoundly human bonds are created among people across the globe, transcending all differences, including religious ones. Of course, as has been emphasized, this can only begin at the levels closest to the person, the family and the community. But it does not end there. It ends with nothing less than a global solidarity; the common good at the local level unites with an ever-expanding sense of the common good until the whole world is embraced. Such solidarity will only be real when the real sources of division are broken down. Dialog among religions, then, is written into social life itself.

Authentic dialog among religions bears three other specific fruits intrinsic to personalism. First, it is clear at this point that the global problems of hunger, poverty, oppression, and disease bear on the conscience of all. The followers of no one religion can solve these problems. We must work together to solve them, but can only do so effectively if we are living in relationship with one another. Second, religions must work together to defend the common human values they share. They must overcome enough of their distrust to defend and promote the family in the face of all the forces arrayed against it. They must join together to prevent, for example, the gross abuses of human life in our time, such as abortion and child prostitution. Third, dialog can actually enrich one's own practice of one's own faith. The exigencies of time, place, and culture have a way of modifying religion in ways inconsistent with the faith. For example, in the United States today, Christianity is in many ways badly out of touch with its contemplative roots. Also, Christians all too frequently defer to the paganism of the surrounding culture. Moreover, they often exhibit a shocking loss of the raw sense of awe in the presence of God. What a vivifying effect contact with Buddhism or Islam can have! Respect for the contemplative dimension is far more vibrant  among Buddhists. A substantial number of people in recent decades knew nothing of the contemplative tradition in Christianity prior to contact with Eastern spirituality. In addition, on a personal note, I will never forget what I saw in the Mohammed Ali mosque in Cairo, Egypt. What reverence the people showed to the Almighty! What awe in the presence of the transcendent God! I could only feel ashamed when I thought of the offhanded attitude toward the sacred prevailing in so many Catholic Churches. Moreover, the Moslem is unafraid to pray or demonstrate his faith in public. I could only think of so many contemporary Catholics who go out of their way never to demonstrate their faith, and would never defend it if attacked. Similarly admirable are the straightforward ways Moslems characterize cultural trends in the West as decadent.

To dialog sincerely with people in other religious traditions is no easy matter. One's respect for the personhood of the other can truly be tested, but in this struggle are tremendous possibilities for human growth. Authentic dialog must be distinguished from two tempting alternatives. The first is simply to adopt a "take it or leave it" attitude. Convinced of the truth of our own faith, we can simply emphasize explaining our own faith to those of other traditions, without

*Yes*

really wanting to listen to what they have to say. This is no dialog; the latter requires the willingness to learn about the other, to enter into a relationship of mutual exchange. Another faulty and related attitude is to enter into dialog solely for the purposes of converting the other. There is nothing wrong with evangelization or traditional missionary activity, but these are not the same as dialog. To enter into dialog in a disingenuous way violates one's own personhood and *Yes* that of the other. One must keep in mind that the purpose of dialog is to break down barriers toward the end of working to gather to solve common problems, and the promotion of this kind of solidarity is also an important expression of one's personhood.[7] *How do we best do this?*

Interreligious dialog is also crucial in our time for the promotion of peace and justice. It is again simply not possible for any one religion in the world today to bring about these ends. They must collaborate. It is a misapprehension of Christianity to allow concerns over evangelization to interfere with this call to solidarity; all such reservations are the result of a misunderstanding of the Incarnation and its implications for the human person. Belief in Christ is belief in His mission, which includes within it the affirmation of all human goods. These are to be vigorously pursued on behalf of all and in union with all people of good will. As the most profound repositories of human values, religions can and must be on the forefront of the promotion of peace. Fortunately, major religious traditions such as Judaism, Islam, Buddhism, and Hinduism embrace peace as a fundamental value, historical failures notwithstanding. Moreover, the religious contribution to peace is indispensable in that it alone fathoms the true depths of peace. Peace is not simply the absence of fighting or the offshoot of a balance of power as the politicians frequently see it. The religions understand that war begins in the depths of the person, and radiates outward from there. In those same depths lie the roots of peace. Moreover, without the broader set of human values and moral strictures that religions promote, no authentic peace is possible.[8]

## The Hard Cores of Culture

The concept of person is not a sufficient basis upon which to form an entire culture. As the person is an openness to the infinite, so the possibilities for cultural developments are countless. It is not the province of personalism per se to explore these possibilities, but to restrict the treatment of culture to the core requirements which do relate to the meaning of personhood itself. Here we must first recall all of what was said in chapter two concerning the ontology of the person which must be the lodestone to which any viable culture must be attached. Of particular significance is the correct understanding of freedom as a special kind of determination belonging uniquely to persons which directs them and makes them capable of realizing the moral good in all its dimensions. Such freedom must, as previously discussed, always attend to the givens which make life in community possible. The culture of the person can only be along the lines of what John Paul II calls "the culture of life," which bears witness to the gift-character of our existence as coming forth from the loving hand of God by proclaiming "the total gift of self" as the ultimate cultural model.[9]

To reflect on the meaning of person brings out more than these deepest ontological cores of culture, important though they be. A thoroughgoing reflection on the meaning of human freedom opens up the entire moral realm for consideration. As this has been well-explored by so many others outside of the explicit context of personalism, we will restrict ourselves here to the foundations of culture alone. *The first and most essential point is that there is a hard, ontological core of culture, grounded in the person himself, consisting in the expression and realization of objective necessities.* The human capacities which allow us to know what is real and true and to bring about the good are what have traditionally been known as virtues. Aristotle defined as "intellectual virtues" the following: understanding, or the capacity to perceive immediately the truth of immediate propositions; science, by which the mind is capable of discovering necessary truths by means of demonstration; wisdom, or the capacity to order the universe of knowledge; art, which is the determination of things to be made by man, following the correct course of reasoning; and prudence, which directs us to know how to choose well, and to realize the good in particular circumstances.[10] Each of these is a stable quality related to objective necessities. For example, to have the virtue of understanding, one must hold definitively that two plus two is equal to four. By the possession of science we follow the demonstrations of geometry and embrace their conclusions with certitude. Prudence tells us that we *must* act in a particular way under a particular set of circumstances. These qualities constitute the hard core of culture.[11]

The moral virtues involve the fulfillment of objective necessities. A long tradition going back to Plato has defined four "cardinal" virtues: wisdom, or the capacity to know how to order the various components of one's life; courage, which maintains the objective hierarchy of goods by preserving the truth concerning what is to be feared; temperance, which regulates the pursuit of pleasure so as to insure the proper ordering of goods to be pursued; and justice, which insures that what is received or given is what is due. Again, each of these involves fulfilling objective requirements. Courage demands that I overcome my feelings of fear and help my neighbor who is being attacked. Temperance demands that I limit my pursuit of pleasure so that I can pursue higher goods. Everyone understands that to possess a virtue means that in many cases one must act in certain ways and resolutely avoid acting in other ways. It is not simply left to chance or opinion.[12]

The hard, ontological core of culture also has implications for the way we understand the relationship between work and culture. As we have just seen, qualities of mind and heart, or virtues, which involve meeting objective requirements, must be the moral basis of any good society. This makes them similar to work, which we also associate with the realization of objective ends. It is fair to say, then, that at the core of culture are activities in their nature closer to work than to indeterminate leisure. It is important to the health of a culture that this relation-

*work is good / results based* [handwritten margin notes]

ship between work and culture be maintained, and that the association be used to dignify work, for work done well and honestly itself promotes the virtue which is the basis of a healthy culture. That is why it is so important to promote healthy forms of work, and to maintain manual labor as the paradigm of human work. Societies that lose respect for farming and other forms of hard work are becoming decadent, because to fail to respect human labor is to fail to respect the fulfillment of objective necessity. The same societies overvalue activities in which the connection between the activity and the fulfillment of real needs is more tenuous. Activities such as farming, plumbing, and carpentry should remain our models for work precisely because they tightly maintain the link between human activity and an objective set of results. When the farmer, plumber, locksmith, or carpenter fails to meet the objective requirements of his work, that failure is readily and often immediately intelligible to any observer, and it is good that it is so. It keeps these people honest and disciplined in their labor, and guarantees that society's needs are actually met via their activities. They cannot get away with failures and do what their professions demand. Contrast that to the situation of professors in the university. Academics can cut many corners in their teaching, waste class time on frivolous activities, propose philosophies that are fundamentally flawed, and go on like this for years without perhaps any widespread discovery of their failures. Stockbrokers counsel thousands of people to place their financial futures in dangerous investments in technology and Internet stocks that lose billions. Investment advisors generate bad advice. Yet, repercussions for these workers are few. It is in the nature of such professions that performance in the sense of accomplishing genuine and morally good ends is difficult to assess, even under healthy social conditions. The kind of work they do should never be held to be superior to that of manual workers.

Wilhelm Roepke has written at length concerning the cultural prerequisites of a market economy. Again, we find a series of definitive moral ends to be achieved. In his own words:

> The market economy . . . implies the existence of a society in which certain fundamentals are respected and color the whole network of social relationships: individual effort and responsibility, absolute norms and values, independence based on ownership . . . responsibility for planning one's own life, proper coherence with the community, family feeling, a sense of tradition and the succession of generations . . . firm moral discipline, respect for the value of money . . . and a firm scale of values. . . . [Moreover,] it is an essential part of a reasonable and responsible way of life . . . to restrain impatience, self-indulgence, and improvidence alike . . . not to live beyond one's means . . . to live one's life as a consistent and coherent whole extending beyond death to one's descendants rather than as a series of brief moments of enjoyment followed by the headaches of the morning after.[13]

Given that there must be some kind of free market in order to preserve personal liberty, the disciplines recommended by Roepke need to be revived. Roepke notes as a negative feature of the contemporary scene the proliferation of debt in the form of consumer credit. All available evidence confirms the growth of this pathology, often encouraged by business firms themselves as a way of boosting sales. Debt as a way of life is both cause and effect of the materialist culture of consumerism.

To assert a hard, ontological core of culture involving the fulfillment of objective necessities is not to deny the role of activities characterized by leisure, creativity, and the absence of necessity. We can take the fine arts to be examples of this component of culture. Indeed, it is a widely held view that culture is associated principally with the latter. This common belief has merit so long as culture is understood to be only this component of activities of free expansion. That is not the way it is being defined here, however. By culture, we mean primarily the moral bases of society, and, secondarily, the element of activities we associate with being refined or "cultured" in the commonly accepted sense of the term. By referring to these activities as secondary and as not necessary, there is no intention of denying the importance of such activities. Artistic activities, contemplation, and leisure reflect the transcendent pole of the person. The ontology of the person is such that he is called both to fulfill objective necessities and to be open to the infinite.[14] Revelation completes the picture here. We say that God creates nature as something definitive with knowable laws, but creation itself is an absolute gratuity, the overflow of divine beneficence, and completely unnecessary on God's part. It is natural, therefore, that the human person, created in the image and likeness of God, must participate in both the realm of necessity and that of free expansion, or openness to the infinite. A healthy culture will be one which maintains a balance between the two kinds of activities, avoiding two extremes. On the one hand is a society that places such an emphasis on the fulfillment of objective requirements that the culture is closed. A culture closed to leisure, art, and contemplation will ultimately be closed to God, and may tend toward self-glorification, even militarism and imperialism. On the other hand, a society which glorifies leisure and refinement will lose the hard, ontological core of culture, moving in the direction of frivolity and nihilism.

Contemporary culture is particularly harmful in that it tends to deny the need to fulfill objective necessities. The situation is particularly perilous in that it proliferates from two sources: popular culture and the intellectual milieu. In both we see the glorification of the negation of the objective moral bases of Western civilization. In the latter, subjectivity and arbitrariness themselves have become embodied in postmodernism. Hard and honest work can and perhaps does to some degree offset these trends, but work under present conditions has problematic features of its own. As mentioned in chapter three, work under conditions of modern capitalism is less clearly related to the fulfillment of genuine human needs. The disjuncture between monetary remuneration and genuine service often seems to be growing, especially when we see the amounts of money going to (a) speculative activities, (b) advertising dubious goods and services, and (c) middlemen who serve corporate centralization and tend to drive out real producers. Under these circumstances, work becomes more related to profit-making than reinforcing the foundations of the moral order. In light of these developments, we have need to be concerned more than ever about what Simon calls "the nihilistic monster which plagues today . . . the oldest civilizations of the West and threatens to deliver them up to barbarism."[15]

Many people could be cited as models of a culture of personalism. I would like here to mention two, one explicitly related to the history of personalism as a theory, the other not. The first is farmer and agrarian author Wendell Berry. No one has written more eloquently about the devastating impacts occasioned by corporate agriculture, the centralization of economic life, and the destruction of local communities in our culture. Yet the major reason he serves as a model is that he has taken personal responsibility to counteract the negative trends by his own life. He himself gave up his academic career to become a farmer. He farms in a way that minimizes dependence on fossil fuels and expensive technology. In this way, he demonstrates the viability of farming as a way of life today. I am sure Berry himself would appreciate it if we added all those who have maintained small farms as further examples of what I call here a personalist culture. The second example is Dorothy Day and, more broadly, the Catholic Worker movement. Dorothy Day especially models the personalist goal to place personal love in the center of our culture, to replace processes and social forces by personal responsibility and commitment to others. Day argued that we needed to take personal responsibility for the poor and give them concrete, personal assistance, not simply turn them over to the agencies of the state. Day also models the universality of personalism, in that she served all and fought for the rights of all with absolutely no restrictions. The broader Catholic Worker movement always held out the broader goal to renew agrarian life and to give the urban poor opportunities to learn farming skills. True, Day wrote and spoke out against the abuses of the economic and political orders, but such activities never undermined or replaced the daily practice of the works of mercy. Hard work and concrete service of the most basic needs of the needy are what make her a model of personalism.[16]

*need to see results → BMO*

### False Solutions: Multiculturalism and Postmodernism

In recent years, particularly within the academic world, what has come to be called multiculturalism has been proposed as the best way to protect rights and promote solidarity. It is a reaction to the domination of Western civilization, or at least elements within it, that have served to oppress peoples of other cultures, both within and beyond the West itself. Multiculturalism, therefore, is a criticism of both Western imperialism and racist or otherwise prejudicial treatment of minorities within the dominant nations. Clearly, many of the specific criticisms are well taken, and no reasonable person need question that much of what was done in the past is to be justified no longer. Surely, no one embracing personalism would want to rationalize slavery, Jim Crow laws, or attempts to extinguish the cultures indigenous to the New World prior to the arrival of Columbus. But there is far more to multiculturalism than simply this, at least in the models predominant in the academic world today. To be challenged are the deeper philosophical roots of this ideology which would carry us far beyond the needed moral critique of the past and the promotion of reform in the present. As William Cavanaugh explains it, the glorification of diversity at the core of multiculturalism is actually an attempt to replace the one—Western culture—by the many; that is, a diversity of cultures.[17] Prior to any philosophical investigation of the validity of such an approach, it must first be stated that such a theory is politically and socially *impossible without serious qualification.* It is so because the legal and political order inherently has to pick and choose among value claims, and establish some kind of hierarchy of claims if only for the purpose of resolving the inevitable disputes which arise. The state can only be "neutral" so long as we remain in the world of thought. In the practical order, there are real conflicts which press for resolution. Unless one wants somehow to claim that the state should resolve disputes over value claims in random fashion—which no one actually proposes—then it is clear that, explicitly or implicitly, the state and other social authorities must have some hierarchical scale of values upon which to weigh competing value claims. Take the issue for abortion, for example. In any specific case, it is either allowed or disallowed. Justifications on both sides are based on competing scales of value claims. Is the value of preserving individual choice the trump card, or the need to protect life? The real world mandates a decision one way or the other. This is not to say that different cultures must always be antithetical. There are of course many cases where different cultures can and do coexist reasonably well. Diverse cultures embrace the same values on many occasions. Moreover, there are cases where each culture can simply choose according to its own respective value system, and peaceful coexistence is possible. However, in cases where we see peaceful coexistence, what is going on is not multiculturalism, that is, the replacement of the one by the many. In the case of common values, peaceful coexistence is clearly the recognition of a one as well as the many. In the case where cultures may differ, with each preserving its own practice, we are dealing with instances of diversity that do not generate the kind of conflict that call for an authoritative, public resolution. For example, diverse courting and marriage practices can coexist in the same space to a significant degree. The point is, however, that there are cases where the very nature of a political community under the authority of law demand an authoritative resolution, and the multicultural paradigm of replacing the one by the many is simply impossible.

Beyond that, Cavanaugh demonstrates that, even on its own terms, multiculturalism is an inadequate resolution of the problems occasioned by cultural diversity. Multiculturalism claims to glorify the diversity of cultures, but it does so only by eviscerating each culture of any universal significance.[18] Indeed, the willingness on the part of a culture to gain acceptance to the multicultural club is to do precisely this. It is clear why multiculturalism does this, for the assertion of universal significance is implicitly a claim to a one which they fear will inevitably dominate the many. Therefore, multiculturalism is implicitly a mandate that each culture consent to the withering effects of the following factors: moral and cultural relativism, consumerism and materialism, and the individualism that underlies the market.[19]

In the final analysis, multiculturalism is actually a misnomer, in that there is a kind of dominant culture being ushered in the back door as the previously dominant culture is being unceremoniously thrown out the front. The new, dominant culture has the following characteristics. First, it consists of a moral and cultural relativism that is progressively more intolerant of cultures that continue to insist on their universal significance, particularly when such insistence issues in the maintenance of moral absolutes. There is thus a world of difference between the reception afforded to a person of Latin American origin willing to renounce constitutive features of his or her culture, particularly Catholicism, and one who intends to maintain those same features. Similarly, African Americans who accept and promote multiculturalism are accepted, while those who become evangelicals and join the pro-life movement are marginalized, viewed as traitors to their race by the white liberals who take it upon themselves to determine who and what beliefs qualify as authentically black. Second, multiculturalism is really multiethnicism amidst the emerging monoculture that multiculturalism itself defines. The pursuit of multiethnicism is indeed central, for it promotes the aura of diversity upon which the political success of the movement depends. The substance of genuine cultural diversity is, however, increasingly absent. Finally, it is important to make the connection between globalized multiculturalism and the globalized economy. Cultures are expected to cooperate with the market and even make themselves marketable commodities. The overriding imperative is to produce, market, and consume. All cultures are welcome so long as they cooperate with the imperatives of the system. Those who offer substantive resistance are to be marginalized. Wendell Berry remarks humorously concerning the hypocrisy of multiculturalism in the academy, "Quit talking bad about women, homosexuals and preferred social minorities, and you can say anything you want about people who haven't been to college, manual workers, country people, peasants, religious people, unmodern people, old people, and so on."[20]

John Francis Burke, in his important book *Mestizo Democracy: The Politics of Crossing Borders*, does an excellent job in demonstrating the possibilities for intercultural collaboration in the political order. Burke is aware that endless appeals to diversity and pluralism do not solve the problems of cultural diversity and conflict. He proposes a model of "unity-in-diversity" based upon the experience of Mexicans living in the Southwest segment of the United States. He argues convincingly that what has taken place there is a *mestizaje*; that is, a mingling of cultures without either one being dominant. One culture learns and borrows from the other and both are transformed into something new in the process. There are doubtless countless examples of this. To cite one from another context, untouchables in India availed themselves of principles of British law to argue against their debilitated status. Burke has highlighted a process which holds out much hope for intercultural cooperation. Imprisoned as we often are in hostile and mutually exclusive ideological camps, we have not even begun to explore the creative and hopeful possibilities that such processes hold out. But there are limits, and I would deny that the model is of universal applicability. Processes of *mestizaje*, insofar as they are reflected in the political arena, must result in some kind of definitive, authoritative policy. Laws cannot be coincidences of opposites. The more that cultures have compatible elements, the more processes of *mestizaje* can mutually transform and enrich. In the Southwest, there are surely differences between the so-called "Anglo" culture and the Mexican. But both cultures were deeply influenced by Christian understandings of many moral issues. Where *mestizaje* cannot work is when the foundations are mutually irreconcilable. For example, moral absolutists and moral relativists are not going to mix and merge. Pro-lifers and pro-choicers are not going to mix and come up with a policy acceptable to both. In the practical order of politics, there will always be a one within which the many will operate.

A particular kind of multiculturalism is in evidence in the move toward religious pluralism endorsed by many contemporary theologians. Concerned over the historical relationship between religious conviction and various forms of intolerance and imperialism, theologians such as John Hick and Paul Knitter propose a pluralist approach to religion which will allegedly maintain the integrity of the various traditions while purifying them of intolerance.[21] Exclusivism must be rejected on theological grounds because, according to Knitter, the "Divine mystery is ever greater than the reality and message of Jesus." This Mystery transcends Christianity and all other faiths. Subordinate to it, "*all* the religions could be, perhaps need to be included in—that is, related to—each other as all of them continue their efforts to discover or be faithful to inexhaustible Mystery or Truth."[22] Not only is the Christian Word incomplete without other words, it is not even accessible, because texts can be understood only within the framework of the "historical life-practice" which obviously transcends the boundaries of a specific religious community.[23] A kind of uniqueness is allowed to the various religions, what Knitter terms "relational uniqueness"; that is, they occupy a specific place in a dialog with other religions. What is unique about Jesus, for example, is his "distinctive contribution to the interreligious dialog."[24]

There is more here than simply a belief that the pluralist perspective somehow operates on some higher ground than commitment to a particular tradition. They are concerned, in Knitter's words, that "traditional theology . . . especially its christological base, served to cloak or condone an unconscious theological desire to maintain superiority, or to dominate and control . . . or . . . to justify the subordination of other cultures and religions."[25] Moreover, belief in dogmas is historically associated with a range of other unacceptable behaviors such as patriarchalism, traditional missionary efforts which explicitly or implicitly degrade others, and capitalism.[26] Hick goes so far as to deny the traditional Christian belief that God is personal.[27]

The kind of religious pluralism advocated by Hick and Knitter involves the assertion of an ultimate Truth or Mystery. Nonetheless, in the practical order, the criticisms just made of multiculturalism retain their force here. The celebration of pluralism comes at the price of denying universal significance to particular religious traditions. Religions are unique only in the sense that they have different messengers and sacred texts, but not with respect to holding any truths not held by other traditions, such a possibility in fact ruled out by the pluralist premise that no particular tradition can have universal truth inaccessible to the others. Truths congregate in the transcendent Truth which is beyond the reach of any particular revelation, and it is to this Truth the pluralist is ultimately committed. The commitment, however, is a peculiar one, in that it consists in neither holding any particular belief nor embracing any religious practice as of ultimate salvific value. In practice, it can only be what Cavanaugh rightly characterizes as a cosmopolitan detachment, a kind of "religious tourism"[28] which, for its lack of concrete, absolute commitment in depth to anything in particular, inevitably encourages religious dilettantes more than committed believers.

A deeper look at the religious pluralist position reveals that it unwittingly plays into the false anthropology of consumerism and individualism which the religious pluralist claims to oppose. For *who* precisely is it that stands above Judaism, Christianity, Islam, Buddhism, and Hinduism, other than the "I," the autonomous self of liberalism, who reemerges here to assert again his sovereignty as the ultimate arbiter of values. It is this "I" who stands above and in judgment on the history and relative merits of the respective religions. It is this "I" who speaks for the "Truth," as it is assumed that none of the committed members of the particular traditions can be relied upon to do so. This "I," standing above the fray of religious difference, is bound ultimately to his own moral, political, and religious views. This is, moreover, a particularly poor basis for solidarity. Specific commitments understood as having a religious basis are essential to keeping people and communities together. The pluralist emphasis on detachment from as opposed to commitment to particular communities of faith feeds right into the individualism the pluralists believe they oppose. This "I" is in the final analysis the empty self of liberalism, trying to find himself by maintaining his sovereignty over truth.

As Paul Griffiths has written, for all their emphasis on renouncing adherence to the traditional dogmas of the various faiths, religious pluralists such as Hick and Knitter do not for all that deny epistemological absolutism. Hick claims to know with certitude that all purported differences among the various religious traditions pertaining to matters of ultimate salvation are in fact misinterpretations. As most committed members of these traditions have actually had disagreements of this kind, they must all be wrong. As with other pluralists, Hick is concerned that the traditional interpretations of the various religions, made by the very members of those traditions, create the kinds of exclusivist attitudes that the pluralists want to eliminate.

> The power of Hick's pluralist convictions here becomes evident. These convictions enable him to do . . . what only the most assured of traditionally exclusivistic apologists is able to do; that is, to judge that certain key doctrines of major religious communities are clearly false, and to do so without engaging them upon their own terms, without discussing their cognitive merits or the epistemic respectability of those who profess them, but rejecting them solely by pointing to a contingent and in many cases weak connection between their profession and certain modes of conduct and attitudes [found] reprehensible.[29]

Postmodernism is pluralism at its extreme. Indeed, it can perhaps be characterized as the ultimate, logical conclusion of pluralist and multiculturalist premises. The stand it takes concerning cultural traditions of all kinds, according to Eagleton, "is one of irreverent pastiche . . . a contrived depthlessness [which] undermines all metaphysical solemnities, sometimes by a brutal aesthetics of squalor and shock."[30] So as to underline its rejection of universal truth, it refers to all philosophies as mere "discourses" or "narratives." It harbors in principle an intense distrust of any and all discourses purporting to be universal, referring to them negatively as "metanarratives." These need to be replaced by heterogeneous belief systems particular to communities which embrace them. In this, postmodernism, according to Harvey, is more or less simply an extreme of the multiculturalism and pluralist positions critiqued above. Two characteristics, however, I do believe to be distinct. One is that postmodernism "abandons all sense of historical continuity and memory," rejecting the idea of progress and taking such liberties with history that it is willing to arrange and rearrange historical fragments so as to support the arbitrary desires of the present.[31] Second, postmodernism's "preoccupation with the fragmentation and instability of language and discourses carries over directly . . . into a certain conception of personality . . . a certain schizophrenic effect." This is the logical result of the epistemological radicalism which denies (a) any inherent connection between words and meanings, and (b) universality or continuity in meaning. Personal identity depends on having a capacity to unify the past, present, and future. Yet postmodernism's fragmentizing epistemology suggests that our consciousness is no more than a series of unrelated and isolated moments.[32]

The positive contribution of postmodernism is to expose the obvious and even hidden ways in which political and religious traditions have oppressed and dominated others. That such oppression has indeed occurred under the banners of exalted themes is something which no just person need deny. Like multiculturalists and religious pluralists, they sometimes get the targets rights. Unfortunately, postmodernism's negation of universals in principle only turns reason against itself and renders postmodernism unqualified to serve as the basis for any adequate philosophy of change. By denying moral foundations, postmodernism can serve to criticize but not to construct. It is incapable of providing either the rationality or the motivation for charting a course for society to follow, much less any motivation for people to unite together and pursue it. As progressive theologian Roberto S. Goizueta explains, the kind of pluralism postmodern pluralism engenders is to relativize all the claims minority groups have been fighting for, thus reinforcing their marginalization. Hispanics and other minorities become in the postmodern understanding merely "one social location." But what they are fighting for is the recognition of the absolute worth of their own traditions, as well as absolute claims such as the preferential option for the poor.[33] Third, postmodernism unwittingly becomes a hyperindividualism. It provides no basis for holding people together aside from their ultimately arbitrary and temporary decisions. There is nothing in human nature or in reality to prompt us to continue to think in any consistent way or remain in the traditions we are born in. This is a formula for endless fragmentation, not solidarity. There is even, as Peukert notes, a certain egoism in all of this, as postmodernism motivates those who feel different to demand that their own distinctiveness be recognized, but does not direct the same people to recognize the distinctive value of their opponents.[34] In conclusion, it is obvious that postmodernism is an inadequate basis for cultural reconstruction, being that it is incompatible with any firm notion of personhood.

## Contemporary Culture: Images of Fragmentation and Integration

The predominant culture in the West today is one of fragmentation at the level of both society and the person. Unfortunately, the disintegrating intellectual tendencies of the modern mind prevent this truth from being widely understood. The morass into which metaphysical skepticism, positivism, empiricism, relativism, and postmodernism have thrown us inhibits us from making connections. Wendell Berry states it well:

> Mostly, we do not speak of our society as disintegrating. We would prefer not to call what we are experiencing social disintegration. But we are endlessly preoccupied with the symptoms: divorce, venereal disease, murder, rape, debt, bankruptcy, pornography, soil loss, teenage pregnancy, fatherless children, motherless children, child suicide, public child-care, retirement homes, nursing homes, toxic waste, soil and water and air pollution, government secrecy, government lying, government crime, civil violence, drug abuse, sexual promiscuity, abortion as "birth control," the explosion of garbage, hopeless poverty, unemployment, unearned wealth.[35]

We tend to conceive of these phenomena as separate, yet all of them are the result of the depersonalization of our political, economic, and cultural life. Once the person fragments, the fissure extends throughout the entire social order.

One of the worst features of this fragmentation is the pervasive "homelessness" of the contemporary world. What I refer to here is only secondarily the sad phenomenon of those who live without established residences, for even those who own houses have become "homeless." "The history of our time," Berry writes, "has been to a considerable extent the movement of the center of consciousness away from home."[36] This movement to which Berry refers is a part of the larger process by which the center of Western culture has moved away from the person. As power gravitates away from the person to the new centers of political, economic, and cultural power, man finds himself correspondingly adrift. The homelessness to which I refer "consists in an abstract and mechanistic pattern of being, thinking, acting, and producing that makes human beings rootless, in a world stripped of its intrinsic creaturely order,"[37] in the words of David Schindler. The result is that the contemporary "successful" person has only an abstract sense of where he is. For him, "Geography is defined . . . by his house, his office, his commuting route, and the interior of the shopping centers, restaurants, and places of amusement—which is to say his geography is artificial; he could be anywhere, and he usually is." Berry refers to this contemporary person as a "vagrant sovereign," who does not know "where" he is morally either. He is vagrant because his devotion to escape restraints and limits is incompatible with the geographically specific, time-consuming limitations of home life. As a successful man, he assumes that there is nothing he can do which he should not; that there is nothing he can use which he should not.[38]

The narrative approach of film and literature captures these realities in a manner superior to philosophical discourse. Latin American writers, living in the world where this fragmentation and the contradictions of globalization are most visible, have generally a far greater sense of what is going on than their North American counterparts. The late Osvaldo Soriano, in his work *A Shadow You Soon Will Be,* captures brilliantly the personal and national fragmentation of his native Argentina.[39] In this work, Soriano recounts the adventures of a young man, a former expatriate, who returns to his native land in search of his identity. Traveling through Patagonia, his train breaks down, and he embarks on a journey on foot, encountering a series of bizarre characters who are all "lost" in terms of their own identity, fractured people in a fractured nation. A leitmotiv of the novel is the pervasive sense of homelessness. The characters are in Argentina, but lack any sense of Argentine identity. Most of them have either recently been in another country or are headed to one. Moreover, none of the characters does meaningful work. One character, Coluccini, is on his way to Bolivia to sell pornographic films. There are various schemers trying to find ways to make money. Some turn to superstition, believing in the predictions of Nadia the fortune-teller. One of the most striking images is that of unemployed gauchos, symbols of Argentine identity, riding their horses to no end or purpose, powerful images of displaced people in a world gone by. Amidst the hopelessness, as the protagonist continues on his journey, most of the basic economic services, such as post offices and gas stations, are either nonexistent or

Art shows

working badly. Of the train station, a symbol of former prosperity, "all that remains is a dirty floor, where some vagabonds and passers-by sleep. The benches were all pulled out, and they did not even leave the bell."[40] There is no productive work in any of the towns through which the protagonist passes. As one who remembers better days for his nation, he can only recall the past with a sense of pain and distance from the present reality. His sense of identity comes to reflect the shattered self of postmodernism. "Everything," he laments, "seems to me to be far away, as if it were happening to another person or if I were observing it in a movie."[41]

Argentine filmmaker Fernando Solanas' production *El Viaje* presents another compelling image of personal and national fragmentation. In this work, we have again a young man going on a journey through Latin America, beginning in the city of Ushuaia on Tierra del Fuego. Traveling north, he discovers that Patagonia is actually a part of England, a powerful image of the threats to cultural identity faced by all these nations. When he arrives in the capital city of Buenos Aires, he discovers that the entire city is flooded by open sewers, and the people make their way around only by boat. In a particularly humorous section, Solanas satirizes the disjuncture between reality and political rhetoric by depicting then-President Carlos Menem, here named "Doctor Ranas" (Dr. Frog), as a frog-man walking on a pair of fins. He indicates his intention to extend the Buenos Aires sewer system with the support of foreign investors. "But," a reporter asks, "haven't we hit bottom?" The president responds, "Not at all. We are sailing full steam ahead. . . . Boys, don't make waves! I'd like to ask you to have faith. You'll come out afloat. Argentines! Dive in and swim!"[42]

What both Soriano and Solanas capture is the way in which the globalizing tendencies undermine the particularities of nations and their cultures. Richard Barnet summarizes these developments well:

> Even in culturally conservative societies in what we still call the Third World, the dinner hour is falling victim to television. In bars, tea-houses, and cafes and in living quarters around the world the same absence of conversation and human interaction is noticeable as family members, singly or together, sit riveted in front of a cathode tube. As in the United States, Europe and Japan, centuries-old ways of life are disappearing under the spell of advanced communication technologies. The cultural products most widely distributed around the world bear the stamp, "Made in the U.S.A.," and almost any Hollywood video is bound to offend . . . values somewhere [in the manner of a] barbarian intrusion.[43]

In the North American context, Wendell Berry has emerged as a prophetic voice denouncing the depersonalization which accompanies the centralizing tendencies of our time. All of Berry's fictional works are set in a small community, Port William, Kentucky, and have local personages for their main characters. In

*Jayber Crow,* the central character is Jayber, the town's barber for thirty years. At the outset, Jayber sets the tome by recalling the past which is no more:

> When I came here and set up shop in January 1937, the place was maybe better off than I have seen it since. Thirty-seven was a Depression year, and I don't ask you to believe the place was flourishing. But it was at least thrifty. People didn't waste anything they knew how to save. . . . There were a lot of patched clothes in those days. But all the commercial places in town were still occupied and doing business. The people of the town still belonged to it economically as well as in other ways. And we still had a doctor, "old" Dr. Markman.⁴⁴

For Jayber, to be the town barber is not primarily to possess a career—that is, a life in which particular people and places do not matter. It is, rather, to live in this particular community, to belong to it, to serve others through his work, with the sense that the service is recognized.

Unfortunately, this quality of life now belongs to the past. Industrialization, technology, and centralization increasingly fragment and undermine the community. This is symbolized in the novel partly by the coming of the interstate highway. Jayber's friend, Milo Settle, owned a garage in town and sold Standard Oil for fifty years until one day the company "would no longer deliver as much gas as he needed for his customers. . . . They were squeezing him out in favor of the new service station on the interstate." Milo's fifty years of service to the community and as a distributor of the firm's oil meant nothing. "The great road," the narrator relates, "moving, it seemed, purely according to its own will, was the mark of an old flaw come newly ordered into the world. Who could doubt that if everything stood in its way, nothing would be left?"⁴⁵ Throughout the text, Berry uses the terms "The Economy" and "The War" as undifferentiated, impersonal entities disconnected from people's needs and feelings. Jayber reflects with indignation, "More even than The Economy and The War, [the interstate] carried the people of Port William into the modern world." On another occasion, the country barber provides the insight, "The Economy no longer wanted the people of Port William to produce . . . eggs. It wanted them to buy eggs."⁴⁶

Social fragmentation is present in abstract or mechanistic ways of being and acting, as in the case of the government inspector who visits the barbershop. Jayber ends up losing his entire livelihood for the lack of hot running water, after thirty years of service. One day, Jayber recalls, "The inspector said that I was in violation of Regulation Number So and So, which required that all barbershops should be equipped with hot running water. I pointed to the urn from which I had just run some hot water. He said that the hot water had to run from a proper faucet at the end of a pipe, not from a spigot of an urn."⁴⁷ In this absurd situation, the barber faces a cold and inhuman inspector who, like all corporations, acts in terms of "contractual relations between self-interested or . . . disinterested individuals."⁴⁸ Jayber reflects: "[H]e was not there as himself. He was the man across the desk, the one I had so dreaded to meet again. But this time . . . it was not a desk but a whole building full of sub-assistant secretaries. He did not speak for himself but for another man behind a desk, who also did not speak for himself."[49] The young inspector is an "instrument" of a larger abstract entity, an "it," empty of humanity.

Among the best hopes for reversing these trends at the cultural level would be a revitalization of traditional cultural influences. The prospects, however, are undermined by the fact that the global culture industries themselves inevitably undermine any kind of serious cultural reform.[50] These industries promote materialism, consumerism, and utilitarian values. If the process of serious cultural formation is one which takes time, then we have good reason to believe that the culture industries undermine culture. All of the available evidence confirms this. For example, let us consider a community which has a serious cultural tradition it could conceivably revive, such as the Catholic community. A typical Catholic family in the United States spends twenty to twenty-five hours per week watching television. Only 3 percent of registered Catholics spend even twenty-five hours per month on religious activities outside of Mass. Most Catholics read no books to develop knowledge of their faith or its history. The little that they do know of their own tradition is largely mediated through the culture industries. Secondly, the culture industries themselves impede the creation of a context within which the Catholic tradition might be appropriated. In the long run, many Catholics will cease even to recognize their own tradition. As Michael Budde writes, "Were television to decontextualize baseball the way it decontextualizes Christianity—presenting nothing but dropped third strikes . . . and emotional debates about the designated-hitter rule—baseball would become unrecognizable (especially if people invested as little time actually playing baseball as they do involved in religiously formative practices)."[51] Moreover, the culture industries create serious obstacles to any serious thought, due to the obsession they create with speed, instant gratification, and sensory inputs. Finally, the industries are symbolic predators, exploiting cultural imagery for commercial purposes, hijacking the meaning of symbols along the way. Consider, for example, that for most people today, the only images of monks derive from commercials designed to sell copy machines and computers. Themes and images such as faith, conversion, and universal brotherhood have been hijacked for primarily commercial purposes. "I'd like to buy the world a Coke" replaces the substance of solidarity. In a broader context of the failure to transmit culture, in either its hard core or in its arts, such practices render cultural reformation even more difficult.

However overwhelming might seem the forces arrayed against the person, personalism can brook no compromise with despair. As stated from the beginning, personalism is about placing the person at the center of civilization, and this can only be done by acts of love, one at a time. As anyone can perform such acts of solidarity, personalism never depends on institutional structure to get started. This was one of the great innovations of Dorothy Day, Peter Maurin, and the Catholic Worker movement. All one needs to do is go out and do the work! There are no screenings or applications. Anyone who wants to can start a Catholic Worker house. Moreover, when engaging in such acts to "build the new within the shell of the old"—as Peter Maurin put it—one knows that it is only by such acts that a personalist society can ever be created. Moreover, as personalism is grounded in what we actually are, we know that no failure is permanent. The forces arrayed against the person and contrary to his nature can never really satisfy him and are ultimately self-destructive. Personalism is forever a radical reassertion of hope.

Personalism, moreover, can only begin at the personal and local level. This is not to deny the value of macrolevel and institutional changes of the kinds discussed in chapters three and four. But such changes would only be to facilitate local initiatives. Although it is the case that macrolevel change is near impossible at the present time, local initiatives are always possible, and they never rely on having some preexisting superstructure. It is a grave error of our time that people have their eyes always on the macrolevel. People of talent who would like to make political challenges often avoid the local level, where they might be able to accomplish something, for the higher reaches of political power, only to discover that in order to arrive at their intended destination, they have to compromise many convictions and appease wealthy interest groups.

Of course, to construct the new within the shell of the old, people must do whatever possible to withdraw from the depersonalizing megastructures. The latter have today become so all-encompassing that possibilities for withdrawal are limited, but there are many things people can do simply by deciding to do so. For example, people can decide to limit their consumption of the products of the global culture industries. There are many small publications supportive of the kinds of changes being advocated here, such as *Orion* magazine. People can, moreover, revitalize elements of their own local cultures. Vibrant churches represent some of the best opportunities for these activities, and there are still many of these left. Churches have the greatest potential for reinvigorating a personalist culture because many of them already represent something of counterculture where families are strong and the broader cultural trends are renounced. The biggest factor limiting the expansion of these trends is poor leadership in the mainstream denominations. The upper clergy are often the most imbued with the negative trends of our time, trained more in a spirit of accommodation to the surrounding intellectual culture. All too often the clergy in the larger denominations are concerned to appease the anti-Christian culture which surrounds them rather than to confront it by building a counterculture. Interestingly, it is the churches that choose the latter approach who are undergoing the growth. The trend symbolizes the fact that secular liberalism is at every level a culture of death, and churches that embrace it die. Even within the Catholic Church, it is the communities, parishes, and movements that embrace a countercultural commitment to tradition that undergo dynamic growth.

One of the most destructive notions present in our intellectual culture is the notion that current trends are inevitable and cannot be reversed. Take, for exam-

ple, what most people would take to be the most hopeless of the changes advocated in this book—that is, the revival of the small farm. Despite the fact that it
is almost impossible to make such a proposal and be taken seriously in any academic setting, agrarian author Gene Logsdon presents evidence that such renewal
is already taking place.[52] According to Logsdon, those who make the easy argument in favor of ever-larger industrial grain farms and animal "factories" do not
know the history of any particular farm, and have no sense of the long-term
changes that have characterized the development of American agriculture. "It is
just as possible," Logsdon writes, "for farming to go from big to small as from
small to big."[53] Logsdon cites John Ikerd of the University of Missouri, who
asserts the validity of "universal cycle theory," which asserts that observed trends
of today are phases of larger historical cycles. Ikerd writes, "If we can look back
over past centuries and around the globe, we can find examples where control of
land become concentrated in the hands of the few only to later become dispersed
in control among the many."[54]

Logsdon claims that there is a "new" agrarianism emerging which holds out
a great deal of promise for healthier and better food production. The government
itself stopped counting farmers in the 1980s, so there are no official statistics to
report. Moreover, much of the new agrarianism is done at the microlevel, and
many of its practitioners derive income from other sources as well. Logsdon sees
small homesteads and garden farms sprouting up in his native Ohio, owned by
many young couples and retirees. The demand for smaller acreages is high, and
younger families with urban jobs will bid more for them than will the megafarm-
ers. According to Logsdon, the new, small-scale farmers:

> are perfecting new/old practices such as deep-bedding systems for
> hogs that are free of factory farm odor and pollution problems; organic
> dairies; meat, milk and egg production that relies on rotational pasture
> systems, not expensive chemicals or machinery; permanent, raised-
> bed vegetable gardens where production per foot is enormously
> increased with hand labor . . . improved food plants from natural selec-
> tion of open-pollinated varieties whose seed can be economically
> saved for the next year's crop. . . .[55]

Much of the new agrarianism is focused on meeting the demand for new or variegated products such as goat cheese, hand-pressed cider, hydroponic spinach,
stone-ground flour from locally grown organic grains, and baby lambs—and this
is only the new products in the New England market![56] Logsdon believes that the
long-term trends favor more farmers, not fewer.

> I can give three reasons for my prediction that the number of food and
> fiber producers . . . is about to increase. One: historically, in all the past
> civilizations I have studied, the denser the population becomes, the
> smaller and more numerous the farms become. Two: financially, the

economies of scale that apparently rule manufacturing do not really apply to any sustainable kind of food production; when you count all the costs, it is cheaper to raise a zucchini in your garden than on your megafarm. And three: socially, people are beginning to understand they really are what they eat and are demanding quality food, which megafarms can't supply.[57]

For Logsdon, all of this represents nothing less than the return of Thomas Jefferson's agrarian ideal in modern guise.[58]

## Religion and Culture

As Christianity introduced the phenomenon of person, authentic religious renewal would be essential to the renewal of a personalist culture. It must be a renewal at a popular level. There are surely elements of this within the Protestant fundamentalist and evangelical camps. This is not simply to endorse these points of view. However, to write off these trends with contempt is of no value. Within what elite culture calls "the religious right" lies a great deal of completely legitimate discontent over trends in the culture and politics of the United States. (Admittedly, within these circles there is an unfortunate tendency to define as "Christian" positions which have no inherent connection with the Gospel—such as opposition to gun control and national health care.) The leaders in the mainstream Protestant and Catholic churches should have educated these people and provided leadership for them. This is, notoriously, what they did not do, which is why one meets within the ranks of the "religious right" a plethora of ex-Catholics, ex-Presbyterians, ex-Methodists, and ex-Lutherans. Although there is evidence of growth within the Catholic Church, much of that growth comes from the influx of Latin Americans whose Catholicism is rife with popular expressions of religion.

Although what has been defined here as a personalist society would benefit greatly from an increase in popular religiosity, there are two dangers within such movements. The first is that it can be manipulated for ideological ends, left or right. We see, for example, in the case of the United States, that popular Protestantism tends to side strongly with conservative views even when there is no clear link between such positions and the Gospel, as on questions of war, income distribution, and possession of weapons. At its worse, this can become a civil religion which uncritically glorifies the United States and its history. On the other side, as in Latin America, you have priests imbued with liberation theology believing that it would be opportune to drive out "the spirit of capitalism" from Latin America, as though it were a form of exorcism. Indeed, in the writings of some liberation theologians, it is hard to find any traditional element of Christian faith not given a socialist reading.[59] The second problem is that popular religion can become superficial and superstitious, as when people engage in certain practices independent of conversion and other elements of faith tradition. For example, one would not want to encourage wealthy people who never give a thought to the poor to seek God's blessing by burying statues of Saint Joseph so that they can make money in real estate. In both cases, the solution to the inevitable shortcomings of popular religiosity is to provide leadership and direction. What seems to have been a decision to abandon it in the North American context has contributed to the disastrous result of exodus from the more traditionally grounded churches and the proliferation of churches that, despite the often good intentions of their members, have little sense of historical continuity or even theological grounding.

The attempt to infuse popular religiosity with social reform should be viewed in the same way as other expressions of popular religion. What is positive should be encouraged and given direction by competent church authorities, who would then be in a good position to provide correction as needed. Much of what went wrong with liberation theology in the Latin American context is that the chasm between the movement and the hierarchy of the church was wider than it needed to be. Popular organizations such as *comunidades de base,* focusing on worker rights, land reform, and other dimensions of social justice, were badly needed. The almost complete dismantling of these organizations, replaced in most cases by nothing comparable, bodes badly for the future. The multinational corporations and banks, in tandem with the International Monetary Fund and the World Bank, dominate the region as never before, and the possibilities of social transformation have never been bleaker, to the detriment of the vast majority. On the other hand, the leaders of these small communities have to bear their share of the blame for failing to employ sound catechesis, for imbuing the movement with more ideology than spirituality.

With the aforementioned reservations in mind, I will tendentiously suggest some lines along which popular religion might develop in Latin America as a way of formulating an authentic culture of resistance to the negative trends of contemporary globalization.[60] All of the previously mentioned reservations concerning such developments should be taken as axiomatic for all of what follows here.

The first essential contribution which the Latin American Christian tradi-  tion has to offer is that of a deep and authentic anthropology which can hold together two equally important notions without obscuring either. These are: (a) the insistence that the person possesses a transcendent dignity which must be respected by the social order, and (b) the insistence that personhood itself is defined by relationship. In the recovery of this Christian understanding of person lies the hope for Latin America. It is deeply associated with the movement for the integral liberation of the Latin American people, where integral means that which touches all dimensions of human existence—material, intellectual, cultural, and spiritual.

One of the greatest contributions made by Latin American theologians is simply to name the problem honestly, to speak of Latin America as it truly is. For clearly, the disease must first be discovered and named before it can be cured.[61] Speaking of his own process of discovering the truth about El Salvador, Jon Sobrino says, with an honesty that refreshes, "The first thing we discovered was that this world is one gigantic cross for innocent people who die at the hands of executioners." This remains to this day one of the most important facts to be said about the world we live in, though it is rarely said so baldly. Sobrino is worth quoting at length here:

> [W]e have come to identify our world by its proper name: sin. . . . We call it by that name because, Christianly speaking, sin is "that which deals death." Sin dealt death to the Son of God, and sin continues to deal death to the sons and daughters of God. One may or may not believe in God, but because of the reality of death, no one will be able to deny the reality of sin. From this basic reality of the cross and death, we have learned to place in its true perspective the massive poverty which draws people to death—death which is slow at the hands of the ever-present structures of injustice, and death which is swift and violent when the poor seek to change their lot. We have learned that the world's poor are practically of no consequence to anyone—not to the people who live in abundance or . . . have any kind of power. . . . [T]he poor have ranged against them . . . the oligarchies, the multinational corporations, the various armed forces, and virtually every government. The First World is not interested in the Third World, to put it mildly. . . . Western human beings have to a great extent produced an inhuman world for those in the Third World. . . . And still, no change seems imminent.[62]

In the writings of Gustavo Gutiérrez, communion among people is rooted in conversion from sin, which creates strong bonds of solidarity. Conversion involves a breaking away from actions and attitudes which contribute to or ignore our personal communion with others, especially those who are despised and cast out. It also involves setting out on a new path, which will include great efforts to create solidarity. It cannot be overemphasized the degree to which Gutiérrez insists on this traditional Christian theme as a prerequisite for any authentic liberation. Of course, Gutiérrez writes, "Conversion implies that we recognize the presence of sin in our lives and our world." It is absolutely essential that those involved in any movement for social justice recognize their "personal connivances with elements that are keeping an inhuman and unjust situation in existence." As Archbishop Romero said, "Nowadays an authentic Christian conversion must lead to an unmasking of the social mechanisms that turn the worker and the peasant into marginalized persons." The personal encounter with God, so emphasized today in circles of Christian individualism, calls for an encounter with the same God in the depths of the suffering of other persons.[63]

At the root of this call to solidarity is more than simple voluntarism. Latin American Christianity has perhaps more than any other rooted this call to solidarity with the poor in the understanding of God's real presence in them. Historically, as Casarella emphasizes, Bartolomé de Las Casas predicated his defense of the Indians on a "new Christology, one that acknowledges the intrinsic dignity of all humanity in light of God's incarnate self."[64] It was this insight, at once theological and anthropological, that prompted his famous words concerning "the crucified Christs of the Indies."[65] Although fully consistent with the classical Christology, to emphasize the presence of the divine person and hence a transcendent source of dignity in those who were considered pagan and uncivilized was certainly not the predominant tendency of Las Casas' time, nor is it today. What Las Casas was asserting is precisely what needs to be asserted now, namely, that God is really and truly present in the poor and the suffering, and it is this presence that is the deepest and truest roots of their personhood.

Las Casas argued further, Gutiérrez notes, that it was blasphemous that these same people disguised their evils as service to God. "[T]his is their excuse," he wrote, "for the destruction of the innocent in order that from their blood they may extract the wealth they hold for their god." The insight is rich. The foreign invaders were, in a strict biblical sense, idolaters, because they placed more value on gold and silver, not only than on God's commands, but on God's real presence in the humanity of the Indians. In fact, the Indians, who did not value gold for its commercial value, thought in some cases that gold actually was the god of the Spaniards. This is what flawed so deeply the first evangelization of the New World.[66] As Gutiérrez argues, the relevance of Las Casas' insight is by no means merely historical. The conquistadors, while frequently using Christianity as part of their rationale, were careful to exclude the Gospel from their thinking about the economy, because they wished to organize the latter for their own interests, excluding the good of most of the inhabitants. The same occurs today, except that those who wish to exploit the region have a somewhat more sophisticated form of idolatry, neoliberalism, which is an elaborate justification for explaining why the Gospel really has nothing to do with the organization of the economy, and why it is just for some to accumulate millions while others languish in hopeless poverty. Like the conquistadors of the sixteenth century, they want to Christianize the culture of the region so as to render it malleable and to create social order; but just as the conquistadors rejected a Gospel critique of their mercantilist system, so today's neoliberals reject a Gospel critique of their liberal system. In doing so, they continue to make a mockery of evangelization, and render the credibility of Christianity understandably low in many circles.

Christian personalism, which emphasizes the ontological roots of human solidarity and transcendent dignity of the person in God, can make a powerful contribution to the struggle for identity and cohesion. Much more, however, is needed. The exploited people need a narrative to lead their way out of their present condition. It has been the accomplishment of theologians such as Gutiérrez and Elizondo to reread the Gospels in light of the specific experience of Latin American Christians. We focus here on Elizondo, who movingly reads the narrative of his people into the life of Christ, and in a way which is completely consistent with the people's own faith and historically lived experience.[67]

Elizondo understands the journey of his people in terms of three principles:

the Galilee experience, the Jerusalem experience, and the Resurrection experience. Galilee, the land where Jesus came from, is for Elizondo "a symbol of multiple rejection." The Jews themselves were scorned by Gentiles, and Galilean Jews were scorned with contempt by the Jews of Jerusalem. Galilee was indeed a cultural and biological *mestizaje* of Phoenicians, Syrians, Arabs, Greeks, Orientals, and Jews. The intellectually oriented faith of Jerusalem had little impact on Galilee. Their way of speaking, considered defective in Jerusalem, led to their occasional banishment from reciting public prayers in Jerusalem. "For the Jews of Jerusalem," Elizondo writes, "Galilean was almost synonymous with fool."[68] Therefore, the theme of "Galilee," which is mentioned sixty-one times in the New Testament, "is the same as the theme of the election of 'what is nothing.' To be a Galilean Jew was in and of itself to be considered ignorant, unsophisticated, and despised. Elizondo writes, "That God had chosen to become a Galilean underscores the great paradox of the Incarnation, in which God becomes the despised and lowly of the world. . . . What the world rejects, God chooses as his very own."[69] This theme becomes the basis of some of the earliest Christian preaching, in which Jesus is interpreted in the words of the psalmist as "the stone rejected by the builders" who "has become the cornerstone."[70]

In his preaching and ministry, Jesus introduces humanity to a new model of existence that is open to all, based on the common Fatherhood of God. All barriers of caste, class, citizenship, religion, and ideology are rejected. His attitude of welcoming the rejected is underlined again and again in the Gospels. Jesus is forming a group, but it is completely universal and ignores customary divisions among people.[71] Of course, this confronts the established order at all levels—religious, political, economic, and cultural. In one sense Jerusalem as the place where Jesus is rejected is the symbol of absolutism, the triple domination of the masses: religious, intellectual, and politico-economic-military.[72] That is why, in the end, the established orders did not hesitate to kill him.

As Elizondo sees it, oppressed peoples must learn to find their identity in the suffering and rejected Christ.[73] Moreover, it is in Jesus' mission from Galilee to Jerusalem that gives to the oppressed their mission to society. For Elizondo, God selects the oppressed people not simply to give them solace but to empower them to confront injustices, transforming themselves and their oppressors in the process.[74] In this context, the Resurrection is not simply a promise of life after death, although it is always that. The meaning of the Resurrection is that the way of universal love is the ultimate victor, even if this victory within history is only partial. Moreover, it means that love is the only way to triumph over evil; the confrontation with evil must mean the willingness to bear suffering rather than simply to retaliate and to seek revenge in the manner of the powerful. The Resurrection, therefore, has a special meaning for the poor and marginated groups such as the Mexican Americans. There is a power greater than that of the oppressors, but it is not the power of the world. The goal is not to destroy anyone, but to invite all to the celebration of new life.

> And so we Mexican-Americans celebrate the joy of what has begun in
> us, and we suffer the pain of the tragedy that the world has not yet dis-
> covered it. In our *posadas* we celebrate the real meaning of our iden-
> tity that remains hidden to the eyes of those who will not see. In our
> personal devotion to *Diosito* we live in intimate communion with the
> ultimate source of life. . . . [T]he Mexican-American celebration of
> suffering, especially on *Viernes Santo* . . . often appears morbid to
> those who fear death and suffering. But to those whose daily life is suf-
> fering and death, only a suffering God on the cross can give meaning
> to the absurdities that life multiplies. If the "enlightened" and "edu-
> cated" scoff at Mexican-American devotion to the virgin mother, it is
> because they have never really experienced the joy of birth. In their
> devotion to *la Morenita,* Mexican-Americans celebrate the suffering
> of childbirth—not unto a creation manipulated and straightened by
> self-interested human designs, but into a new creation open to the effu-
> sive dynamism of the Spirit.[75]

Clearly, the Galilean journey is about creating justice where it does not
exist. In the process, Christian theology has yet another indispensable contribution, perhaps best understood in the light of the Book of Job. In his book-length
study of this biblical text, Gutiérrez uncovers an essential theme which the detrac-
tors of his work have always carefully failed to notice. In addition to the prophetic
denunciation of injustice and the call for justice, there is also the language of contemplation, the recognition of God's mystery and transcendence. God is free, His
love is gratuitous, and He cannot be pigeonholed by any anthropocentrism. The
language of justice alone, as understood by human beings, has not the final say.
Gutiérrez writes, "We in Latin America are also convinced . . . that in the liberation process we are creating our own idols for ourselves . . . [;] justice can become
an idol if it is not placed in the context of gratuity." This means opening one's self
up to the sufferings of others and commitment to work to eliminate unjust sufferings because of the gratuitousness of God's love. In the absence of this sense of a
gift freely given, the struggle for justice easily degenerates into an idolatry characterized by, on the one hand, anger and even hatred for those who stand in the
way, and, on the other, a need to justify the demand for justice by exalting the
virtues of poor people. Through the maintenance of a contemplative respect for
God's transcendence, the struggle for justice will keep alive those dimensions of
truth which purely secular approaches tend to ignore: the need to forgive and to
be forgiven, the primacy of interpersonal love, the sense of one's own contribution to social injustice, and the realization that justice is pursued ultimately
because of the gratuity of divine love, not the merits of any social group. God
wants justice, but the order of creation allows for the exercise of human freedom
which permits injustice. This order must be respected, even though it means that
the possibility of more injustice remains.[76]

Many of the central themes necessary for the creation of a Latin American identity and solidarity are contained in the narrative of the *Nican Mopohua*, which describes the event of Our Lady of Guadalupe and Juan Diego, and is the subject of a marvelous little volume by Elizondo.[77] In it, Elizondo shows that Christianity in Latin America is not simply part of European imperialism. In fact, "those whom the builders of this world's empires had maligned and rejected, re-created the gospel at every level of human existence." There is an evangelization, to be sure, but it is based on "beauty, recognition, respect for 'the other,' and friendly dialog." Juan Diego was given what the people of Latin America (and everywhere) today still need; that is, "beautiful and transforming alternatives to the present-day world situation of violence, filth, misery, enslavement, and earthly damnation."[78] Moreover, after Guadalupe, the Indians could spread *their faith based upon their experience, their testimonies, and in their language.*

There are three levels of transformation associated with the Guadalupe event.[79] Together, they promote dignity and identity for individual persons, as well as the highest degree of solidarity. First, Juan Diego is transformed from a wounded, disintegrated social outcast into a healthy, confident, and integrated man. The evangelization process imposed by the Spaniards left people like Juan Diego homeless in two worlds; on the one hand, he was to the Spaniards a mere "mission Indian," inferior in all respects; on the other, he was no longer a part of the Indian culture either. If not for the appearance of the Virgin of Tepeyac, he would have had a split and tortured sense of identity; as Elizondo puts it, he would have been a "coconut: brown on the outside, white on the inside."[80] She makes of him the carrier of a divine message to be given to the religious leaders. In a real, spiritual sense, Juan Diego becomes more important than the bishop. He is for-ever a changed man. But not he alone, for he becomes the messenger calling for the resurrection of a dying people, who now come to life as the new Christian people. In the Lady's healing of Juan Diego's uncle, Juan Bernardino, Elizondo reads a divine guarantee of the continuity of the life of his people, which was transmitted through the maternal uncle. Finally, the church itself is converted in the person of the bishop and his household. They move from a self-confident, eth-nocentric approach to faith to one of awe, humility, and willingness to accept an Indian as God's messenger to them. The Virgin places the Indians on a par equal to the Spaniards and calls for their collaboration. In the process, the Indians are ennobled, affirmed in their identity by the messenger from heaven.

### Notes

1. The following summary of Von Balthasar's treatment of the one and the many is from Hans Urs Von Balthasar, *The Glory of the Lord,* Vol. 1, *Seeing the Form,* trans. Erasmo Leiva-Merikakis (San Francisco: Ignatius Press, 1982), 496-506.

2. See, for example, John Rawls, *Political Liberalism* (New York: Columbia University Press, 1993); and Richard Rorty, "The Priority of Democracy to Philosophy," *The Virginia Statute for Religious Freedom,* ed. Merrill D. Peterson and Robert C. Vaughan (Cambridge: Cambridge University Press, 1988).

3. Brian Tierney, *Religion, Law and the Growth of Constitutional Thought: 1150-1650* (Cambridge: Cambridge University Press, 1992); *The Idea of Natural Rights* (Atlanta: Scholars Press, 1997).

4. Moral neutrality can exist only in contexts where people refrain from making choices among competing value claims. This simply does not occur in politics, which requires practical choices. To claim moral neutrality in one's politics is simply to announce one's ignorance of one's value preferences or to assume contrary to fact that no value choices other than one's own are possible. For a more developed argument along the same lines, read J. Budziszewski, *True Tolerance: Liberalism and the Necessity of Judgment* (New Brunswick: Transaction Publishers, 1992).

5. Vatican Council II, *Dignitatis Humanae*, no. 2.

6. John Paul II, *Redemptor Hominis*, no. 17.

7. The foregoing discussion of the value of religious dialog draws on Francis Arinze, *Meeting Other Believers: The Risks and Rewards of Interreligious Dialog* (Huntington: Our Sunday Visitor, 1997).

8. Francis Arinze, *Religions for Peace: A Call for Solidarity to the Religions of the World* (New York: Doubleday, 2002).

9. John Paul II, *The Gospel of Life*, no. 86.

10. This explanation of the intellectual virtues relies on Yves R. Simon, *Work, Society and Culture*, ed. Vukan Kuic (New York: Fordham University Press, 1971), 159-167. Simon contends that, with the exception of prudence, these attributes are not actually virtues, even on Aristotle's own terms, because virtues involve the correct or good human use of things. Clearly, one could make evil use of the foregoing qualities, with the exception of prudence. I could, for example, use science to kill innocent people, which would not be virtuous.

11. Yves R. Simon, *Work, Society and Culture*, 163.

12. This is not to say that virtues do not involve the use of judgment, or that there is simply one right answer for every moral question. Aristotle and the tradition coming down from him recognized that virtue involved the pursuit of a certain "mean" between two extremes, but that mean is always relative to us. Hence the correct behavior in a given case may well depend on who is acting. Subjectivity matters. The virtuous mean with respect to the consumption of alcohol relates to one's size and weight. With respect to courage, the demands of virtue may well depend on one's physical characteristics and abilities. For a full treatment see Yves R. Simon, *The Definition of Moral Virtue*, ed. Vukan Kuic (New York: Fordham University Press, 1986).

13. Wilhelm Roepke, *A Humane Economy: The Social Framework of the Free Market* (Lanham: University Press of America, 1960), 98, 100.

14. Yves R. Simon, *Work, Society and Culture*, 168-169.

15. Yves R. Simon, *Work, Society and Culture*, 186. It is worth noting that Simon made this observation over forty years ago. One can only imagine what he would say about contemporary developments.

16. For a summary of Dorothy Day's life and work, see William Miller, *A Harsh and Dreadful Love* (New York: Liveright, 1973).

17. William Cavanaugh, "Balthasar, Globalization and the Problem of the One and the Many," *Communio* 28 (Summer 2001): 330.

18. William Cavanaugh, "Balthasar, Globalization and the Problem of the One and the Many," 333.

19. William Cavanaugh, "Balthasar, Globalization and the Problem of the One and the Many," 331-332.

20. Wendell Berry, *Sex, Economy, Freedom and Community* (New York and San Francisco: Pantheon Books, 1992), xv.

21. See, for example, Monika Hellwig, "Christology in the Wider Ecumenism," in Gavin D'Costa, ed., *Christian Uniqueness Reconsidered* (Maryknoll: Orbis Books, 1990), and other articles in the same volume; John Hick and Paul F. Knitter, eds., *The Myth of Christian Uniqueness* (Maryknoll: Orbis Books, 1987; London: SCM, 1987); John Hick, *God Has Many Names* (Philadelphia: Westminster Press, 1982); and Paul F. Knitter, *Jesus and the Other Names: Christian Mission and Global Responsibility* (Maryknoll: Orbis, 1996).

22. Paul Knitter, *Jesus and the Other Names*, 9.

23. Paul Knitter, *Jesus and the Other Names*, 158.

24. Paul Knitter, *Jesus and the Other Names*, 85.

25. Paul Knitter, *Jesus and the Other Names*, xiii.

26. John Hick, "The Non-Absoluteness of Christianity," in John Hick and Paul Knitter, eds., *The Myth of Christian Uniqueness*, 16-36.

27. John Hick, *God Has Many Names*, 108.

28. William Cavanaugh, "Balthasar, Globalization and the Problem of the One and the Many," 337.

29. Paul J. Griffiths, "The Uniqueness of Christian Doctrine Defended," in D'Costa, ed., *Christian Uniqueness Reconsidered*, 161.

30. Terry Eagleton, quoted in David Harvey, *The Condition of Postmodernity* (Oxford: Basil Blackwell, 1989), 7-8.

31. David Harvey, *The Condition of Postmodernity*, 54.

32. David Harvey, *The Condition of Postmodernity*, 53.

33. Roberto S. Goizueta, *Caminemos con Jesus: Toward a Hispanic/Latino Theology of Accompaniment* (Maryknoll: Orbis Books, 1995), 171.

34. H. Peukert, quoted in Gustavo Gutiérrez, "Donde dormirán los pobres?" in Gustavo Gutiérrez, ed., *El rostro de Dios en la historia* (Lima: Centro de Estudios y Publicaciones, 1996), 44, note no. 52.

35. Wendell Berry, *The Hidden Wound* (New York: North Point Press, 1989), 131.

36. Wendell Berry, *The Unsettling of America: Culture and Agriculture* (San Francisco: Sierra Club Books, 1996), 53.

37. David Schindler, "Homelessness and the Modern Condition: The Family, Community, and the Global Economy," *Communio* 3 (2000), 415.

38. Wendell Berry, *The Unsettling of America*, 53-54.

39. Osvaldo Soriano, *Una sombra ya pronto serás* (México, D.F.: Editorial Diana, S.A., 1992).

40. Osvaldo Soriano, *Una sombra ya pronto serás*, 26.

41. Osvaldo Soriano, *Una sombra ya pronto serás*, 24.

42. Quotes from the film *El Viaje* are from Peter Winn, ed., *Americas* (Berkeley and Los Angeles: University of California Press, 1992), 432-433.

43. Richard Barnet and John Cavanagh, *Global Dreams: Imperial Corporations and the New World Order* (New York: Simon and Schuster, 1994), 16.

44. Wendell Berry, *Jayber Crow* (Washington, D.C.: Counterpoint, 1999), 4.

45. Wendell Berry, *Jayber Crow*, 282.

46. Wendell Berry, *Jayber Crow*, 275.

47. Wendell Berry, *Jayber Crow*, 290.

48. Wendell Berry, *Jayber Crow*, 420.

49. Wendell Berry, *Jayber Crow,* 290.

50. The following discussion of the ways in which culture industries undermine culture is drawn from Michael Budde, *The (Magic) Kingdom of God: Christianity and Global Culture Industries* (Boulder: Westview Press, 1997), 67-96. Budde's focus is on Christianity, but the same arguments he makes concerning the negative impacts of the global culture industries apply more broadly to any culture.

51. Michael Budde, *The (Magic) Kingdom of God,* 85.

52. The following is based on Gene Logsdon, *Living at Nature's Pace* (White River Junction, Vt., and Totnes, England: Chelsea Green Publishing Company, 2000), 246-257.

53. Gene Logsdon, *Living at Nature's Pace,* 247.

54. John Ikerd, quoted in Gene Logsdon, *Living at Nature's Pace,* 255.

55. Gene Logsdon, *Living at Nature's Pace,* 255.

56. Gene Logsdon, *Living at Nature's Pace,* 108.

57. Gene Logsdon, *Living at Nature's Pace,* 107.

58. Gene Logsdon, *Living at Nature's Pace,* 110.

59. See, for example, José Porfirio Miranda, *Marx and the Bible* (Maryknoll: Orbis Books, 1974).

60. I focus exclusively on Latin America here simply because I see no real possibility for popular religion in the Northern Hemisphere to develop such a culture. The few possibilities that do exist are within the Latin American cultures which derive their inspiration from south of the border.

61. The following is taken from Jon Sobrino, *The Principle of Mercy: Taking the Crucified People from the Cross* (Maryknoll: Orbis Books, 1994), 4-7.

62. Jon Sobrino, *The Principle of Mercy,* 4-7.

63. Gustavo Gutiérrez, *We Drink from Our Own Wells* (Maryknoll: Orbis Books, 1984), 95-99.

64. Peter Casarella, "Solidarity as the Fruit of Communion, 'Post-Liberation Theology,' and the Earth," *Communio* 27 (Spring 2000): 117.

65. Quoted in Gustavo Gutiérrez, *Las Casas* (Maryknoll: Orbis Books, 1995), 62.

66. Gustavo Gutiérrez, *Las Casas,* 438-442.

67. The following is based on Virgilio Elizondo, *Galilean Journey: The Mexican-American Promise* (Maryknoll: Orbis Books, 1983).

68. Virgilio Elizondo, *Galilean Journey,* 53.

69. Virgilio Elizondo, *Galilean Journey,* 53.

70. Virgilio Elizondo, *Galilean Journey,* 53.

72. Virgilio Elizondo, *Galilean Journey,* 64.

72. Virgilio Elizondo, *Galilean Journey,* 70.

73. Virgilio Elizondo, *Galilean Journey,* 103.

74. Virgilio Elizondo, *Galilean Journey,* 103.

75. Virgilio Elizondo, *Galilean Journey,* 125.

76. Gustavo Gutiérrez, *On Job: God-Talk and the Suffering of the Innocent* (Maryknoll: Orbis Books, 1987), 72-81; *The Density of the Present: Selected Writings* (Maryknoll: Orbis Books, 1999), 141.

77. Virgilio Elizondo, *Guadalupe: Mother of the New Creation* (Maryknoll: Orbis Books, 1997), 81-99.

78. Virsilio Elizondo, Guadalupe, 115, 120-121.

79. The following is taken from Virgilio Elizondo, *Guadalupe,* 109-110, 88-98.

80. Virgilio Elizondo, *Guadalupe,* 109.

# Conclusion

The crisis of our time is one of declining respect for the human person by the dominant political and economic institutions which increasingly revolve around a variety of utilitarian and materialistic processes. As a result, people rightfully feel displaced politically and economically. They see the substance of democracy being hollowed out, while at the same time perceive the government to be more intrusive. Although omnipresent, government seems less able to deliver inexpensive, quality services to improve the lives of all the citizens living under it, nor even able to guarantee clean water, air, or a health-promoting food supply. Economically, we have constructed a system which relies very heavily on job creation, as ownership becomes concentrated. Yet, the logic of the multinational firms whose performance we increasingly use to measure the health of "the economy" is to displace high-wage workers with low-wage workers. At the time of this writing, we are having an economic "recovery" that no longer even includes increases in employment, given the number of jobs created in other nations. Yet, the nations to which the manufacturing jobs have shifted are themselves in crisis, frequently insolvent and effectively in receivership to foreign banks and international lending institutions. In no nominally democratic nation in the world today can it be said that meaningful popular sovereignty is on the rise. In all such nations, power is effectively in the hands of central governments working in conjunction with corporations and monied interest groups. A disgruntled attitude of disaffection toward government predominates, and understandably so.

At the root of all of this is the loss of the sense of the person as the center around which the social order should be constructed. At times, even the sense of who the person is seems to be declining. In this book, we have seen that the concept of person arose specifically as a consequence of Christianity. Originally developed to explain the doctrines of the Trinity and the person of Jesus Christ, the concept of person applied also to the human being created in the image and likeness of the tripersonal God. The person so understood has two poles: He is both (a) a responsible, autonomous center of activity, and (b) intrinsically oriented to the most profound solidarity with all other persons. He is radically directed to pursue his own good in union with others and to place the common good of the entire society above his own individual good. Above all, the person

199

is transcendent, and it is only in this transcendence, his spiritual nature directed toward God, that these poles come together. It is only the person as transcendent that explains how man as spiritual transcends the entire political and economic order, yet as material must sacrifice himself for the common good of all. As we have also seen, it is the person as transcendent which explains further ontological features of human nature, particularly that we are creatures of faith, reason, and freedom. Without the orientation to the spiritual and transcendent, to the service of truth, reason loses its end and destroys itself precisely by absolutizing itself, this in conjunction with the false sense of freedom which heralds the entry of the nihilistic monster which threatens to overwhelm us.

The political order should properly reflect the constitution of the person, preserving the proper senses of autonomy, solidarity, and transcendence. Perhaps the most important development along these lines was the Jesuit doctrine of popular sovereignty, which declared resolutely that power belongs originally and by nature to the people as a whole; no regime can usurp this original jurisdiction. This doctrine served further to preserve the notion that all government must serve the preexisting society, and is therefore limited in its power and scope. On the other hand, the theory of authority reflects the solidaristic nature of persons in political community. The common good is real, and no mere summation of properly individual goods. Authority exists for the sole purpose of being the agent which determines the specific material content of that common good. Properly constituted, authority serves both to promote solidarity in concrete ways and to preserve the legitimate autonomy of persons and the multiple goods they rightly pursue.

The regime which best preserves the centrality of the person is one in which popular sovereignty flows from the bottom up, respectful of that principle of subsidiarity which preserves the autonomy of the person, the family, local communities, and those authorities closest to the person. Ideally, practices of direct democracy should be preserved as far as possible. Far from causing confusion, the institution of something along the lines of Jefferson's ward republics would actually simplify contemporary local government. The principle always to be preserved is to allow people input into the decisions which impact their lives through representation whenever they cannot participate directly in decision-making processes.

Rights are central to any valid theory and practice of democracy today. The origin of the concept of natural rights was the natural law, and the connection between the two is necessary. Neither in the theoretical nor practical orders can one construct a coherent theory of rights without a corresponding theory of obligations. The former cannot somehow be said to be more natural than the latter. For good reasons, natural law as natural obligation developed first. Rights without the moral context provided by natural law have no real foundations, and ultimately become indistinguishable from mere desires, reducing the political order to a series of incompatible rights claims with no rational basis upon which to make reasoned judgments. Ultimately, rights claims in such a context merely mask a Nietzschean will to power. In addition, a personalist theory of rights is buttressed by distinguishing features of the Christian tradition, particularly that each and every person is created in the image and likeness of God, worthy of and claiming our love. Rights must be linked to the building of what John Paul II has repeatedly called the "civilization of love." Without this deeper ethical demand, there is always the danger that rights in practice will emphasize the rights of those who are propertied and already established.

The personalist approach to political economy can only be a call to decentralization in an era of centralization. The large corporations, the performance of their stocks, and their "growth" have become the recognized measures of economic performance. This is an absurdity, as 60 percent of people in the United States own no stock. Equally absurd is the "consumer confidence index" which is based on a nonrandom pool of upper-income people. A personalist economy is one which focuses on the economy of the household. Personalists believe that the healthiest economy compatible with a free and democratic society is one with the widest diffusion of ownership. There should be a strong preference, reflected in our tax laws, for smaller enterprises. There also needs to be a renewal of small-scale farming. Most of our communities are dying due to declines in economic self-sufficiency. The very idea that we can claim that our nation is great while conceding the destruction of most of our communities is a sad commentary on what our conception of the nation is. The connection between vibrant, economically viable communities and democracies has long been noted, and the failure to do so today reflects the impoverished concept of democracy we have come to accept.

A personalist economy would save property and the market by subjecting them to common-sense moral principles. The primary motive of production is use. When it becomes profit, the economy will be riddled with genuine human inefficiencies: the performance of services which are in fact illusory; speculative activities and exchanges wherein all the benefit goes in one direction; and unequal exchanges. Any morally sound analysis of the current global economy would confirm the proliferation of all of these while millions go hungry. Moreover, as so well-argued by John Paul II, labor must always have priority over capital. The worker must participate in the direction and organization of the work he performs.

Culturally, the theologically grounded concept of person provides the only authentic basis for both unity and diversity. For something to be universal, it must have meaning universally. The particular derives its meaning from its participation in the universal. To vacate all cultures of universality in the name of promoting diversity strips both concepts of their meaning. This seems to be the unfortunate trend at the basis of much of what is referred to in academic circles as multiculturalism and religious pluralism. Both of these concepts and movements are indeed vital, but only when authentically appropriated. When seen aside from the Christian solution, namely, that the particular can indeed embody universal meaning, these movements tend to do more harm than good, glorifying diversity for its own sake. This often takes the ahistorically one-sided forms of denying Christianity's enormous and singular contributions to civilization while glorifying the proposals of its enemies.

Culture, moreover, must have a hard ontological core if it is to ground a successful civilization. The two most important dimensions are virtues and work. The great threat of our time is the loss of the sense of both to various forms of utilitarianism and relativism. Virtue is to be reserved for dispositions which are unqualifiedly good in the moral sense. Moreover, work must be related to the fulfillment of genuine human needs. When people put in enormous hours of effort simply to make money, work itself is demeaned.

Narratives are important to any healthy society, a way to instruct and renew society in its fundamental values. Authors from both North and South America, such as Wendell Berry and Osvaldo Soriano, capture well the fracturing and disintegration characteristic of our times. In order for narratives to play an integrating role, they need to be known and subsist in the popular culture. Popular religiosity is an excellent source for the people's narratives. What is needed in our time is that elites cease to distance themselves from this dimension of culture, and find in it instead a source of renewal.

It is not likely that the current social malaise will be resolved soon. The entrenched forces in the political, economic, and cultural arenas have too much at stake to allow profound change. Personalism, however, is quintessentially a philosophy of hope; it calls all to undertake personal responsibility for change, and to work within existing institutions to change them. The impersonal forces which govern us do so only because some people believe that to do so is to their advantage, and others acquiesce. Almost all of the institutional changes suggested in this book have been tried in the past and proven to be workable. It is simply a question of having the initiative and courage to act on what in our inmost depths we already know to be true.

# Bibliography

Adair, Douglas G. *The Intellectual Origins of Jeffersonian Democracy: Republicanism, the Class Struggle, and the Virtuous Farmer.* Edited by Mark E. Yellin. Lanham, New York, Oxford: Lexington Books, 2000.

Aquinas, Thomas. *On the Truth of the Catholic Faith: Summa Contra Gentiles.* Translated by Anton Pegis. New York: Doubleday Image Books, 1955-57. *See also* Pegis, Anton.

Arinze, Cardinal Francis. *Meeting Other Believers: The Risks and Rewards of Interreligious Dialog.* Huntington: Our Sunday Visitor Publishing Division, Inc., 1998.

_____. *Religions for Peace: A Call for Solidarity to the Religions of the World.* New York: Doubleday, 2002.

Agar, Herbert, and Allen Tate, eds. *Who Owns America? A New Declaration of Independence.* Wilmington: ISI Books, 1999.

Aristotle. *Nicomachean Ethics.* Translated by J.A.K. Thompson. London: Penguin Books, 1976.

Ashford, Robert. "Louis Kelso's Binary Economy." *The Journal of Socio-Economics* 25, no. 1 (1996): 1-25.

Bales, Kevin. *Disposable People: New Slavery in the Global Economy.* Los Angeles: University of California Press, 1999.

Barnet, Richard, and John Cavanaugh. *Global Dreams: Imperial Corporations and the New World Order.* New York: Simon and Schuster, 1994.

Beabout, Gregory R., et al. *Beyond Self-Interest: A Personalist Approach to Human Action.* Lanham, New York, Oxford: Lexington Books, 1999.

Belloc, Hilaire. *Economics for Helen.* London: Arrowsmith, 1924.

Brockman, James R. *Romero: A Life.* Maryknoll: Orbis Books, 1999.

Budde, Michael. *The (Magic) Kingdom of God: Christianity and Global Culture Industries.* Boulder: Westview Press, 1997.

Berry, Wendell. *Another Turn of the Crank.* Washington, D.C.: Counterpoint Press, 1999.

_____. *A Continuous Harmony: Essays Cultural and Agricultural.* New York: Harvest Books, 1972.

_____. *The Hidden Wound.* New York: North Point Press, 1989.

_____. *Home Economics.* New York: North Point Press, 1987.

_____. *Jayber Crow.* Washington, D.C.: Counterpoint, 2000.

_____. *Sex, Economy, Freedom and Community.* New York: Pantheon Books, 1993.

_____. *The Unsettling of America: Culture and Agriculture.* San Francisco: Sierra Club Books, 1996.

_____. *What Are People For? Essays.* New York: North Point Press, 1990.

Birzer, Bradley J. *J.R.R. Tolkien's Sanctifying Myth: Understanding Middle-Earth.* Wilmington: ISI Books, 2002.

Brohawn, Dawn K., ed. *Every Worker an Owner: A Revolutionary Free Enterprise Challenge to Marxism.* Arlington: Center for Economic and Social Justice, 1987.

Budziszewski, J. *The Revenge of Conscience: Politics and the Fall of Man.* Dallas: Spence Publishing Co., 1999.

_____. *True Tolerance: Liberalism and the Necessity of Judgment.* New Brunswick, N.J.: Transaction Publishers, 1992.

Burke, John Francis. *Mestizo Democracy: The Politics of Crossing Borders.* College Station: University of Texas A&M Press, 2002.

Comblin, José. *Called for Freedom: The Changing Context of Liberation Theology.* Translated by Phillip Berryman. New York: Orbis Books, 1998.

Cavanaugh, William T. "Balthasar, Globalization, and the Problem of the One and the Many." *Communio* 28 (Summer 2001): 324-347.

Chesterton, G.K. Collected Works, Vol. IV: *What's Wrong With the World?* San Francisco: Ignatius Press, 1987.

_____. Collected Works, Vol. V: *The Outline of Sanity.* San Francisco: Ignatius Press, 1987.

Clarke, Norris. "John Paul II: The Complementarity of Faith and Philosophy in the Search for Truth." *Communio* 26 (Fall 1999): 557-570.

_____. *Person and Being.* Milwaukee: Marquette University Press, 1993.

Dagger, Richard. *Civic Virtues: Rights, Citizenship, and Republican Liberalism.* Oxford: Oxford University Press, 1997.

Dallmayr, Fred, ed. *Border Crossings: Toward a Comparative Political Theory.* Lanham, New York, London: Lexington Books, 1999.

Dawson, Christopher. *Dynamics of World History.* New York: Sheed and Ward, 1962.

Day, Dorothy. *Loaves and Fishes: The Story of the Catholic Worker Movement.* San Francisco: Harper and Row, 1963.

_____. *The Long Loneliness.* San Francisco: Harper and Row, 1952.

_____. *Selected Writings.* Maryknoll: Orbis Books, 1994.

_____. *Therese.* Springfield: Templegate Publishers, 1979.

D' Costa, Gavin, ed. *Christian Universalism Reconsidered.* New York and San Francisco: Pantheon Books, 1992.

De Lubac, Henri. *A Brief Catechesis on Nature and Grace.* Translated by Brother Richard Arnandez. San Francisco: Ignatius Press, 1984.

_____. *Catholicism: Christ and the Common Destiny of Man.* San Francisco: Ignatius Press, 1988.

_____. *The Drama of Atheist Humanism.* San Francisco: Ignatius Press, 1995.

_____. *The Mystery of the Supernatural.* New York: Crossroads, 1998.

_____. *Theology in History.* San Francisco: Ignatius Press, 1996.

Donohue-White, Patricia, et al. *Human Nature and the Discipline of Economics: Personalist Anthropology and Economic Methodology.* Lanham, New York, Oxford: Lexington Books, 2002.

Elizondo, Virgilio. *Galilean Journey: The Mexican-American Promise.* New York: Orbis Books, 1985.

_____. *Guadalupe: Mother of the New Creation.* Maryknoll: Orbis Books, 1985.

Ederer, Rupert J., ed. *Heinrich Pesch on Solidarist Economics.* New York: University Press of America, 1998.

Ferree, William J. *Introduction to Social Justice.* Edited by Michael D. Greaney. Arlington: Center for Economic and Social Justice, 1997.

Figgis, J. Neville. *The Theory of the Divine Right of Kings.* Cambridge: Cambridge University Press, 1896.

Forest, Jim. *Love Is the Measure: A Biography of Dorothy Day.* Maryknoll: Orbis Books, 1997.

Fortin, Ernest. *Classical Christianity and the Political Order.* Edited by Brian Benestad. Lanham and London: Rowman & Littlefield Press, 1996.

Fuller, Timothy and John P. Hittinger, eds. *Reassessing the Liberal State: Reading Maritain's Man and the State.* Washington, D.C.: The Catholic University of America, 2001.

Galot, Jean. *The Person of Christ.* Rome: Gregorian University Press, 1980.

Gilson, Etienne. *Christian Philosophy: An Introduction.* Toronto: Pontifical Institute of Medieval Studies, 1993.

_____. *The Christian Philosophy of Saint Thomas Aquinas.* Translated by L.K. Shook, C.S.B. Notre Dame: University of Notre Dame Press, 1956.

Goizueta, Roberto. *Caminemos con Jesus: Toward a Hispanic/Latino Theology of Accompaniment.* Maryknoll: Orbis Books, 1995.

Greider, William. *One World: Ready or Not: The Manic Logic of Global Capitalism.* New York: Simon and Schuster, 1997.

_____. *Secrets of the Temple: How the Federal Reserve Runs the Country.* New York: Simon and Schuster, 1988.

Guardini, Romano. *Power and Responsibility.* New York: Sheed and Ward, 1957.

Gutiérrez, Gustavo. *The Density of the Present: Selected Writings.* Maryknoll: Orbis Books, 1999.

_____. *Las Casas.* Translated by Robert R. Barr. Maryknoll: Orbis Books, 1995.

_____. *On Job: God-Talk and the Suffering of the Innocent.* Translated by Matthew J. O'Connell. New York: Orbis Books, 1987.

_____. *El rostro de Dios en la historia.* Lima: Centro de Estudios y Publicaciones, 1996.

_____. *Theology of Liberation*. Rev. ed. Translated and edited by Sister Caridad Inda and John Eagleson. Maryknoll: Orbis Books, 1988.

_____. *The Truth Shall Make You Free: Confrontations*. New York: Orbis Books, 1990.

_____. *We Drink from Our Own Wells: The Spiritual Journey of a People*. Translated by Matthew J. O'Connell. Maryknoll: Orbis Books, 1997.

Glendon, Mary Ann. *Rights Talk*. New York: Free Press, 1991.

Hanson, Victor Davis. *Fields Without Dreams: Defending the Agrarian Idea*. New York: Free Press, 1996.

_____. *The Land Was Everything: Letters from an American Farmer*. New York: Free Press, 2000.

Hart, Gary. *Restoration of the Republic: The Jeffersonian Ideal in 21st-Century America*. Oxford and New York: Oxford University Press, 2002.

Harvey, David. *The Condition of Postmodernity*. Oxford: Basil Blackwell, 1989.

Hicks, John. *God Has Many Names*. Philadelphia: Westminster, 1982.

Hicks, John and Paul Knitter, eds. *The Myth of Christian Uniqueness*. Maryknoll: Orbis Books; London: SCM, 1987.

Hightower, Jim. *If the Gods Had Meant Us to Vote, They Would Have Given Us Candidates*. New York: Perennial Publications, 2001.

Ivereigh, Austen. *Catholicism and Politics in Argentina:1810-1960*. New York and Oxford: Oxford University Press, 1996.

John Paul II (Karol Wojtyla). *The Acting Person*. Dordrecht, the Netherlands and Boston: D. Riedl, 1979.

_____. Encyclical Letter *Centesimus Annus*. 1991.

_____. Encyclical Letter *Dives in Misericordia*. 1980.

_____. Encyclical Letter *Ecclesia in America*. 1999.

_____. Encyclical Letter *Evangelium Vitae*. 1995.

_____. Encyclical Letter *Fides et Ratio*. 1998.

_____. Encyclical Letter *Laborem Exercens*. 1981.

_____. Encyclical Letter *Veritatis Splendor*. 1993.

Keane, Eamons. *The Brave New World of Therapeutic Cloning*. Front Royal, Va.: Human Life International Press, 2001.

Kelso, Louis, and Mortimer Adler. *The Capitalist Manifesto*. New York: Random House, 1958.

Kelso, Louis, and Patricia Hetter. *Democracy and Economic Power: Extending the ESOP Revolution*. Lanham: University Press of America, 1991.

_____. *Two-Factor Theory: The Economics of Reality*. New York: Random House, 1967.

Knitter, Paul F. *Jesus and the Other Names: Christian Mission and Global Responsibility*. Maryknoll: Orbis Books, 1996.

Komonchok, Joseph. "Subsidiarity in the Church: The State of the Question." *The Jurist* 48 (1988): 298-300.

Korten, David C. *When Corporations Rule the World*. San Francisco: Berrett-Koehler Publishers, Inc., and Kumarian Press, 2001.

Kurland, Norman. *Community Investment Corporation (CIC): A Vehicle for Economic and Political Empowerment of Individual Citizens at the Community Level.* Arlington: Center for Economic and Social Justice, 1971.

_____. *The Federal Reserve Discount Window: An Untapped Off-Federal Budget Source of Expanded Bank Credit for Accelerating Private Sector Growth.* Arlington: Center for Economic and Social Justice, 1995.

_____. *An Illustrated Guide for Statesmen: A Two-Pronged Strategy for Implementing ESOP Privatizations in a Developing or Transforming Economy.* Arlington: Center for Economic and Social Justice, 1991.

Kuic, Vukan. *Yves R. Simon: Real Democracy.* Lanham, New York, and Oxford: Rowman & Littlefield, 1999.

Lairson, Thomas D., and David Skidmore. *International Political Economy: The Struggle for Wealth and Power.* New York: Harcourt Brace College Publishers, 1993.

Leo XIII. Encyclical Letter *Aeterni Patris.* 1879.

Levinson, Sanford. *Constitutional Faith.* Princeton: Princeton University Press, 1988.

Logsdon, Gene. *Living at Nature's Pace: Farming and the American Dream.* White River Junction: Chelsea Green Publishing Company, 2000.

MacIntyre, Alasdair. *After Virtue: A Study in Moral Theory.* Notre Dame: University of Notre Dame Press, 1981.

_____. *Whose Justice? Which Rationality?* Notre Dame: University of Notre Dame Press, 1988.

Maritain, Jacques. *The Person and the Common Good.* New York: Scribners, 1947.

Miller, John H., ed. *Curing World Poverty: The New Role of Property.* St. Louis: Social Justice Review and Center for Economic and Social Justice, 1994.

Miller, William. *A Harsh and Dreadful Love: Dorothy Day and the Catholic Worker Movement.* New York: Liveright, 1973.

_____. *Dorothy Day: A Biography.* San Francisco: Harper and Row, 1982.

Moulton, Harold G. *The Formation of Capital.* Washington, D.C.: Brookings Institution, 1935.

Neuhaus, Richard John. *Doing Well and Doing Good: The Challenge to the Christian Capitalist.* New York: Doubleday, 1992.

Novak, Michael. *The Catholic Ethic and the Spirit of Capitalism.* New York: Free Press, 1993.

Pegis, Anton, ed. *Basic Writings of Saint Thomas Aquinas.* New York: Random House, 1945.

Peterson, Merrill D. *Jefferson: Writings.* New York: Library of America, 1984.

Petras, James, and Henry Veltmeyer. *Globalization Unmasked: Imperialism in the 21st Century.* New York: Zed Books, 2001.

Portier, William. "Are We Serious When We Ask God to Deliver Us from War?" *Communio* 23 (Spring 1996): 47-61.

Pontificio Consejo Justicia y Paz. *Para una mejor distribución de la tierra: El reto de la reforma agraria.* Buenos Aires: Paulinas de Asociación Hijas de San Pablo, 1998.

Quasten, Johannes, ed. *Patrology.* 4 Vols. Allen, Tex.: Christian Classics, 1994.

Rager, John. *The Political Philosophy of Robert Bellarmine.* Reprint ed. Spokane: Our Lady of Siluva, 1995.

Ratzinger, Joseph. *Behold the Pierced One.* Translated by Graham Harrison. San Francisco: Ignatius Press, 1986.

_____. *Called to Communion: Understanding the Church Today.* San Francisco: Ignatius Press, 1996.

_____. *Church, Ecumenism and Politics.* New York: Crossroads, 1988.

_____. "Concerning the Notion of Person in Theology." *Communio* 17:3 (Fall 1990): 439-453.

_____. *Introduction to Christianity.* Communio Books and Ignatius Press, 1990.

_____. *The Meaning of Christian Brotherhood.* San Francisco: Ignatius Press, 1966.

Rawls, John. *A Theory of Justice.* Cambridge: Harvard University Press, 1971.

_____. *Political Liberalism.* New York: Columbia University Press, 1993.

Rifkin, Jeremy. *The End of Work: Decline of the Labor Force and the Dawn of the Post-Market Era.* New York: G.P. Putnam's Sons, 1995.

Roepke, Wilhelm. *A Human Economy: The Social Framework of the Free Market.* Lanham: University Press of America, 1960.

Rorty, Richard. "The Priority of Democracy to Philosophy." In Merrill D. Peterson and Robert C. Vaughan, eds., *The Virginia Statute for Religious Freedom.* Cambridge: Cambridge University Press, 1988.

Rourke, Thomas R. *A Conscience as Large as the World.* Lanham, New York, and Oxford: Rowman & Littlefield, 1997.

_____. "Contemporary Globalization: An Ethical and Anthropological Evaluation." *Communio* 27:3 (Fall 2000): 490-510.

_____. "The Death Penalty and the Ontology of the Person." *Communio* 25:3 (Fall 1998): 397-413.

_____. "Egalitarian Economics." *Yves R. Simon: Philosophy and Social Justice.* Edited by Jack Carlson. Washington, D.C.: Catholic University of America Press, forthcoming, 2004.

_____. "Globalization: A Theological and Political Assessment." *Journal of Peace and Justice Studies* 14:1 (Spring 2004): 5-24.

_____. "Michael Novak and Yves Simon on the Common Good and Capitalism." *Review of Politics* 58:2 (Spring 1996): 229-258.

Sacred Congregation for the Doctrine of the Faith. *Instruction on Certain Aspects of the "Theology of Liberation."* 1984.

_____. *Instruction on Christian Freedom and Liberation.* 1986.

Santelli, Anthony J. Jr., et al. *The Free Person and the Free Economy: A Personalist View of Market Economics.* Lanham, New York, and London: Lexington Books, 2002.

Schindler, David L. *Heart of the World, Center of the Church: Communio Ecclesiology, Liberalism and Liberation.* Grand Rapids: William B. Eerdmans, 1996.

_____. "Homelessness and the Modern Condition." *Communio* 27:3 (2000): 411-430.

Schmitz, Kenneth L. *At the Center of the Human Drama: The Philosophical Anthropology of Karol Wojtyla/Pope John Paul II.* Washington, D.C.: Catholic University of America Press, 1993.

Sigmund, Paul. *Liberation Theology at the Crossroads: Democracy or Revolution?* New York and Oxford: Oxford University Press, 1990.

_____, ed. *Saint Thomas Aquinas on Politics and Ethics.* New York: W.W. Norton and Co., 1998.

Simon, Yves R. *Freedom of Choice.* Edited by Peter Wolff. New York: Fordham University Press, 1969.

_____. *The General Theory of Authority.* Notre Dame: University of Notre Dame Press, 1980.

_____. *Philosophy of Democratic Government.* Notre Dame: University of Notre Dame Press, 1993.

_____. *Practical Knowledge.* New York: Fordham University Press, 1999.

_____. *The Tradition of Natural Law.* New York: Fordham University Press, 1992.

_____. *Work, Society and Culture.* Edited by Vukan Kuic. New York: Fordham University, 1971.

Sobrino, Jon. "The Winds of Santo Domingo and the Evangelization of Culture." In *Santo Domingo and After: The Challenges for the Latin American Church,* edited by Gustavo Gutiérrez, et al. London: Catholic Institute for International Relations, 1993.

_____. *The Principle of Mercy: Taking the Crucified People from the Cross.* Maryknoll: Orbis Books, 1997.

Soriano, Osvaldo. *Una sombra ya pronto serás.* Mexico, D.F.: Editorial Diana, 1992.

Suárez, Francisco. "De Legibus Ac Deo Legislatore." In *Classics of International Law,* edited by James Scott Brown. London: Clarendon Press, 1949.

Tierney, Brian. *The Idea of Natural Rights: Studies on Natural Rights, Natural Law and Church Law, 1150-1625.* Atlanta: Scholars Press, 1997.

_____. *Religion, Law and the Growth of Constitutional Thought: 1150-1650.* Cambridge: Cambridge University Press, 1982.

Vatican Council II Documents. *Gaudium et Spes.* 1965.

Vitoria, Francisco. *De indis.* In *Francisco Vitoria: Political Writings,* edited by Anthony Pagden and Jeremy Lawrance. Cambridge: Cambridge University Press, 1991.

Von Balthasar, Hans Urs. *The Glory of the Lord: A Theological Aesthetics.* Edited by Joseph Fessio and John Riches. Translated by Erasmo Leiva-Merikakis. San Francisco: Ignatius Press; New York: Crossroads, 1961-1969.

_____. "On the Concept of Person." *Communio* 13:1 (Spring 1986): 18-26.

_____. *Theo-Drama: Theological Dramatic Theory.* Translated by Graham Harrison. San Francisco: Ignatius Press, 1990-1996.

_____. *Unless You Become Like This Child.* Translated by Erasmo Leiva-Merikakis. San Francisco: Ignatius Press, 1991.

Walsh, Michael, and Brian Davies. *Proclaiming Justice and Peace: Papal Documents from Rerum Novarum Through Centesimus Annus.* Mystic, Conn.: Twenty-Third Publications, 1994.

Wood, Adrian. *North-South Trade, Employment, and Inequality.* Oxford: Oxford University Press, 1994.

Wootton, David, ed. *Modern Political Thought: Readings from Machiavelli to Nietzsche.* Indianapolis and Cambridge: Hackett Publishing, Inc., 1996.

# Index

Made in the USA
Middletown, DE
15 January 2019